W9-BWM-278

Published by:

Frommer Media LLC

ISBN 978-1-62887-242-2 (paper), 978-1-62887-243-9 (e-book)

Editorial Director: Pauline Frommer
Editor: Holly Hughes
Production Editor: Heather Wilcox
Photo Editor: Meghan Lamb
Cartographer: Elizabeth Puhl

For information on our other products or services, see www.frommers.com.

Frommer Media LLC also publishes its books in a variety of electronic formats. Some content that appears in print may not be available in electronic formats.

Manufactured in China

5 4 3 2 1

About This Guide

Organizing your time. That's what this guide is all about.

Other guides give you long lists of things to see and do and then expect you to fit the pieces together. The Day by Day guides are different. These guides tell you the best of everything, and then they show you how to see it *in the smartest, most time-efficient way.* Our authors have designed detailed itineraries organized by time, neighborhood, or special interest. And each tour comes with a bulleted map that takes you from stop to stop.

Looking to explore the old-fashioned Arabian souks of the old city or to visit contemporary landmarks, such as the Burj Al Arab or Burj Dubai? Wanting to find the best shops or the coolest places to eat and drink? Whatever your interest or schedule, the Day by Days give you the smartest routes to follow. Not only do we take you to the top attractions, hotels, and restaurants, but we also help you access those special moments that locals get to experience—those "finds" that turn tourists into travelers.

The Day by Days are also your top choice if you're looking for one complete guide for all your travel needs. The best hotels and restaurants for every budget, the greatest shopping values, the wildest nightlife—it's all here.

Why should you trust our judgment? Because our authors personally visit each place they write about. They're an independent lot who say what they think and would never include places they wouldn't recommend to their best friends. They're also open to suggestions from readers. If you'd like to contact them, please send your comments our way at feedback@frommers.com, and we'll pass them on.

Enjoy your Day by Day guide—the most helpful travel companion you can buy. And have the trip of a lifetime.

About the Author

Gavin Thomas is a freelance travel writer specializing in Arabia and Asia. He first visited Dubai in 2005, when the Burj Dubai was simply a big hole in the ground and the Dubai Marina was nothing but a forest of cranes. He looks forward to making many more visits to this ever-changing metropolis.

An Additional Note

Please be advised that travel information is subject to change at any time—and this is especially true of prices. We therefore suggest that you write or call ahead for confirmation when making your travel plans. The authors, editors, and publisher cannot be held responsible for the experiences of readers while traveling. Your safety is important to us, however, so we encourage you to stay alert and be aware of your surroundings.

Star Ratings, Icons & Abbreviations

Every hotel, restaurant, and attraction listing in this guide has been ranked for quality, value, service, amenities, and special features using a **star-rating system.** Hotels, restaurants, attractions, shopping, and nightlife are rated on a scale of zero stars (recommended) to three stars (exceptional). In addition to the star-rating system, we also use a **kids icon** to point out the best bets for families. Within each tour, we recommend cafes, bars, or restaurants where you can take a break. Each of these stops appears in a shaded box marked with a coffee-cup-shaped bullet ☕.

The following **abbreviations** are used for credit cards:

AE	American Express	DISC	Discover	V	Visa
DC	Diners Club	MC	MasterCard		

Frommers.com

Now that you have this guidebook to help you plan a great trip, visit our website at **www.frommers.com** for additional travel information on more than 4,000 destinations. We update features regularly to give you instant access to the most current trip-planning information available. At Frommers.com, you'll find scoops on the best airfares, lodging rates, and car rental bargains. You can even book your travel online through our reliable travel booking partners. Other popular features include:

- Online updates of our most popular guidebooks
- Vacation sweepstakes and contest giveaways
- Newsletters highlighting the hottest travel trends
- Online travel message boards with featured travel discussions

A Note on Prices

In the "Take a Break" and "Best Bets" sections of this book, we have used a system of dollar signs to show a range of costs for 1 night in a hotel (the price of a double-occupancy room) or the cost of an entree at a restaurant. Use the following table to decipher the dollar signs:

Cost	Hotels	Restaurants
$	under $100	under $10
$$	$100–$200	$10–$20
$$$	$200–$300	$20–$30
$$$$	$300–$400	$30–$40
$$$$$	over $400	over $40

An Invitation to the Reader

In researching this book, we discovered many wonderful places—hotels, restaurants, shops, and more. We're sure you'll find others. Please tell us about them, so we can share the information with your fellow travelers in upcoming editions. If you were disappointed with a recommendation, we'd love to know that, too. Please write to: Contact@FrommerMedia.com

15 Favorite
Moments

15 Favorite Moments

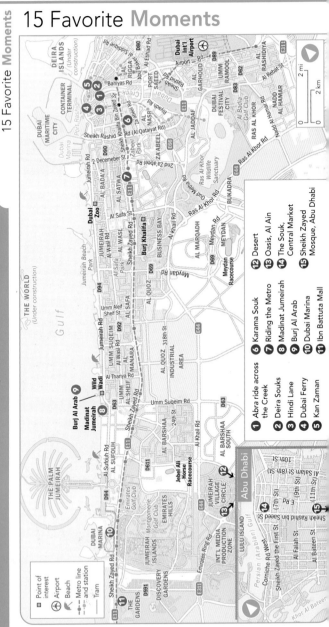

1. Abra ride across the Creek
2. Deira Souks
3. Hindi Lane
4. Dubai Ferry
5. Kan Zaman
6. Karama Souk
7. Riding the Metro
8. Madinat Jumeirah
9. Burj Al Arab
10. Dubai Marina
11. Ibn Battuta Mall
12. Desert
13. Oasis, Al Ain
14. The Souk, Central Market
15. Sheikh Zayed Mosque, Abu Dhabi

Previous page: View of the Marina at dusk.

ubai, it often seems, is not so much a conventional city as a fascinating urban experiment in which almost anything can happen—and frequently does. This is the place where some of the world's most spectacular developments are taking shape, but it is also a city whose heart still beats to the traditional rhythms of the Arabian bazaar, lending the place a unique character.

① Riding an _abra_ across the Creek. Hop aboard a traditional _abra_ (water taxi) for the brief but thrilling ride across the breezy waters of the Creek, with views of tangled souks, wind towers, and minarets to either side—a marvelous panorama of old Dubai, and unforgettable at any time of the day or night. _See p 28._

② Getting lost in the Deira Souks. Getting disoriented is half the fun, whether in the backstreets of the Spice or Gold souks or in the seemingly endless Covered Souk, with its labyrinth of tangled alleyways and tiny shops. If you don't get lost the first time, go back until you do. _See p 32._

③ Hunting for religious curios in Hindi Lane. A fascinating enclave of Indian life tucked away in the depths of Bur Dubai, this is the closest you can get to visiting India without actually going there. Explore picturesque little stalls selling assorted religious bric-a-brac and a pair of fascinatingly secretive little Hindu temples. _See p 43._

④ Cruising on the Dubai Ferry from Bur Dubai to the Marina. Escape the traffic and see the city from an entirely fresh angle during this marvelous 75-minute ride down

the coast aboard the sleek new Dubai Ferry. _See p 166._

⑤ Enjoying an after-dark shisha at Kan Zaman. Loll back in your seat, watch the lights twinkling over the Creek, and puff on a fragrant shisha (waterpipe) while the dulcet Arabian warblings of Um Kalthoum or Fairuz fill the night air. Pure Dubai heaven. _See p 91._

⑥ Shopping for designer fakes at Karama Souk. Penny-pinching fashionistas can't do better than head to the legendary Karama Souk, home of the "authentic" Dubai fake, with top-quality replica gear at budget prices. Just don't expect it to last quite as long as the real thing. _See p 64._

⑦ Zipping around on the metro. Not just a brilliantly efficient and inexpensive way of getting from A to B, the elevated lines of the Dubai Metro also offer peerless views of the city's futuristic skyline and massed towers—the stretch down Sheikh Zayed Road is particularly dramatic. _See p 11._

⑧ Marveling at Madinat Jumeirah. The most superbly over-the-top of

Taking a ride on an abra boat on Bay Creek.

Interior of Ibn Battuta Mall, where each salesroom is decorated in the style of a different country.

all Dubai's mega-developments, this vast faux-Arabian city is a fabulous place for an idle stroll or a cocktail at sunset, with splashes of wonderful ersatz traditional architecture framing surreal views of the futuristic Burj Al Arab beyond. *See p 15.*

⑨ Gazing at Burj Al Arab. Nothing is quite like Dubai's iconic Burj Al Arab, quite simply the world's most sensational building of recent years. It's jaw-dropping from all angles and at any time of the night or day. *See p 119.*

⑩ Exploring the Dubai Marina. A fabulous forest of skyscrapers now stands where a few years ago there was nothing but empty desert. Nowhere showcases the incredible scale, speed, and ambition of Dubai's ongoing expansion as much as the incredible Marina development—the nearest you'll get to seeing history, literally, in the making. *See p 58.*

⑪ Stopping by Ibn Battuta Mall. Supersized kitsch is one of the things Dubai does best, and nowhere more so than at the surreal Ibn Battuta Mall, themed in extravagant pan-Islamic designs after the travels of the legendary Moroccan traveler. Take it all in over a Starbucks coffee in the grandiose Iranian courtyard at the heart of the mall—the world's weirdest cappuccino experience. *See p 68.*

⑫ Experiencing the desert at dusk. Ignore the roar of dune-bashing four-wheel-drives and the squeal of distant quad bikes. The desert at dusk is always unforgettable, as the sands turn a rich, deep gold, the light magically thickens, and one feels strangely and wonderfully insignificant amid the interminable sand dunes, stretching away as far as the eye can see. *See p 169.*

⑬ Walking through the oasis at Al Ain. You could wander for hours through the oasis at Al Ain, a miraculously peaceful forest of date palms, which feels hundreds of miles from the modern city outside. *See p 138.*

⑭ The Souk, World Trade Center, Abu Dhabi. Proving that not all Emirati developments have to be either massive skyscrapers or chintzy scraps of faux-Arabian pastiche, this Foster + Partners creation lays down a template for a whole new kind of Gulf architecture, blending traditional Middle Eastern motifs and postmodern minimalism into a magical, and marvelously original, whole. *See p 149.*

⑮ Discovering the Sheikh Zayed Mosque, Abu Dhabi. This landmark mosque is one of the world's most spectacular places of Islamic worship—awesomely huge from the outside and extravagantly decorated within. *See p 150.* ●

The Best **in One Day**

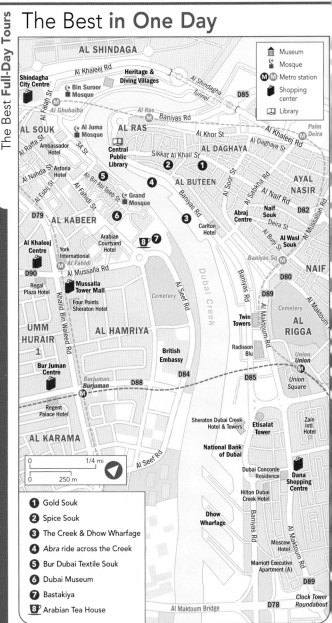

Museum
Mosque
M Metro station
Shopping center
Library

1 Gold Souk
2 Spice Souk
3 The Creek & Dhow Wharfage
4 *Abra* ride across the Creek
5 Bur Dubai Textile Souk
6 Dubai Museum
7 Bastakiya
8 Arabian Tea House

Previous page: Sheikh Zayed Mosque.

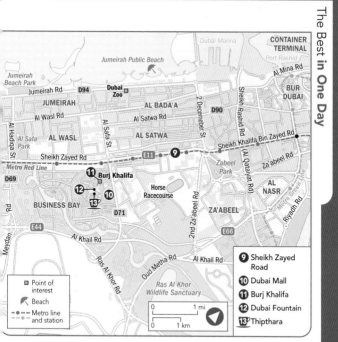

Begin amid the souks of old Dubai, which offer a memorable taste of traditional Gulf life. Then take a boat over the Creek before heading south to the futuristic Sheikh Zayed Road, Downtown Dubai, and neck-cricking Burj Khalifa, the world's tallest building. START: **Gold Souk, Deira. Catch a taxi, or take the metro to Al Ras station on the Green Line.**

① ★★★ Gold Souk. At the heart of the vibrant trading district of Deira, the Gold Souk is a perfect introduction to a city that prides itself on all things brash and ostentatious. The souk—a long, wooden roofed arcade of small shops full of gold jewelry—offers everything from suave European designs to fabulously ornate traditional Arabian pieces, plus the elegant Emirati-style gold bangles featured prominently in many storefronts. Prices are cheap, too. For more information see p 33, ①. ⏱ *30 min. Most shops open 10am–10pm.*

② ★★ Spice Souk. Hidden away just south of the Gold Souk is the city's atmospheric Spice Souk, with a cluster of tiny shops squeezed into the narrowest of alleyways, their presence signaled by the photogenic sacks of herbs and spices piled up outside. You'll probably smell the souk before you actually see it. The shops here are run by Iranian traders—an engaging and friendly bunch, who are always happy to explain the sometimes mysterious substances on offer, ranging from everyday cooking spices to prized Omani

Herbs and spices in the Spice Souk.

frankincense and rose-petal tea. For more information, see p 34, ❷.
🕐 20 min. Most shops open 10am–10pm.

❸ ★★★ **The Creek & Dhow Wharfage.** Exit the south side of the Spice Souk, and you'll find yourself at the edge of the Creek (*Al Khor* in Arabic), the broad sea inlet that provides the city center with refreshing sea breezes and many of its most memorable views. The Creek was the reason for Dubai's existence in the first place and still serves as an important

shipping conduit, busy with boats day and night.

The stretch of waterfront south of the Spice Souk, known as the Dhow Wharfage, is where you'll get the strongest sense of the city's traditional maritime trading past. Dozens of fine old wooden dhows can generally be seen here, moored in front of the glass-fronted high-rises that line this side of the Creek—one of the city's most incongruous yet photogenic sights. Many boats are almost museum pieces but still see regular service plying the Arabian Gulf to neighboring emirates and over to Iran, Pakistan, and India. The adjacent waterfront promenade serves as an impromptu loading and unloading area, with a bewilderingly eclectic array of cargo—enormous waterside piles of anything from washing machines to contraband cigarettes stacked in great cardboard-box towers. 🕐 20 min. Baniyas Rd.

❹ ★★★ **kids** *Abra* **ride across the Creek.** Despite all its high-tech modern attractions, Dubai's most unforgettable (and

Unloading an old dhow at the Dhow Wharfage.

Abra ride on Dubai Creek.

inexpensive) ride is still the 5-minute trip across the Creek by *abra*, the old-fashioned wooden passenger ferries that zip to and fro between the districts of Deira and Bur Dubai—the most fun you can have in the city for just one dirham. Catch a boat at the Deira Old Souk Abra Station in front of the Spice Souk and ride with an interesting cross-section of Dubaian society, from Emiratis in flowing white *dish-dashas* to expatriate Pakistani day-laborers and camera-toting tourists. From midstream, there are wonderful views to either side of central Dubai's eclectic skyline of high-rises, minarets, and wind towers, underlaid by the rough, coral-walled outline of old souks and wooden dhows. See also p 28, **❾**.
🕐 *5 min. AED 1 per person.*

❺ ★★ Bur Dubai Textile Souk. Jump off your *abra*, and you'll find yourself at the north end of the Textile Souk (also known as the Bur Dubai Old Souk). This is easily the best-looking traditional bazaar in

the city, an attractively restored old-fashioned structure with wooden roof (keeping things pleasantly cool during the heat of the day) and rough-walled old shops made from coral and gypsum stone, topped with the occasional wind tower.

Ancient textile market Bur Dubai Textile Souk.

Grand Mosque and minaret in Bur Dubai.

Despite the Arabian architecture, the souk has a pronounced subcontinental flavor. Most of the shops are owned by Indians whose ancestors settled in Bur Dubai in the 19th century and who continue to dominate the commercial life of the area, selling reams of flowery cloth along with assorted low-grade souvenirs, pashminas, and inexpensive clothes.

At the far (eastern) end of the souk, a narrow alleyway leads into fascinating **Hindi Lane** (see p 43, ⑥). Beyond, you'll find the imposing **Grand Mosque** (see p 42, ④), with its towering minaret dominating the skyline of old Bur Dubai. Immediately next door is the **Diwan,** the original seat of Dubai's government, although you can't get any closer than the impressively high railings that enclose it on all sides. ⏱ 20 min. Most shops open 10am–10pm, some closed 1–4pm.

❻ ★★ **Dubai Museum.** Immediately in front of the Grand Mosque stands the city's oldest building, the quaint Al Fahidi Fort.

Looking more like a lopsided sandcastle than a military stronghold, the fort was built around 1800 to protect the landward side of the fledgling town from attack. It subsequently served as an ammunition store and then the town jail before being converted into the Dubai Museum in 1971.

The fort's picturesque courtyard houses a few old-time boats and a traditional barasti (palm-thatch) hut. Most of the museum displays are housed in an absorbing series of underground galleries, offering a comprehensive insight into virtually every aspect of Emirati culture, customs, and commerce, complete with short films, sound effects, spooky life-size mannequins, and excellent displays. See also p 23, ❶. ⏱ 45min. Al Fahidi St. ☎ 04-353-1862. http://bit.ly/DubaiMus. Admission AED 3 (AED 1 for kids 5 & under). Sat–Thurs 8:30am–8:30pm; Fri 2:30–8:30pm.

❼ ★★★ **Bastakiya.** Tucked away behind the Diwan and Grand Mosque, the tiny Bastakiya quarter

Al Fahidi Fort (1787), home to the Dubai Museum, is the city's oldest building.

The old merchant quarter of Bastakiya.

(or Al Fahidi Historical Neighborhood, as it's now officially known) is the most perfectly preserved traditional area in Dubai. The area was first settled in the 1920s by Iranian traders from Bastakiya, in Iran; their high, windowless stone houses were clustered around a disorienting labyrinth of alleyways built deliberately narrow to provide shade during even the hottest parts of the day. They also introduced the distinctive wind towers (see p 25) that stand atop every house in the district, which subsequently were adopted as an integral element of local architecture throughout the old city.

Like most of old Dubai, Bastakiya fell into dereliction during the 1970s and 1980s and only narrowly escaped demolition before being extensively restored. The whole quarter still has a slightly deserted and museum-like atmosphere, although growing numbers of guesthouses, cafes, art galleries, and museums are slowly breathing life back into this fascinating area. See also p 23, ②. ⏱ *30 min.*

8 **Arabian Tea House.** Right by the main entrance into Bastakiya, the Arabian Tea House is one of central Dubai's most appealing lunch spots, tucked into a pretty garden. It offers an appetizing selection of mainly Arabian-style sandwiches, salads, and light meals, accompanied by refreshing fruit juices. *Bastakiya (next to the main entrance on Al Fahidi St).* ☎ *04-353-5071.*

9 ★★ **Ride the metro south along Sheikh Zayed Road.** Walk up to the Al Fahidi metro station on the Green Line and ride the metro to the Burj Khalifa/Dubai Mall station on the Red Line (change at BurJuman). The most memorable stretch of Dubai's state-of-the-art metro system, this 20-minute elevated railway ride offers spectacular views of the massed skyscrapers of Sheikh Zayed Road—an utterly surreal contrast to the traditional souks and wind-towered houses of the old city.

En route, you'll pass the soaring **Emirates Towers** (see p 52, ④)

View of modern skyscrapers from Dubai's Metro.

and other postmodern landmarks, such as the quirky, Big Ben–inspired **Al Yaqoub Tower** (see p 52) and the *wai*-shaped **Dusit Thani** hotel (see p 120).

⑩ ★★ Dubai Mall. Alight at Burj Khalifa/Dubai Mall station and follow the air-conditioned walkway into the Dubai Mall, the centerpiece of the stunning **Downtown Dubai** development.

The largest mall on the planet, the vast **Dubai Mall** is stuffed with more designer outlets and other retail opportunities (see p 67) than you could visit in a month of Sundays. The mall is also home to the **Dubai Aquarium** (see p 45, **④**), an Olympic-size **ice rink** (see p 79); assorted kids' attractions (see p 47, **⑤**); and the **Dubai Dino,** a beautifully preserved 150-million-year-old skeleton of a Diplodocus longus, discovered in 2008 in Wyoming. ⏱ *90 min.* ☎ *800/38224-6255. www.thedubaimall.com.*

Sun–Wed 10am–11pm; Thurs–Sat 10am–midnight.

⑪ ★★★ Burj Khalifa. Exit the back of the Dubai Mall, and you'll emerge onto the promenade around **Burj Khalifa Lake,** ringed by modern Dubai's most jaw-dropping modern landmarks. Just over the lake on your left is the Arabian-style **Souk al Bahar** (see p 39, **⑩**), while to your right rises the incomparable **Burj Khalifa,** the world's tallest building (see p 54, **⑧**).

Few visitors miss the chance to visit the Burj's **At the Top** observation deck. Ride the world's fastest lifts up to the 124th floor (456m) to enjoy peerless views, with the whole of downtown Dubai and beyond spread out below. Almost microscopic figures can be seen walking the pavements beneath; even the huge skyscrapers of Sheikh Zayed Road seem reduced to puny insignificance. To get even closer to the top, sign up for the (seriously pricey) "Burj Khalifa Sky Experience," which takes you to a second observation deck on the 148th floor (555m)—although, apart from the one-upmanship of saying you've been to the very summit of the world's tallest building, it doesn't really justify the extra expense. *At least 1 hr. Prices vary according to time of day, rising during late-afternoon/sunset "prime hours." At the Top AED 125–AED 200 if pre-booked (children ages 4–12 AED 95–AED 120; free for kids 3 & under); AED 300 (all ages) immediate admission. At the Top Sky Experience (must be prebooked) AED 300–AED 500. ☎ 04-888-8124. www.burj khalifa.ae.*

⑫ ★★ Dubai Fountain. Set within Burj Khalifa Lake, the show-stopping Dubai Fountain is the world's largest: 275m long,

illuminated with 6,600 lights, studded with water jets shooting more than 140m into the air (as high as a 46-story building). The fountain performs every evening, with jets, swirls, and watery flourishes "dancing" in time to Arabian, Hindi, and Western pop hits. Enjoy it for free from the lakeside promenade. *Daily 6–11pm every 30 min., plus afternoon shows Sat–Thurs at 1pm & 1:30pm. Free.*

⑬ Thipthara. For arguably the best views of the Dubai Fountain and Burj Khalifa, book dinner at the upmarket Thipthara, located in a quaint wooden pavilion overlooking the lake and serving up delicious Royal Thai cuisine, with the emphasis on top-notch seafood creations. *The Palace Hotel. ☎ 04-428-7961. $$$.*

Dubai Fountain from At the Top of the Burj Khalifa.

The Best in Two Days

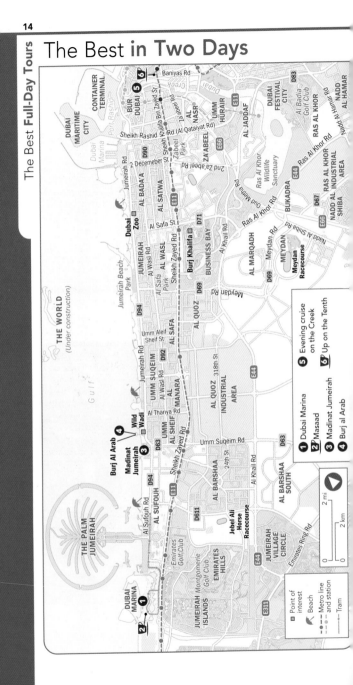

THE WORLD
(Under construction)

Gulf

THE PALM JUMEIRAH

Legend:

■ Point of interest
Beach
Metro line and station
Tram

0   2 mi
0   2 km

1 Dubai Marina
2 Masaad
3 Madinat Jumeirah
4 Burj al Arab
5 Evening cruise on the Creek
6 Up on the Tenth

Map labels:

DUBAI MARINA
JUMEIRAH ISLANDS
Jumeirah Montgomerie Golf Club
Emirates Golf Club
EMIRATES HILLS
Jebel Ali Horse Racecourse
JUMEIRAH VILLAGE CIRCLE
Emirates Ring Rd
AL BARSHAA
AL BARSHAA SOUTH
24th St
Umm Suqeim Rd
AL QUOZ INDUSTRIAL AREA
318th St
AL SHEIF
UMM AL SHEIF
Al Thanya Rd
Al Sufouh Rd
Sheikh Zayed Rd
AL SUFOUH
Madinat Jumeirah
Burj Al Arab
Wild Wadi
UMM SUQEIM
Al Wasl Rd
UMM AL MANARA
AL SAFA
Umm Aleif Sheif St
AL WASL
Al Safa Park
Jumeirah Beach Park
JUMEIRAH
Jumeirah Rd
AL QUOZ
Al Khail Rd
Meydan Rd
AL MARQADH
MEYDAN
Meydan Racecourse
Nadd Al Shiba Rd
BUKADRA
RAS AL KHOR INDUSTRIAL AREA
NADD AL SHIBA
Ras Al Khor Rd
Ras Al Khor Wildlife Sanctuary
RAS AL KHOR
RAS AL KHOR
NADD AL HAMAR
Nadd Al Hamar Rd
Al Badia Golf Club
DUBAI FESTIVAL CITY
AL JADDAF
Oud Metha Rd
2nd Za'abeel Rd
ZA'ABEEL
Zabeel Park
AL NASR
UMM HURAIR
Sheikh Khalifa Bin Zayed St
Baniyas Rd
Dubai Creek
BUR DUBAI
Port Rashid
DUBAI MARITIME CITY
CONTAINER TERMINAL
Dubai Marina
Sheikh Rashid Rd (Al Qataiyat Rd)
2 Decemeber St
AL SATWA
AL BADA'A
Burj Khalifa
BUSINESS BAY
Dubai Zoo
Al Safa St

After Day One's sights, your second day in Dubai takes in the bristling high-rises of the Dubai Marina; then the magnificent Madinat Jumeirah, Dubai's most evocative Arabian-style development; and the Burj al Arab, its most iconic modern landmark. Return to the old city for a dinner cruise aboard a traditional wooden dhow. START: **Marina Mall metro station on the Red Line.**

❶ ★★ **Dubai Marina.** Perhaps modern Dubai's most remarkable conjuring trick, the Dubai Marina area was largely untouched desert a decade ago. That's almost impossible to believe nowadays as you stand amid its forest of high-rises, shiny shops, swanky restaurants, and moored million-dollar boats.

The centerpiece of the development, the Marina itself, was created out of an artificial sea inlet. Attractive pedestrian promenades enclose the marina and connect with **The Walk**, its appealing beachfront promenade, passing assorted architectural landmarks (see p 58) en route.

There's plenty to do here. Fashionistas can explore the tony designer boutiques of the **Marina Mall** (see p 153), while sun-lovers can head to the beach itself, with its spacious white sands and a range of **watersports** (see p 80). Take to the water on one of many old-style dhows that putter around the marina (see p 28), or head out

to sea aboard the **Dubai Ferry** (see p 166).

❷ **Masaad.** This cute little cafe makes for a great lunch stop on the beachfront promenade, with inexpensive and flavorsome Lebanese-style fare including mezze, salads, and sandwiches, plus kebabs and grills. *The Walk, Jumeirah Beach Residences.* ☎ *04-362-9002. $.*

Catch a taxi from the Marina up to Madinat Jumeirah (around AED 20).

❸ ★★★ **Madinat Jumeirah.** There's a definite touch of Hollywood about the enormous Madinat Jumeirah leisure complex, one of modern Dubai's most spectacular landmarks. From a distance, the whole thing looks like a gigantic and slightly outlandish film set, framed by palm trees and topped by hundreds of wind towers, like the ultimate desert mirage. The Madinat is designed as a miniature, self-contained Arabian

Yachts in Dubai Marina.

Work in Progress

The spectacular speed with which the Dubai Marina was built is one of Dubai's great recent success stories, while the nearby Palm Jumeirah (see p 57), slightly longer in the making, is now also virtually complete. Other Dubai mega-projects have been less successful, however. Two further gigantic "palm" islands, the **Palm Jebel Ali** (south of the city) and the **Palm Deira** (adjoining the old city), have both been on hold since the 2008 financial crisis—although large areas of land have already been reclaimed. Meanwhile, the fanciful **The World** development—an artificial archipelago in the shape of a map of the world—has been long finished, but almost all its constituent islands remain totally undeveloped, and apparently forgotten. Elsewhere, the epic **Dubailand** project—originally planned to hold the world's largest theme park, plus a record-busting collection of mega-malls and uber-hotels—has barely gotten off the ground, although construction continues to rumble along at a snail's pace. A few of its attractions, including the zany Dubai Miracle Garden (see p 49) are finally now open.

city, complete with two top-notch hotels (**Mina A'Salam,** p 124, and **Al Qasr,** p 118) and its own Oriental-style bazaar, the **Souk Madinat Jumeirah** (p 39, ⑪). It may be a little bit cheesy, but it's all done with such panache and at such lavish expense that it's hard not to be at least slightly impressed.

At the far end of the souk, a long string of eating and drinking establishments lines the waterfront. From here, walkways and miniature bridges weave confusingly through the complex, offering superb views and plenty of opportunities for getting interestingly lost. (Head to the entrance of the Al Qasr hotel for a

Views of Madinat Jumeirah hotel.

The Burj Al Arab.

great view across the innumerable wind towers.) The Madinat is also the best place for views over to the Burj Al Arab (see p 56, ⑩), its sail-shaped outline surreally framed by the Madinat's traditional Arabian-style buildings. ⏲ *1 hr.* ☎ *04-366-8888. www.madinatjumeirah.com.*

④ ★★★ **Afternoon tea at the Burj al Arab.** The sail-shaped Burj al Arab was the landmark that first really put Dubai on the global map (see p 56, ⑩), and it remains Dubai's most memorable, most beautiful, and most all-around astonishing building—best seen from the Madinat Jumeirah, or from Umm Suqeim public beach just to the north. If you want to see the spectacular **interior,** you'll have to buy a drink or a meal (see p 56). Most visitors opt for the sumptuous afternoon teas served either in the Sahn Eddar lounge or the Skyview Bar—one of the city's most memorably hedonistic experiences.

Catch a taxi back to the Mall of the Emirates metro station (around AED 12), then ride the metro back to the old city.

⑤ ★★ **Evening cruise on the Creek.** After a day exploring the

skyscrapers and supersize developments of modern Dubai, return to the Creek to take another look at the old city—this time from the water and after dark. Dozens of tour companies (see p 169) offer evening dinner cruises along the Creek, most of them aboard traditional-style wooden dhows. Arabian- and Western-style food is served, plus soft drinks. En route, you'll drift gently past local waterfront landmarks, such as the futuristic Golf Club (Dubai's answer to the Sydney Opera House), the minimalist glass-fronted tower of the Dubai Chamber of Commerce, and the adjacent National Bank, with its huge, sail-shaped facade, as well as the souks, wind towers, and minarets of the old city, prettily illuminated by night. ⏲ *2 hr. Book in advance. See p 169 for a list of tour operators & packages available.*

⑥ **Up on the Tenth.** The perfect place for an after-dinner digestif, Up on the Tenth serves spectacular views of the Creek along with a decent drinks list and live jazz nightly (except Tues). *Radisson Blu Dubai Deira Creek, Baniyas Rd. $$$.*

The Best **in Three Days**

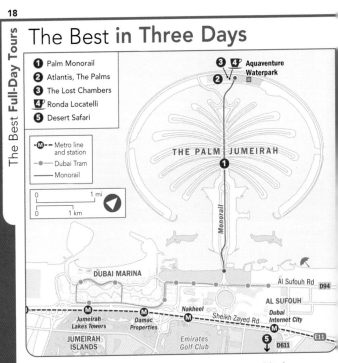

1 Palm Monorail
2 Atlantis, The Palms
3 The Lost Chambers
4 Ronda Locatelli
5 Desert Safari

-M-- Metro line and station
-●- Dubai Tram
—— Monorail

0 ___ 1 mi
0 ___ 1 km

3 **4** Aquaventure Waterpark
2

THE PALM JUMEIRAH

1

Monorail

DUBAI MARINA

Al Sufouh Rd   D94

AL SUFOUH

Nakheel   Sheikh Zayed Rd   Dubai Internet City

Jumeirah Lakes Towers   Damac Properties   Emirates Golf Club

JUMEIRAH ISLANDS   **5**   D611   E11

Start Day 3 with a monorail ride across the world's largest artificial island and explore the huge Atlantis resort. Then head into the desert for an afternoon of dune-bashing and sand-skiing, rounded off with a meal under the stars. START: **Palm Jumeirah station on the Dubai Tram. Follow signs through the car park (5min walk) to the Palm Monorail.**

1 ★★ **Palm Monorail.** Sticking out from the coast of southern Dubai, the vast Palm Jumeirah—the world's largest artificial island—is one of the modern city's more hit-or-miss developments (see p 57, **12**). Still, the 15-minute ride across the island on the elevated Palm Monorail is spectacular, with sweeping views of the palm-shaped development and mainland skyscrapers beyond. *Palm Monorail 15dh, or 25 return. Services 10am–10pm daily, 2–3 departures hourly. www.palm-monorail.com.*

2 ★ **Atlantis, The Palm.** At the far end of the island, the monorail ends at the 2,000-room Atlantis resort, modeled after its sister resort in the Bahamas. The gargantuan Atlantis looks like a set from an outlandish fantasy film, with two towering wings centered on a vaguely Islamic-looking arch, all painted a uniform shade of frozen-shrimp pink ("like the tomb of Liberace," as the UK's *Sun* newspaper described it). It's one of the few places in Dubai that actually lives up to the city's popular image as the Land That Taste

Atlantis Hotel.

Forgot—although you've got to be at least slightly impressed by its sheer size and uninhibited bling.

It's worth going inside the hotel to gape at the madly overcooked decor, complete with gold-plated pillars and vast **Lost Chambers** underwater "ruins" (see below). The resort offers several attractions, including the state-of-the-art **Aquaventure** water park (see p 80) and the chance to swim with dolphins at **Dolphin Bay** (see p 81). ⏱ *1 hr.*

www.atlantisthepalm.com. *For accommodations, see p 119.*

❸ ★★ The Lost Chambers. Archeologists will be delighted to learn that the legendary city of Atlantis (last seen, according to Plato, sometime around 10,000 BC in the western Mediterranean) has finally been rediscovered—in the waters beneath Dubai. This, at least, is what the guides at the Lost Chambers would have you believe. (Some of them even seem to believe it themselves.) Dubai's

The Lost Chambers.

Jeeps on safari in Pink Rock Desert.

hokiest attraction, the Chambers consists of a maze of underwater passageways and chambers in the bowels of the resort, with glass-walled viewing tunnels leading through a series of submerged "ruins." The real attraction is the stunning array of 65,000-odd marine creatures living quietly amid the pseudo-Atlantean relics. Note, however, that you can save yourself the admission fee and admire the lagoon's marine life for free from a viewing area in the hotel lobby. *Atlantis, The Palm.* ☎ *04-426-1040. www.atlantisthepalm.com. Admission adults AED 100, children ages 3–11 AED 70, free for kids 2 & under. Daily 10am–10pm.*

4 **Ronda Locatelli.** At this relaxed Italian restaurant run by super-chef Giorgio Locatelli, prices are above-average even for Dubai, but the good wood-fired pizzas (AED 75–AED 90) won't blow the budget. *Atlantis, The Palm.* ☎ *04-426-2626. $$.*

5 ★★ **Afternoon and eve-ning desert safari.** Most visitors to Dubai fit in a trip to the desert at some point in their stay. All sorts of packages are available, but by far the most popular option is a combined afternoon and evening excursion. Be forewarned: The desert around Dubai is far from unspoiled, and the tourist crowds and flotillas of four-wheel-drives make the desert a surprisingly busy—and noisy—place. It's all good, harmless fun, however. Most tours include the same mix of activities: You start off with around 45 minutes' energetic dune-bashing—being driven at high speed across the dunes, with exhilarating swoops up and down steep ridges of sand—with perhaps some sand-skiing or sand-boarding added on. Then you're driven to a desert camp, where you (and a couple hundred other tourists) can experience various traditional Arabian activities, including smoking *shisha*, getting henna-painted, dressing up in local costumes, or riding a camel. After this comes a buffet supper, followed by music and the inevitable belly dancer. ⏱ *6–7 hr. (includes dinner). Book in advance. For a list of tour operators, see p 169.* ●

Old Dubai

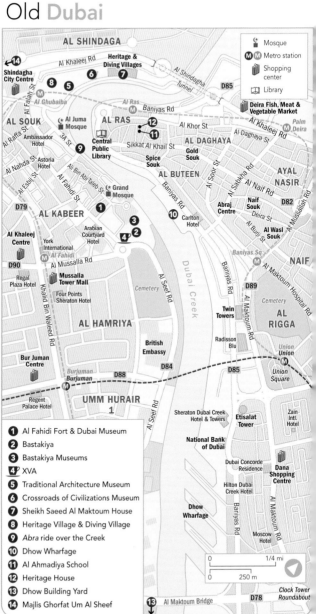

Legend:
- (* Mosque
- Ⓜ M Metro station
- 🛍 Shopping center
- 📖 Library

AL SHINDAGA

Al Khaleej Rd

Heritage & Diving Villages

Al Shindaga Tunnel

D85

Shindagha City Centre

⑧ ⑤ ⑥ ⑦ ⑭

Al Falahi St

Al Ghubaiba

Al Ras

Baniyas Rd

Deira Fish, Meat & Vegetable Market

AL SOUK

Al Raffa St

Ambassador Hotel

Astoria Hotel

3A St.

Al Nahda St

Al Esbij St.

(* Al Juma Mosque

AL RAS

⑫

Al Khor St

Palm Deira

Al Khaleej Rd

Central Public Library

Sikkat Al Khail St

⑪

AL DAGHAYA

Al Daghaya St

⑨

Spice Souk

Gold Souk

AL BUTEEN

Al Soor Rd

Al Sabkha Rd

AYAL NASIR

Ali Bin Abi Taleb St

Al Fahidi St

(* Grand Mosque

Baniyas Rd

Al Naif Rd

Abraj Centre

Naif Souk

Deira St

D82

D79

AL KABEER

①

③

Arabian Courtyard Hotel

④ ②

⑩

Carlton Hotel

Al Buteen St

Al Wasi Souk

York International

Ⓜ Al Fahidi

Al Mussalla Rd

Al Khaleej Centre

D90

Mussalla Tower Mall

NAIF

Regal Plaza Hotel

Four Points Sheraton Hotel

Cemetery

Al Seer Rd

Dubai Creek

Baniyas Rd

Baniyas Sq.

Ⓜ Al Maktoum

D89

Al Maktoum Rd

Cemetery

AL RIGGA

Al Mussallah Rd

Al Hospital Rd

AL HAMRIYA

British Embassy

Twin Towers

Radisson Blu

Union

Ⓜ Union

Bur Juman Centre

Burjuman D88

D84

D85

Union Square

Ⓜ Burjuman

UMM HURAIR 1

Al Seer Rd

Regent Palace Hotel

Sheraton Dubai Creek Hotel & Towers

Etisalat Tower

Zain Intl. Hotel

National Bank of Dubai

Dubai Concorde Residence

Dana Shopping Centre

Hilton Dubai Creek Hotel

Dhow Wharfage

Baniyas Rd

Al Maktoum Rd

Moscow Hotel

① Al Fahidi Fort & Dubai Museum
② Bastakiya
③ Bastakiya Museums
④ XVA
⑤ Traditional Architecture Museum
⑥ Crossroads of Civilizations Museum
⑦ Sheikh Saeed Al Maktoum House
⑧ Heritage Village & Diving Village
⑨ Abra ride over the Creek
⑩ Dhow Wharfage
⑪ Al Ahmadiya School
⑫ Heritage House
⑬ Dhow Building Yard
⑭ Majlis Ghorfat Um Al Sheef

0 ____ 1/4 mi
0 ____ 250 m

Clock Tower Roundabout

⑬ Al Maktoum Bridge   D78

Previous page: The Jumeirah Mosque.

ontrary to popular belief, Dubai wasn't built yesterday. The old city dates back to the early days of the 19th century, and although much of the traditional architecture was swept away during the modernizing rush of the 1960s and 1970s, a considerable number of characterful old buildings survive. START: **Shindagha, Bur Dubai.** Taxi or Green Line metro to Al Ghubaiba station.

1 ★★ kids **Al Fahidi Fort & Dubai Museum.** Dating back to around 1800, Al Fahidi Fort is the oldest building in Dubai. Inside, the **Dubai Museum** serves as a brilliant first stop if you're looking for an introduction to all things Arabian. The museum is entered via the fort's courtyard, where you'll find a few traditional wooden boats and a small *barasti* (palm thatch) hut complete with primitive canvas wind tower. The surrounding rooms hold exhibits on Emirati music and folklore, including an entertaining film of Emirati men performing the traditional stick dance.

All this, however, is a mere appetizer for the museum's excellent sequence of underground galleries. Atmosphere is provided by a series of carefully re-created traditional buildings, including various shops—a carpenter's, a potter's, a blacksmith's—all inhabited by

An exhibit in the Dubai Museum.

slightly spooky life-size mannequins posed drinking tea, standing behind the counters of their shops, or hammering away in their workshops. Context and background information are provided by an excellent series of displays covering all relevant cultural bases—Islam, architecture, falconry, dates, wind towers, and so on. ⏱ *45 min. See p 10,* **6**.

2 ★★★ **Bastakiya.** The Bastakiya area (now officially renamed the Al Fahidi Historical Neighborhood) is where you'll get the best sense of what Dubai looked like 50 years ago, with its fascinating tangle of tiny alleyways running between traditional sand-colored houses topped with distinctive wind towers. (See "Wind Towers: The Original A/C" on p 25.) If you want to explore the area at greater length, walking tours of the district are available—see "Cultural Tours in Bastakiya," p 26. ⏱ *15 min. See p 10,* **7**.

3 ★ **Bastakiya Museums.** A number of Bastakiya's old houses have been opened as low-key museums. In almost all cases, the exhibits are extremely modest, but admission is free, and it's a great opportunity to nose around inside some characterful old houses. Easily the most interesting is the **Coffee Museum** (Sat–Thurs 9am–5pm), showcasing an enjoyable collection of antique coffee grinders, roasters, packaging, and other coffee-related paraphernalia dating back to the

A Walk along the Creek

This is far and away my favorite walk in Dubai. Nothing gives as fine a sense of the city's history and maritime past as this breezy and invigorating stroll along the Bur Dubai side of the Creek.

Start at the Shindagha end of the Creek, by the **Diving Village and Heritage Village** (see p 27, **7**), then walk along the waterfront, passing the **Sheikh Saeed Al Maktoum House** (see p 26, **6**). From here, a narrow walkway hugs the waterfront, leading to the entrance to the **Textile Souk** (see p 37, **6**). Head to the far end of the souk, then turn left to reach the waterfront again. Follow the waterfront as it skirts **Bastakiya** (see p 23, **2**) on your right, while further Creek views open up ahead.

early 19th century. You can also sample different types of traditional coffee—Arabic, Turkish, Ethiopian—and there's a cute upstairs cafe.

Continue through Bastakiya toward the Creek to reach the **Coins House** (Sat–Weds 8am–1pm), also worth a look for its well-presented selection of Abbasid, Umayyad, Ottoman, and other Islamic coins dating back to A.D. 79. Close by are the **Philately House** (Sat–Thurs 8:30am–5:30pm), **Architectural Heritage Society** (Sat–Thurs 8am–2pm), and the **Architectural Heritage House**

(Sat–Thurs 8am–2pm), a surprisingly grand mansion with florid painted columns, elaborately cusped arches, and finely carved windows. Follow the signs. 🕐 *45 min. Bastakiya. Free admission.*

4 **XVA**. This is a gorgeous little cafe, hidden away in an old traditional house in the backstreets of Bastakiya. Finding it is half the fun. Choose from a small but tasty selection of (meat-free) Arabian-style salads, sandwiches, and light meals. *Bastakiya.* ☎ *04-353-5383.*

Bastakiya district and wind towers.

Traditional Architecture Museum.

❺ ★ Traditional Architecture Museum. Tucked away close to the Creekfront behind the small Bin Zayed Mosque, this museum gives a good overview of the historic architecture of Dubai and the rest of the UAE. Exhibits cover such topics as the making of mud-brick walls, mangrove-pole roofs, decorative gypsum effects, and many other essential elements of traditional Emirati architecture before the age of the skyscraper. ⓘ *20 min.* *Shindagha.* ☎ *04-392-0093.* *http://bit.ly/TradArchMus. Free admission. Sun–Thurs 7:30am–2:30pm.*

Wind Towers: The Original A/C

Dubai can be hellishly hot, as anyone who has visited the Gulf in the scorching summer months knows. Nowadays, one survives the blasting heat by ducking into air-conditioned malls, restaurants, and hotels. But before universal air-conditioning, the inhabitants of Dubai were forced to come up with novel ways of countering searing summer temperatures.

Their solution was the so-called wind tower (*barjeel*), often described as the world's oldest form of air-conditioning. Each of these elegant towers, which top most of Dubai's old buildings (as well as numerous modern creations constructed in ersatz Arabian style), is open on all four sides. Passing breezes are captured by the tower and funneled downward into the house below, producing a slight but perceptible fall in temperature and encouraging air to circulate—all the more crucial in buildings that were built almost entirely without exterior windows to guard the privacy of those within.

Cultural Tours in Bastakiya

Bastakiya offers a rare opportunity to scratch the surface of Dubai and explore the city's old traditions and history—and to meet local Emiratis as well. **The Sheikh Mohammed Centre for Cultural Understanding** (www.cultures.ae) runs various programs from its office on the edge of the quarter, including walking tours of Bastakiya (Sat, Sun, Tues, and Thurs at 10:30am [9am on Mon]; AED 65) and "cultural" breakfasts, brunches, lunches, and dinners (Sat–Thurs; AED 80–AED 100). You learn something about local traditions of hospitality and have a chat with the center's Emirati staff and local volunteers. Prebooking is required for all these activities; call ☎ **04-353-6666.**

⑥ ★★ Sheikh Saeed Al Maktoum House. Dubai's finest traditional house, the imposing Sheikh Saeed Al Maktoum House commands a wonderful position on the Creekfront as it bends toward the city center. From 1896 to 1958, this was home to the ruling Maktoum family, including four sheikhs. Each added a new wing (plus wind tower) to the original building, gradually expanding it to its current generous dimensions, with dozens of rooms on two stories around a large sandy courtyard.

The house now contains various historical exhibits. Pride of place goes to a fascinating collection of Dubai photographs from the 1940s and 1950s, showing the old town when it was no more than a modest scatter of wind-towered houses and

Ancient Islamic School, Heritage Village.

barasti huts in the desert. You'll also find atmospheric scenes of local life and photographs aboard the boats of pearl divers and fishermen. The pictures—wonderful works of art in their own right—bring home the extraordinary transformation wrought in Dubai in less than a lifetime. ⏱ *30 min. Shindagha.* ☎ *04-226-0286. http:// bit.ly/SaeedHouse. Adults AED 3, children under 10 AED 1. Sat–Thurs 8am–8:30pm; Fri 3–9:30pm.*

❼ ★ Heritage Village & Diving Village. A short walk along the Creek from the Sheikh Saeed Al Maktoum House brings you to the so-called Heritage Village. Inside, low-rise traditional buildings cluster around a large courtyard. Several of those at the back of the courtyard have been turned into shops selling the usual souvenirs and Arabian curios. The whole complex is usually fairly quiet except during the cooler winter months (especially during the Dubai Shopping Festival; see p 101), when there are

sometimes evening performances of traditional Emirati dances and locals set up small stalls selling coffee and traditional snacks.

Just past the Heritage Village lies the smaller and even quieter Diving Village. Again, events are occasionally staged here during the cooler winter months, although most of the time, the atmosphere is fairly sleepy. ⏱ *15 min. Shindagha.* ☎ *04-393-7151. http://bit.ly/Heritage VillageDubai. Free admission. Heritage Village Sun–Thurs 8:30am–10:30pm; Fri–Sat 4:30–10:30pm.* ☎ *04-393-5725. http://bit.ly/DivingVillage. Diving Village Sun–Thurs 8am–10pm; Fri–Sat 4–10pm.*

❽ ★★ Crossroads of Civilizations Museum. Housed in one of Shindagha district's many traditional courtyard houses just a couple of minutes' walk from the Creek, this marvelous little museum is one of the city's hidden gems. Showcasing items from the private collection of Ahmed Obaid Al Mansoori, the museum's exhibits range from

Traditional Arabian Houses

The traditional Arabian house is inward looking, built around a central courtyard that provides fresh air and an enclosed outdoor space for those living within. By contrast, the exterior walls are usually lacking in all but a few small windows to protect the privacy of those within as well as to keep rooms pleasantly cool.

Walls were built using coral stone (*fesht*)—which has excellent natural insulating qualities in the heat of summer—bound together with layers of pounded gypsum, a kind of proto-cement. (Away from the coast, in such places as Al Ain, adobe bricks, made from a mixture of mud and straw, were used instead.) Mangrove poles wound with rope were placed inside walls to help strengthen them and were also used as roofing material, along with planks of Indian teak in more elaborate houses. Walls were built thick and windows small to keep out the heat, while houses were also built close together, perhaps partly for security but also to mutually supply shade.

3rd-century B.C. Mesopotamia to 17th-century China, with assorted Grecian, Roman, Egypt, Seljuk, and Sassanian artifacts along the way. Just about everything on display is of enormous interest, from excellently preserved Sumerian and Babylonian statuettes to wooden mummy masks, Ming porcelain, Islamic astrolabes, and a superb piece of the lavish *kiswa* (a cloth used to cover the Kaaba shrine in Mecca's Grand Mosque) given by Ottoman ruler Suleiman the Magnificent in 1543. ⏱ *45 min. Shindagha.* ☎ *04-393-4440. www. themuseum.ae. AED 30. Sat–Thurs 10am–4pm.*

❾ ★★★ Abra ride over the Creek. Crossing the Creek, drivers can choose between four road bridges or the Shindagha tunnel at the mouth of the estuary. But for pedestrians, there's only one way across: on one of the traditional wooden water taxis, or *abras*, that scuttle across the Creek at all times of day and night.

Boats leave stations on either side of the Creek every few minutes, carrying around 15 passengers per trip. It takes about 5 minutes to make the wonderfully breezy and scenic crossing, with marvelous views of the skyline of central Dubai en route. Picturesque and old-fashioned as they are, the *abras* still play a vital role in Dubai's transportation system, ferrying more than 20 million people across the Creek each year. Around 150 boats are in service, operated by boatmen from India, Bangladesh, Pakistan, and Iran. It remains far and away the cheapest and most enjoyable ride in the city and is worth experiencing several times, by day and night. ⏱ *5 min. AED 1 per person. See p 8,* ❹*, and p 170.*

❿ ★★ Dhow Wharfage. In the heart of the city, the dhow wharfage provides an intriguing link between modern Dubai and its maritime past. True to its entrepreneurial traditions, there's still a thriving import-export trade between Dubai

Dhows of Dubai

The word "dhow" doesn't refer to a particular type of boat. It's actually a generic name for all the various types of wooden boats that formerly sailed between Arabia and East Africa and around the Indian Ocean. These traditionally included a mix of large oceangoing vessels, medium-size dhows for offshore fishing and pearl diving, and small boats (such as *abras*; see p 170) that were used exclusively on the Creek or along the coast. Traditional oceangoing dhows were distinguished by their triangular-shaped lateen sails and by their unusual method of "stitched" construction (planks of wood in the hull were not nailed into place but literally sewn together with various types of cord or fiber). Although nails, rivets, and diesel engines have now replaced the lateen sails and stitched construction, in other respects the boats at the dhow wharfage today have scarcely changed in design for a century.

Traditional abra *ferry.*

and other ports in the region, with dhows taking goods up and down the Gulf to neighboring emirates (particularly Sharjah) as well as farther afield to Pakistan, India, and nearby Iran. At any one time, you'll find dozens of traditional wooden dhows moored along the Creekside while crews load and unload huge piles of merchandise—anything from sacks of spices and slabs of fizzy drinks to TV sets, washing machines, and cars. There's also another dhow wharfage farther south in Deira, with ranks of moored dhows surreally framed against the

Al Ahmadiya School.

Exhibit at Heritage House.

modernist outlines of the National Bank and Dubai Chamber of Commerce. *See p 8,* ❸.

⓫ ★★ Al Ahmadiya School. One of the most enjoyable bolt holes in old Dubai, Al Ahmadiya School offers a peaceful retreat from the bustling souks outside as well as an example of educational egalitarianism in action. This was one of the first schools in Dubai, founded in 1912 by local pearl merchant and philanthropist Sheikh Mohammed bin Dalmouk. Students from all walks of life came to study here, with poor pupils (benefitting from subsidized school fees) rubbing shoulders with wealthy fellow citizens, such as the future Sheikh Rashid, father of modern Dubai. More than 800 pupils were enrolled by 1962, when the overcrowded school relocated to larger premises.

The school is now one of Deira's few surviving traditional buildings:

an intimate two-story structure designed around a small sandy courtyard, with intricately cusped and carved arches on lower and upper levels, topped by a pair of wind towers. The actual exhibits are fairly modest: a couple of old classrooms with rows of wooden chairs and desks, some touch screens outlining the history of the school, and a short but intriguing film. You'll also find the inevitable mannequins in traditional dress, including a rather grumpy-looking elderly teacher admonishing three young pupils with a long wooden cane. ⏱ *15 min. Al Ahmadiya St.* ☎ *04-226-0286. http://bit.ly/ Ahmadiya. Free admission. Sat–Thurs 8am–7:30pm; Fri 2:30–7:30pm.*

⓬ ★ Heritage House. Almost next door to the Al Ahmadiya School, the former home of Sheikh Mohammed bin Dalmouk (the founder of Al Ahmadiya) has been turned into a museum of Emirati life in the old days before oil and tourists turned Dubai upside down.

Originally constructed around 1890, the house was bought in 1910 by Sheikh Dalmouk, one of the city's wealthiest pearl merchants. Carefully re-created traditional interiors give a good idea of what Dubai used to look like and how social life was conducted. There's a sequence of traditional rooms, including men's and ladies *majlis* (meeting rooms in which friends would gather to drink coffee and share news), along with bedrooms, kitchen, bathrooms, and so on, all furnished as they would have been a century or so ago (and populated with the life-size mannequins so beloved by Dubai's museum curators). The building is centered on a large courtyard—a standard feature of Gulf houses—providing air and open space as well as room for a few fruit trees and space for goats and chickens (not to mention children) to exercise in privacy. ⏱ *15 min. Al Ahmadiya St.* ☎ *04-226-0286. http://bit.ly/Heritage HouseDubai. Free admission. Sat– Thurs 8am–7:30pm; Fri 2:30–7:30pm.*

Go to nearby Al Ras metro station and catch a train to Creek station, at the end of the Green Line.

⓭ ★ **Dow-building yard.** For another fleeting glimpse into Dubai's historic maritime traditions, head to the old dhow-building yard at Jaddaf. Exiting the Creek metro station, you'll see the yard directly ahead next to the water, usually with the wooden shells of a few dhows in various stages of completion along the shore. Be aware that it's a working boatyard rather than a tourist attraction, although the (mainly Indian) dhow-builders and carpenters are usually happy for visitors to have a look around and watch them at work—a rare chance to see firsthand the highly skilled and labor-intensive efforts that go into the making of a traditional Arabian dhow. ⏱ *20 min. Jaddaf.*

Now take another taxi (around AED 30) south to Jumeirah. Go past Safa Park, then head south along the Jumeirah Road, past Jumeirah Beach Park (closed until late 2016) until you reach the Emirates Islamic Bank. Turn left down 17 Street (aka Al Mehemal Street) to:

⓮ ★ **Majlis Ghorfat Um Al Sheef.** Marooned amid the endless identikit villas of southern Jumeirah, the quaint little Ghorfat Um Al Sheef offers an interesting throwback to older and simpler times. The *majlis* (meeting house) was built in 1955 and used by the visionary Sheikh Rashid, the father of modern Dubai, as a summer retreat at a time when Jumeirah was no more than a small fishing village. The small, quaint two-story building is constructed in traditional fashion with coral and gypsum walls and wooden roofs. The *majlis* itself is upstairs, its walls lined with cushions on which the great and good of Dubai would once have reposed while plotting the city's dramatic transformation during the 1960s. ⏱ *20 min. 17th St., off Jumeirah Rd.* ☎ *04-226-0286. http://bit.ly/Ghorfat. AED 3, children under 6 AED 1. Sun–Thurs 8:30am– 10:30pm; Fri–Sat 3–10pm.*

Souks

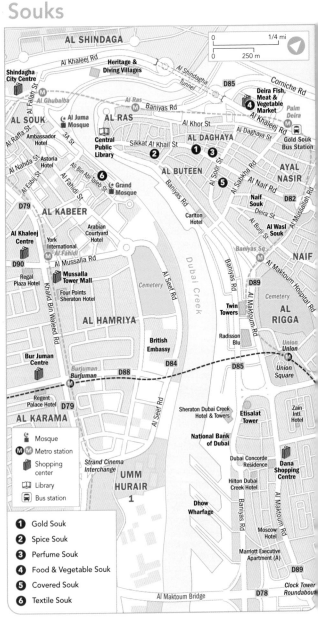

0	1/4 mi
0	250 m

AL SHINDAGA

Al Khaleej Rd

Heritage & Diving Villages

Al Shindagha Tunnel

D85

Corniche Rd

Deira Fish, Meat & Vegetable Market ❹

Palm Deira

Shindagha City Centre 🏬

Ⓜ Al Ghubaiba

Baniyas Rd

Ⓜ Al Ras

Al Khor St

Al Khaleej Rd

Al Daghaya St

Gold Souk Bus Station 🚌

AL SOUK

❋ Al Juma Mosque

3A St

AL RAS

Sikkat Al Khail St

AL DAGHAYA

Al Sood St

Al Sabkha Rd

AYAL NASIR

Al Raffa St

Al Falah St

Ambassador Hotel

📖 Central Public Library

❶ ❸

❷

Al Nahda St

Astoria Hotel

AL BUTEEN

Al Naif Rd

D82

Al Esbij St

Ali Bin Abi Taleb St

❻

❋ Grand Mosque

Baniyas Rd

❺

Naif Souk

Deira St

D79

Al Fahidi St

AL KABEER

Arabian Courtyard Hotel

Al Fahidi

Carlton Hotel

Al Burj St

Al Wasi Souk

NAIF

Al Khaleej Centre 🏬

Ⓜ York International

Al Mussalla Rd

Baniyas Sq

Al Maktoum Hospital Rd

Al Mussallah Rd

D90

🕌 Mussalla Tower Mall

Four Points Sheraton Hotel

Al Seef Rd

Baniyas Rd

D89

Al Maktoum Rd

Cemetery

AL RIGGA

Regal Plaza Hotel

Khalid Bin Waleed Rd

AL HAMRIYA

Dubai Creek

Twin Towers

Radisson Blu

D85

Union Ⓜ Union

Union Square

Bur Juman Centre 🏬

British Embassy

D84

Burjuman

Ⓜ Burjuman

D88

Regent Palace Hotel

D79

AL KARAMA

Al Seef Rd

Sheraton Dubai Creek Hotel & Towers

Etisalat Tower

Zain Intl. Hotel

National Bank of Dubai

Strand Cinema Interchange

UMM HURAIR 1

Dubai Concorde Residence

Hilton Dubai Creek Hotel

Dana Shopping Centre 🏬

Al Maktoum Rd

Dhow Wharfage

Baniyas Rd

Moscow Hotel

Marriott Executive Apartment (A)

D89

Al Maktoum Bridge

D78

Clock Tower Roundabout

Legend:
- 🕌 Mosque
- Ⓜ Ⓜ Metro station
- 🏬 Shopping center
- 📖 Library
- 🚌 Bus station

❶ Gold Souk
❷ Spice Souk
❸ Perfume Souk
❹ Food & Vegetable Souk
❺ Covered Souk
❻ Textile Souk

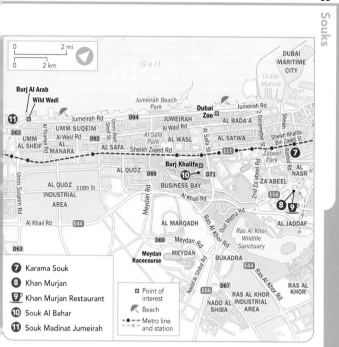

7 Karama Souk

8 Khan Murjan

9 Khan Murjan Restaurant

10 Souk Al Bahar

11 Souk Madinat Jumeirah

☐ Point of interest

🏖 Beach

–•–•– Metro line and station

Dubai's massive wealth was built on trade rather than oil, and for all the modern city's mega-malls and designer shops, the frills-free souks of old Dubai still give you the best sense of the city's commercial pulse and mercantile traditions. Much of the old city center remains a fascinating maze of interconnecting bazaars.
START: **Gold Souk, Deira. Taxi or Green Line Metro to Al Ras station.**

1 ★★ **Gold Souk.** It was gold rather than oil that powered the economy of old Dubai. Severe restrictions on the import of gold in Iran and India during most of the last century encouraged numerous traders to set up shop here, and even today the gold trade generates enormous sums of cash. In 2012, gold sales contributed almost $70 billion to the city's economy, accounting for 25% of the world's annual gold trade (with diamonds worth an additional $40–45 billion). Nowhere is the city's love affair with the precious metal more evident

than in the Gold Souk, with 300 or so shops clustered along a quaint, wooden-roofed main drag and spilling into the surrounding streets. The sheer quantity of gold on display is staggering, each window crammed with gleaming necklaces, rings, and bangles. It's estimated that, at any one time, the shops here contain around 10n tons of gold.

The Gold Souk is still the best place to see Dubai's multicultural commercial machine in top gear, thronged with a cosmopolitan array of shoppers from Africa, Europe,

Gold Souk.

and Asia. Streams of Indian touts sell designer fakes, their constant offers of "Copy watch? Copy bag?" providing the souk's distinctive soundtrack.

For more on shopping for gold here and elsewhere in Dubai, see the box below. ⏱ *30 min. See p 7,* ❶.

❷ ★★★ **Spice Souk.** Dubai's Spice Souk is the old city at its most captivating and authentic. Tucked away behind the Gold Souk, the souk has dozens of diminutive shops, packed into a small grid of narrow alleyways with overflowing sacks of herbs and spices piled outside. The souk is famed for its

Shopping for Gold in Dubai

Lenient import duties and generous government subsidies mean Dubai is one of the cheapest places in the world to buy gold. The obvious place to start shopping is the Deira **Gold Souk** (p 7, ❶); it's also worth exploring the streets north of here and along the Corniche opposite the Gold Souk bus station. You might also want to visit the **Gold and Diamond Park** (p 66) near the Mall of the Emirates.

Gold jewelry is sold by weight rather than workmanship—a piece is tossed on the scales and the cost calculated according to the day's gold price (which is displayed in all shops). At that point, you can start bargaining. Most gold shops in Dubai are run by Indians, who are well practiced in the art of bartering. Expect to knock off around a third of the initial quoted price, depending on how determined you are and how desperate the shopkeeper is for a sale.

frankincense, mainly from Oman and Yemen and sold in a half dozen different varieties—little lumps of reddish or honey-colored crystalline matter. You can also buy cheap frankincense burners here. Other local specialties include rose petals (used to make a flowery herbal tea), dried lemons (used in many Iranian dishes), and Iranian saffron, one of the world's most expensive spices. You'll also find plentiful supplies of everyday spices as well as other products ranging from alum—a clear rock crystal used as a natural skin balm and aftershave—to so-called natural Viagra. ⏱ *30 min.* See p 7, ❷.

❸ ★ **Perfume Souk.** Although there's no actual souk building, the so-called Perfume Souk comprises a cluster of shops along Sikkat Al Khail Road and up Al Soor Street at the east end of the Gold Souk. Look for lines of shops with windows full of beautiful little glass perfume bottles, many of them collectables in their own right. The

Dates in the Spice Souk.

shops here sell a mix of Western perfumes (not necessarily genuine) along with richly aromatic local scents, including oil-based attar perfumes with such characteristic ingredients as the highly prized oud (derived from the fragrant agar-wood, or aloe). ⏱ *10 min. Sikkat Al Khail Rd. & Al Soor St. Most shops 10am–10pm; some closed 1–4pm.*

❹ ★★ **Food & Vegetable Souk.** Marooned on the far side of the busy Deira Corniche road (walk

Spices on sale in the Spice Souk.

Fish salesman showing the catch of the day.

over the footbridge near the Gold Souk bus station), the large, open-sided Food and Vegetable Souk is where Dubai's foodies and restaurateurs go to source the city's freshest and finest ingredients. The souk is divided into three main sections: the meat souk, with its dangling carcasses; the salty fish souk, with all sorts of fish and seafood laid out on slabs; and the fruit and vegetable souk, with colorful piles of produce heaped on small stalls. The last section is also where you'll find the souk's considerable number of date-sellers seated behind huge piles of succulent fruit (see "Save the Date!" below). Early morning is

Save the Date!

Dates are an integral part of Arabian life. Cultivated in ancient Egypt and Mesopotamia, they provided one of the key means of sustenance for the region's Bedouin nomads. Dates keep well in the heat and provide a concentrated sugar rush as well as high levels of vitamin C. Before the discovery of oil, they were the region's most important export.

Dozens of different types of date range widely in size and color from dark brown to pale honey. The best are treasured and savored by local connoisseurs, much as fine wines are in France. Although dates are grown all over the Gulf, expert date-fanciers consider those produced in Saudi Arabia to be generally the finest.

the best time to visit, when the fish market is in full swing. Things are usually a lot quieter in the afternoon, although there's still plenty to see. ⏱ *20 min. Al Khaleej Rd. (Deira Corniche). Daily 7:30am–11pm.*

⑤ ★ Covered Souk. East of the Perfume Souk down Sikkat Al Khail Road is Deira's rambling Covered Souk, as it's known (even though it's not actually covered at all). This draws only a fraction of the visitors of the Gold and Spice Souks, but it has its own particular charm, with tiny alleyways lined with shoebox shops selling an eclectic array of low-grade toys, kitchenware, clothing, and cloth. The souk is easily the best place to get lost in Deira—you probably will, whether you want to or not. It rambles for a considerable distance southeast to the Al Sabkha bus station and then continues on the far side of the road

Shopping in the ancient covered textile souk Bur Dubai in the old city center of Dubai.

(where it's known as Al Wasl Souk, site of electronics and mobile phone shops). Things get livelier after dark, when the area becomes a sea of multinational visitors ranging from Indians, Africans, and Russians to the occasional tourist (usually lost) and local Emirati women hunting for cut-price *abayas* (traditional black gowns). ⏱ *20 min. Btw. Sikkat Al Khail Rd. & Baniyas Sq. Most shops open 10am–10pm, some closed 1–4pm.*

⑥ ★★ Textile Souk. The centerpiece of Bur Dubai is the Textile Souk (also known as the Bur Dubai Old Souk)—the best-looking traditional bazaar in the city, with carefully restored coral and gypsum buildings lined up under a traditional wooden roof. It's blissfully cool and shady even in the noonday heat. Look up and you'll see the remains of elaborate latticed windows, old-fashioned Islamic lamps hanging from the roof, and finely decorated wooden beams. (At the far end of the souk, check out a fine alleyway flanked by no fewer than eight wind towers.) It's one of Dubai's prettiest museum pieces, although the flavor of the place is more Indian than Arabian. Nearly all the shops are owned by Bur Dubai's long-established group of subcontinental traders, who sell flowery fabrics alongside cheap clothes and tacky souvenirs. Alarmingly misshapen toy camels and cheap coffee pots come standard, although a couple of stalls do sell more authentic Arabian antiques.

It's also worth wandering through the lanes immediately behind the main Textile Souk, where you'll find other traditional buildings, some of them with graceful wooden balconies and decorative stone flourishes. ⏱ *20 min. See p 9,* ⑤.

Now take a taxi south (about AED 15) or catch the Green Line metro from the Al Fahidi station to the ADCB station (on the Red Line— change at the BurJuman station) to reach:

❼ ★ Karama Souk. Ersatz Arabian souks, pastiche palaces, faux festivals . . . spend enough time in Dubai, and you might begin to think that faking it is what this city does best. Nothing, however, beats a visit to the original home of the "authentic" Dubai fake, Karama Souk. This city institution offers a fascinating insight into the commercial counterfeiting that still underpins large parts of Dubai's black economy.

Located in the low-income, predominantly Indian suburb of Karama, the souk itself is nothing but an open-air concrete shell full of shops manned by persistent swarms of traders who, depending on your point of view, are either an entertaining part of the Karama scene or a consummate pain in the backside. The hilariously incompetent designer fakes of former years (think Addibas, Hugo Bros, and Channel) are a thing of the past, due to half-hearted government crackdowns, but the underlying ethos remains unchanged. Shelves groan under the weight of borderline brand names and suspicious sportswear, all retailing for a fraction of the price of the real thing, while shopkeepers assail visitors with promises of copy watches, bags, sunglasses, and DVDs.
🕐 *30 min. Karama. Most shops open 10am–1pm, some closed 1–4pm.*

Now take a taxi south (about AED 12) or catch the metro from the ADCB station (Red Line) to the Dubai Healthcare City station (on

Khan Murjan Souk.

the Green Line—change at BurJuman) to the Wafi complex.

❽ ★★ Khan Murjan. Attached to the Egyptian-themed Wafi shopping center (p 69), the Khan Murjan bazaar is one of Dubai's most eye-catching Arabian-style developments. Built on two underground levels, this so-called legendary 14th-century souk (the original is in Baghdad) is divided into four quarters—Egyptian, Turkish, Moroccan, and Syrian—centered around a bustling courtyard restaurant. It might sound like a recipe for pan-Arabian kitsch of the worst kind, but the whole thing has been done with such tremendous panache that it's hard not to be impressed. It's worth a visit, if only to admire the sumptuously decorated inlaid marble floors and walls, intricately worked wooden balconies and doors, and huge Moroccan lanterns. A superb array of top-end handicraft and souvenir shops (p 62) also makes it a great (if relatively pricey) place to shop. ⓘ *1 hr. Wafi, Oud Metha.* ☎ *04-324-4555. www.wafi. com. Daily 10am–10pm; Thurs–Fri until midnight.*

9 **Khan Murjan.** This beautifully decorated courtyard restaurant, constantly packed with local and expat Arabs, has a vibrant atmosphere and—despite the kitsch concept—a strange sort of Arabian authenticity. Stop here for a good range of pan-Arabian food, including classic Egyptian, Iranian, and Moroccan dishes. *Khan Murjan Souk, Oud Metha.* ☎ *04-327-9795.*

Now take a taxi south (around AED 20) or catch the metro from the Dubai Healthcare City station (Green Line) to the Burj Khalifa/ Dubai Mall station (Red Line— change at BurJuman). Walk to the far end of the Dubai Mall to reach the:

10 ★ **Souk Al Bahar.** At the back of the huge Dubai Mall, the low-key Souk Al Bahar lacks the Orientalist dazzle and fantasy of Khan Murjan and the Souk Madinat Jumeirah, but it compensates with a prime location overlooking the spectacular Dubai Fountain (see p 13, **12**) and facing the soaring Burj Khalifa (see p 12, **11**). The views from the souk's exterior terraces and restaurants are among the most memorable in the city, while its vaguely Moroccan-looking interior offers a fair spread of handicraft (and other) shops, along with several attractive restaurants—a nice spot for a meal, coffee, or sundowner. ⓘ *20 min. Downtown Dubai.* ☎ *04-362-7011. www.soukal bahar.ae. Sat–Thurs 10am–10pm; Fri 2–10pm.*

Now take another taxi south (about AED 35) to:

11 ★★★ **Souk Madinat Jumeirah.** Part of the enormous Madinat Jumeirah complex (p 15, **3**), this was the first—and is perhaps still the best—of Dubai's modern Arabian-style souks. The inside of the souk feels more or less Moroccan, with narrow alleyways topped with ornate wooden roofs and hung with multicolored lanterns. Near the main entrance, a cluster of upscale curio and souvenir shops spills their contents into the passageways in a picturesque clutter of Arabian and Asian artifacts—anything from oversize antique coffee pots to bronze statues of Hindu gods. Outside at the back of the souk, beautiful walkways and terraces meander around the Madinat's waterways, with stunning views over the complex's Arabian-style hotels and over to the futuristic Burj al Arab. It's touristy but undeniably fun, particularly after dark, when huge crowds descend on the restaurants and bars. ⓘ *1 hr.* ☎ *04-366-8888. www.madinatjumeirah.com. Daily 10am–11pm.*

Souk Madinat Jumeirah.

Religious Dubai

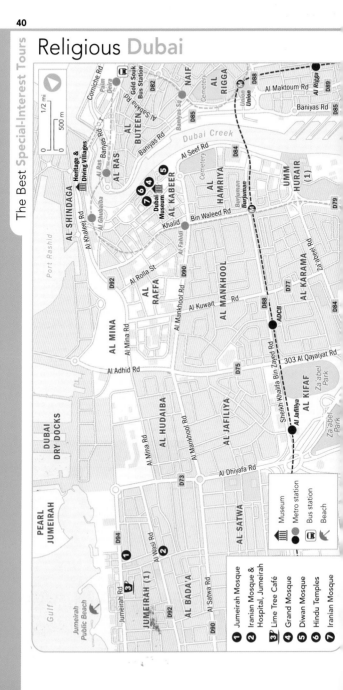

1 Jumeirah Mosque
2 Iranian Mosque & Hospital, Jumeirah
3 Lime Tree Café
4 Grand Mosque
5 Diwan Mosque
6 Hindu Temples
7 Iranian Mosque

Museum
Metro station
Bus station
Beach

Religion in Dubai means essentially one thing: Islam. For all its modern accouterments, Dubai is still a traditional place. In older parts of the city, the spires of minarets still outnumber high-rise towers, while five times a day the air fills with calls to prayer from hundreds of mosques. START: Jumeirah Mosque, Jumeirah Road opposite Palm Strip shopping mall.

① ★★ Jumeirah Mosque.
Dominating the northern end of the Jumeirah Road, the majestic Jumeirah Mosque is one of the largest and finest in the city, built in traditional Fatimid (Egyptian) style in 1979, with a pair of slender minarets and a trio of domes decorated with fine geometrical carvings. Popular morning tours of the Jumeirah Mosque offer a rare chance for non-Muslims to peek around the inside of one of the city's mosques. It's well worth visiting just for a look at the richly decorated interior, although the real point of the tour is cultural rather than architectural. An entertaining local Emirati guide unravels some little-understood (by non-Muslims, at least) customs of

Islamic worship before answering questions on any aspect of Islamic and Emirati life and beliefs. If you've been hankering to know how local Emirati men keep their robes so white, now's your chance to find out. Visitors are requested to dress conservatively; women should cover their hair. 🕐 *1 hr.* 📞 *04-353-6666. www.cultures.ae. Tours Sat–Thurs at 10am. AED 10, free for children under 12 (no pre-booking necessary). Modest dress required (traditional dress can be borrowed on arrival at the mosque).*

② ★ Iranian Mosque & Hospital, Jumeirah. A short walk from the Jumeirah Mosque, this beautiful Iranian mosque has a striking

The Jumeirah Mosque.

The Iranian Shia Mosque in Bur Dubai.

facade and dome covered in richly decorated blue tiles. The Iranian Hospital on the other side of the road sports some similarly impressive tiling. ⏱ *10 min. Al Wasl Rd.*

3 **Lime Tree Café.** Join the local expat ladies-who-lunch at this classic Jumeirah cafe, serving a delicious array of sandwiches, salads, and cakes. *Jumeirah Rd., next to Jumeirah Mosque.* ☎ *04-325-6325. www.thelimetreecafe.com.*

Now take a taxi north from the Iranian Mosque to Bur Dubai and the Grand Mosque (around AED 15).

4 ★ **Grand Mosque.** Close to the Creekside, between the Textile Souk (p 9, **5**) and the Dubai Museum, the imposing Grand Mosque is one of the largest in the UAE, with space for more than 1,000 worshippers. The original Grand Mosque was built in 1900 but demolished in 1960 to make way for a new mosque. This second mosque was, in turn, demolished in 1998,

and the present building (which apparently follows the style of the original 1900 building) was constructed in its place. It's an impressive, if rather austere, edifice, its size unrelieved by much in the way of decoration apart from a Quranic flourish over the main entrance. The bumpy roofline is topped with 9 large domes and 45 smaller ones—not to mention a 70m (230-ft.) minaret, the tallest in Dubai, which dominates the skyline of the old city. ⏱ *10 min. See p 37,* **6**.

5 ★ **Diwan Mosque.** Attached to the Diwan, the original seat of Dubai's government, the distinctive Diwan Mosque provides another Creekside landmark, its snowy-white minaret competing for eye-space with that of the nearby Grand Mosque. Although not as big as the Grand Mosque, in many ways it's a more appealing building, with its unusually flattened onion dome and slender minaret. Non-Muslims are allowed inside the mosque during the walking tours of Bastakiya organized by the Sheikh Mohammed

Grand Mosque.

Muslim Mores in Dubai

Dubai may seem completely Westernized and liberal, but don't be fooled—anything *doesn't* go here. Despite a massive influx of Western tourists and expats, the city is anxious to preserve its Islamic traditions. Misdemeanors, such as public displays of drunkenness or nudity or the slightest suspicion of drug use or possession (p 167), are likely to get you into serious trouble. Foreigners are also regularly prosecuted for making "offensive" gestures (such as raising one or two fingers) that would pass almost unnoticed in the West. If you want a stronger taste of the region's austere religious traditions, visit the emirate of Sharjah (see p 128), just 10km down the road, where hardline Islamic laws include a total prohibition on alcohol as well as strict rules concerning relations between unmarried couples. The upside of all this is that Dubai and the rest of the UAE remain exceptionally safe, with extremely low crime levels as well as a healthy tradition of religious and cultural tolerance.

Centre for Cultural Understanding (see p 26). ⏱ *5 min.*

❻ ★★ Hindu Temples. Tucked away at the far end of the Textile Souk behind the Grand Mosque (❹) is one of Dubai's most intriguing and unexpected sights, a tiny alleyway (sometimes called "Hindi Lane") lined with quaint Indian stalls selling all manner of religious paraphernalia.

The focal point of the lane is its improvised Hindu-cum-Sikh temple, one of the very few in Dubai. The temple is actually built upstairs over the shops: Follow one of the staircases up to the Hindu temple, a simple little affair with improvised shrines to Shiva and other deities. A further set of steps leads up to a small Sikh temple (*gurudwara*)—basically just another room with a modest shrine.

A second, slightly larger and more conventional Hindu temple, the Shri Nathji—dedicated to the blue-skinned god Krishna—can be found at the end of the lane, directly behind the Grand Mosque. There's

no sign—just follow the crowds of worshippers carrying offerings of fruit and flowers. ⏱ *20 min. Bur Dubai. The temples are generally open daily 6am–noon & 5–10pm.*

❼ ★ Iranian Mosque. Just behind the Textile Souk, Bur Dubai's beautiful Iranian Shia Mosque is another of the old city's hidden treasures. The mosque's entire facade and onion-shaped dome are covered in a riot of colorful Persian faience tiles: an azure blue background decorated in intricate floral patterns and curvilinear swirls and flourishes, picked out in yellow, red, green, and white. Rosettes are embellished with elegant Quranic calligraphic flourishes.

Slightly farther down the road (opposite the Time Palace Hotel) you'll also find another Iranian Shia Mosque—a plain sand-colored structure, but with an eye-catching array of small, bulbous domes adorning its flat roof. ⏱ *10 min. Bur Dubai.*

The Best Special-Interest Tours

Dubai for Kids

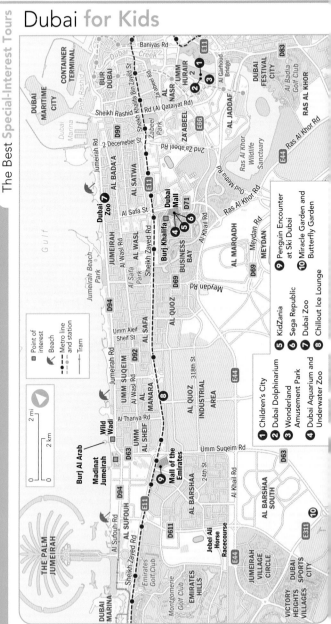

- **1** Children's City
- **2** Dubai Dolphinarium
- **3** Wonderland Amusement Park
- **4** Dubai Aquarium and Underwater Zoo
- **5** KidZania
- **6** Sega Republic
- **7** Dubai Zoo
- **8** Chillout Ice Lounge
- **9** Penguin Encounter at Ski Dubai
- **10** Miracle Garden and Butterfly Garden

- Point of interest
- Beach
- Metro line and station
- Tram

0 — 2 mi
0 — 2 km

Dubai is brilliant for kids—although entrance prices can put quite a dent in the family budget. The beach is the main draw, with a range of watery activities; other attractions include water parks, skiing, ice skating, and dolphinariums, plus traditional pursuits, such as desert safaris and *abra* rides. All the big malls provide air-conditioned, child-oriented diversions as well.

1 ★★ Children's City. A vivid red-yellow-and-blue construction in the middle of Creek Park, Children's City is a well-thought-out piece of edutainment. It's a kind of kids' museum-cum-activity center, with lots of interactive exhibits and touch screens covering all sorts of subjects—science, space travel, computers, the human body, nature, and international culture— plus a planetarium and play area for toddlers. *Creek Park, Gate #1. ☎ 04-334-0808. www.childrencity. ae. Adults AED 15, children ages 2–15 AED 10, family ticket AED 40 plus AED 5 per person entrance fee for Creek Park. Sat–Thurs 9am–8pm; Fri 3–9pm.*

2 ★★ Dubai Dolphinarium. Very close to Children's City, the Dubai Dolphinarium is another guaranteed kid-pleaser. The main draws are entertaining shows in a big state-of-the-art auditorium featuring six resident bottle-nose dolphins and six seals, which have been trained to perform all the usual acrobatics. You can also swim with the dolphins (advance reservations required). "Exotic bird shows" feature parrots, cockatoos, and so on daily at 12:15pm, 2pm, 4:15pm, and 7:15pm (50 AED, or 30 AED for children ages 2–11). *Next to Gate #1, Creek Park, Garhoud. ☎ 04-336- 9773. www.dubaidolphinarium.ae. Adults AED 120 standard/140 VIP; children ages 2–11 AED 70 stan- dard/100 VIP, plus AED 5 per person entrance fee for Creek Park. Shows Mon–Sat 11am, 3pm & 5pm.*

3 ★ Wonderland. One of the city's older attractions, Wonderland is a bit dated but still a decent place for some old-fashioned family fun. It's divided into two sections. The **Theme Park** (the largest in the UAE) has more than 30 rides and attractions, including a roller- coaster, roto-shake, bumper boats and cars, and the noisy mega-disco. The second section, the **Splashland** water park, offers a modest but enjoyable selection of rides, water- slides, rapids, and pools. It's not in the same league as the Wild Wadi (p 82) and Aquaventure water parks (p 80), but the entrance price is much more reasonable. *Creek Park (entrance by Garhoud Bridge). ☎ 04-324-3222. www. wonderlanduae.com. AED 150, chil- dren ages 2–4 AED 75 (discounts sometimes available if you book online). Theme park daily 10am–mid- night; water park daily 10am–8pm.*

4 ★★ Dubai Aquarium and Underwater Zoo. Situated in the Dubai Mall, the Dubai Aquarium doesn't quite know whether it's a serious marine attraction or a glori- fied piece of mall furniture. Its most impressive feature is the huge **Aquarium** dominating the mall's entrance, with its extraordinary dis- play of gliding rays, scary sharks, enormous (and ugly) groupers, and colorful swirls of smaller fish. You can buy a ticket to walk through the 50m-long underwater Aquarium Tunnel, where rays swoop over your head and a shark's toothy grin may loom within an inch of your face.

Other Child-Friendly Attractions

As well as the places listed in this section, numerous other fab attractions around Dubai will appeal to kids. These include **Ski Dubai** (p 80), **Wild Wadi** water park (p 82), **Aquaventure** water park (p 80), the **Lost Chambers** (p 19) and the **Dubai Ice Rink** (p 79). Families who are also traveling to Abu Dhabi should know about the vast **Ferrari World** theme park (see p 151) and **Yas Waterworld** water park (see p 151), both on Abu Dhabi's Yas Island.

Kids will also love the **Wonder Bus** tour (the bus that becomes a boat—see p 170), or they might enjoy a double-decker bus ride around the city with the **Big Bus Company** (p 170). And what child could resist an *abra* ride on the Creek (p 8, ④) or a desert safari (p 20, ⑤)?

For information on activities at Dubai's best beaches and parks, see p 77 and 79.

However, you won't really see much more in the tunnel than you can from the free viewing area outside. The **Underwater Zoo** upstairs is home to piranhas, weird-looking stonefish, poison-dart frogs, octopuses, and the zoo's star resident, King Croc, a 5m-long saltie from Australia. Various other activities include glass-bottom boat tours, a "behind-the-scenes" tour, and visits to see croc- and shark-

Aquarium in Dubai Mall.

Ice rink in Dubai Mall.

feeding, plus assorted diving and snorkeling packages. *Dubai Mall. www.thedubaiaquarium.com.* ☎ *04-448-5200. Packages AED 100–AED 250. Sun–Wed 10am–11pm; Thurs–Sat 10am–midnight.*

❺ ★★ KidZania. One of Dubai's most novel children's attractions, KidZania is a kind of miniature city where kids get to be grown-ups for the day. Little ones get the chance to role-play more than 80 adult jobs—firefighter, journalist, doctor, police officer, and so on—dressing up and performing tasks associated with their chosen job while earning "KidZo" currency with which to play and shop as they go. *Dubai Mall.* ☎ *04-448-5222. www.kidzania.ae. AED 95, children ages 4–16 AED 140, ages 2–3 AED 95, free for kids 1 & under. Sun–Thurs 10am–10pm; Fri–Sat 10am–11pm.*

❻ ★ Sega Republic. Noisy techno-fun is the order of the day at this Sega-inspired indoor mini-theme park, with assorted attractions—bumper cars, rope-climbs, jungle rollercoaster, and so forth—to get the adrenaline pumping, along with a vast array of arcade and video games. *Dubai Mall.* ☎ *04-448-8484. www.segarepublic.com. Individual attractions AED 15–AED 30; all-inclusive passes from AED 175. Sun–Wed 10am–11pm; Thurs–Sat 10am–1am.*

❼ ★ Dubai Zoo. Probably the most dated attraction in the city, the Dubai Zoo is home to a random menagerie of animals including giraffes, lions, chimps, and bears as well as some examples of rare Arabian wildlife, such as Arabian wolves and oryx. Kids will probably enjoy it, although the zoo's impossibly overcrowded conditions, with animals penned in small cages behind heavy double-mesh wire fences, are far from ideal. *Jumeirah Beach Rd., Jumeirah.* ☎ *04-349-6444. Admission AED 2. Wed–Mon 10am–5:30pm; closed Tues.*

Child-Friendly Hotels

The beach hotels are the place to go if you have kids. Many of the larger places (including all five listed below) have well-staffed children's clubs featuring free daily entertainment programs. Clubs usually accept children ages 4 and up, and parents are free to drop off their kids in the club, so long as the parents remain somewhere in the hotel. Under 4s are sometimes accepted if parents stay in attendance. Babysitting services (added charge) are also available in most of the big hotels.

Here are five of the best places for children:

Atlantis (p 18, ❷). This kitsch mega-resort has a great range of kids' attractions, including **Dolphin Bay** (p 81), **Aquaventure** (p 80), and the **Lost Chambers** (p 19, ❸). All are free to hotel guests.

Jumeirah Beach Hotel (p 57, ⓫). Probably the best all-around family hotel in Dubai, with a superb beach, pools, and brilliantly equipped kids' club. Guests get unlimited complimentary entry to **Wild Wadi** water park (p 82).

Le Royal Méridien (p 123). Huge grounds, an enormous beach, watersports, and plenty of kids' facilities.

Mina A'Salam (p 124). Well-set-up resort hotel with a big beach, pools, and watersports. Guests get unlimited complimentary entry to **Wild Wadi** water park (p 82).

Sheraton Jumeirah Beach (p 126). Smaller and less well-equipped than the places above, but very family-friendly and usually the cheapest of the beachfront resorts.

❽ ★ **Chillout Ice Lounge.** Likely to appeal more to younger kids, "the Middle East's first sub-zero lounge" consists of a smallish room at a temperature of –6°C, furnished with ice seats, sculptures, and myriad icicles dangling from the ceiling. It's a novel idea,

Tortoise at Dubai Zoo.

Miracle Garden.

although there's nothing really to do once you're inside except admire the decor. Admission includes a hot drink and the use of thermal clothing during your visit. *Times Square Center, Sheikh Zayed Rd. ☎ 04-341-8121. www.chilloutindubai.com. AED 75, children ages 5–12 AED 35. Sat–Wed 10am–10pm; Thurs–Fri 10am–midnight.*

❾ ★★ Ski Dubai Penguin Encounter. The world's first interactive penguin encounter gives kids (and, indeed, adults) a rare chance to get within a flipper's width of Antarctica's cutest creatures. The 40-minute group encounters include close-up underwater viewing and the chance to interact with at least two resident Gentoo and King Penguins. More exclusive small-group interactions (minimum four people) are also available. The cheesy but fun "March of the Penguins" can be seen at various times of day (check website for latest timings) for free from the mall viewing area. *Mall of the Emirates. www.skidxb.com. Daily noon–9pm. AED*

175; "exclusive" encounters AED 500. No cameras (although official souvenir photos of your visit are available to buy). Warm clothing & gloves provided.*

❿ ★★ Miracle Garden and Butterfly Garden. The world's largest flower garden (with some 45 million plants), the eye-popping Miracle Garden offers a horticultural fantasy likely to appeal to the whole family. It's one of Dubai's most colorfully surreal sights, filled with striped flower beds, fanciful topiary, and outlandish floral designs, all changed annually. Past creations have included a display of flower-festooned cars and an 18m-high replica of the Burj Khalifa. The attached Butterfly Garden is home to around 15,000 of the delicate winged creatures in nine climate-controlled domes. *Dubailand. ☎ 04-422-8902. www.dubaimiraclegarden.com. Miracle Garden Sun–Thurs 9am–9pm; Fri–Sat 9am–11pm, closed late May to Sept. AED 30. www.dubaibutterflygarden.com. Butterfly Garden daily 9am–6pm. AED 50.*

Futuristic Dubai

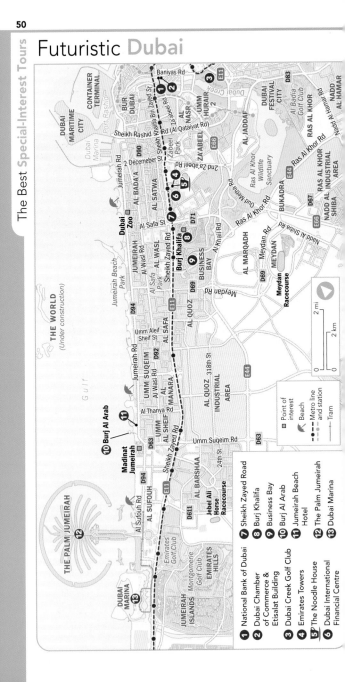

1 National Bank of Dubai
2 Dubai Chamber of Commerce & Etisalat Building
3 Dubai Creek Golf Club
4 Emirates Towers
5 The Noodle House
6 Dubai International Financial Centre
7 Sheikh Zayed Road
8 Burj Khalifa
9 Business Bay
10 Burj Al Arab
11 Jumeirah Beach Hotel
12 The Palm Jumeirah
13 Dubai Marina

Whatever Dubai does, it does to excess, and nowhere is this more evident than in the city's futuristic architectural creations. The surreal skyline may look like the doodlings of a mad scientist, but few can resist its distinctive array of good, bad, and downright weird. START: **Baniyas Road. Taxi or Green Line Metro to Baniyas Station.**

❶ ★★ National Bank of Dubai. Dominating the eastern end of the Deira Creekside, the National Bank of Dubai was one of the first of Dubai's modernist landmarks. At 125m (410 ft.) high, this was the fifth-tallest building in Dubai when originally completed, and although it's since been dwarfed by more recent projects, it remains one of Dubai's most attractive modern buildings. The huge curved front, covered in a gold-colored glass curtain wall, evokes the shape of a wind-filled sail; it also serves as an enormous mirror reflecting the Creek below—particularly magical as it catches the rays of the setting sun (best seen from the Bur Dubai

National Bank of Dubai building on Dubai Creek.

side of the Creek). ⏱ *10 min. to view outside. Baniyas Rd.*

❷ ★ Dubai Chamber of Commerce & Etisalat Building. Right next door to the National Bank is another of Deira's signature modern constructions, the **Dubai Chamber of Commerce** (1995). Probably the most minimalist building in the UAE, it seems to be made entirely out of black glass, topped by a distinctively abstract triangular roof—particularly striking (and photogenic) when seen framed by the masts of the old wooden boats moored at the nearby Dhow Wharfage (p 8, ❸).

Close by is another well-known Dubai skyscraper, the **Etisalat Tower** (1986), designed by Canadian architect Arthur Erikson. It's instantly recognizable, thanks to the unusual globe, looking rather like a supersize golf ball, perched on its roof. That iconic golf ball has become the architectural symbol of Etisalat across the region, with similar balls now topping the company's other Dubai building at the north end of Sheikh Zayed Road as well as the two Etisalat buildings in Abu Dhabi. ⏱ *10 min. to view outside. Baniyas Rd.*

Take a taxi (about AED 12) to:

❸ ★★ Dubai Creek Golf Club. One of Dubai's oldest modernist icons, the relatively diminutive Dubai Creek Golf Club (1993) is proof that, even in a city of megaprojects, size isn't necessarily everything. The shape of the building pays oblique homage to Dubai's

Sheikh Zayed Road Landmarks

The main section of Sheikh Zayed Road, bounded at its north by the Emirates Towers and at its south by the Burj Dubai, is Dubai at its most brazenly futuristic. A long parade of supertall skyscrapers stands shoulder to shoulder along the strip, staring down at the traffic on the 14-lane highway below like a troupe of giraffes regarding a scrum of hyperactive beetles. From north to south, here are some of the strip's most distinctive towers:

World Trade Centre: At 39 stories, this was the city's first genuine high-rise when it opened in 1979.

Fairmont Dubai: Crowned with four little turrets, this large hotel is illuminated in constantly changing colors after dark.

The Tower: This triangular-topped edifice is enlivened with whimsical steel protuberances, like the fronds of an enormous metal palm tree.

Al Yaqoub Tower: Next door to The Tower, Al Yaqoub looks like a supersize remake of London's Big Ben, minus the clock.

Chelsea Tower: Atop this intriguing skyscraper, an enormous needle hangs suspended from a square white frame.

Rose Rotana Hotel: Once the world's tallest hotel (that honor now belongs to the JW Marriott Marquis; see p 107), this pencil-thin tower is crowned with a small globe that glows after dark.

Dusit Thani Hotel: One of the oldest buildings on the strip, this hotel was inspired by the traditional Thai wai greeting, with joined palms.

maritime past, with three triangular canopies looking rather like the wind-filled sails of a traditional dhow (or perhaps an enormous

Aerial view of Dubai Creek Golf Club.

Bedouin tent). Visitors are free to wander around and admire the exterior of the building. It's also worth having a look at the beautiful Park Hyatt hotel and yacht club a few minutes' walk down the road. ⏱ *10 min. Dubai Creek Golf Club, Garhoud.*

Take a taxi (about AED 25) to:

❹ ★★★ **Emirates Towers.** A pair of monumental steel-and-glass colossi looming over the northern end of Sheikh Zayed Road, the superb Emirates Towers (p 123) look like a couple of sci-fi space rockets crash-landed in the heart of the city. Impressively huge (the larger tower was the world's 10th highest building when finished in 2000), the towers are also among

Dubai's most beautiful modern architectural creations, with their distinctive triangular summits and the constant play of intense desert light and shadow on their aluminum-clad facades.

The larger tower (355m) houses the offices of Emirates airline and isn't open to the public. The smaller tower (309m) is home to the Jumeirah Emirates Towers hotel. You can visit the lobby of the hotel tower to have a look at the glass elevators whizzing up and down inside the futuristic atrium. ⓘ *20 min. Sheikh Zayed Rd.*

5 **The Noodle House.** A Sheikh Zayed Road institution, this restaurant is enduringly popular among local office workers thanks to its quick-fire service and delicious pan-Asian food, served at long communal tables. *Emirates Blvd.* ☎ *04-319-8088.*

6 ★ **Dubai International Financial Centre.** Immediately south of the Emirates Towers, the Dubai International Financial Centre—home to the Dubai Stock Exchange—is centered on the striking The Gate building, a kind of postmodern office block–cum–triumphal arch. You're free to go in and wander through the enormous hollowed-out center of the building, although photography is prohibited. ⓘ *15 min. Sheikh Zayed Rd.*

7 ★★ **Sheikh Zayed Road.** Depending on your tastes, the skyscraper row along Sheikh Zayed Road is either crass modernism on an unforgivably epic scale or a thrilling vision of what the 21st-century planet might look like. Although many of its towers are relatively unimaginative, there are enough touches of architectural whimsy to give the road a certain off-beat character. (See "Sheikh Zayed Road Landmarks," p 52.) You can enjoy fine views of the skyscrapers as you ride up or down the metro, whose gleamingly metallic pod-shaped stations add a further futuristic touch to the road's sci-fi scenery. ⓘ *40 min.*

The Gate at Dubai International Financial Centre.

Sheikh Zayed Road.

8 ★★★ **Burj Khalifa.** Even in a city of endless world records and innumerable superlatives, the Burj Khalifa skyscraper stands out by a mile. Far and away the world's tallest man-made structure, the Burj clocks in at a jaw-dropping 828m tall—if you've ever wondered what a kilometer-high building might look like, the Burj is pretty close. Impossibly tall and slender, the tower is visible for a dozen miles in every direction and dwarfs every other building in the vicinity, piercing the Dubai skyline like an enormous needle-fine shard of glass.

Skyscraper City

Dubai is now, without question, the tallest city on the planet, currently home to 20 of the world's 100 highest buildings, with a further 4 in Abu Dhabi. (Traditional high-rise hotspots New York and Hong Kong, by comparison, boast just seven and six top-100 edifices apiece.) Dubai's top-100 landmarks include the **Burj Khalifa** (#1, at 828m), the **Emirates Towers** (joint #38 and #88, at 355m and 309m), the two towers of the new **JW Marriott Marquis Hotel** (joint #38, 355m), the Big Ben–shaped **Al Yaqoub Tower** (#68, 328m), and the memorably twisted **Cayan Tower** (#92, 306m).

The scale of Dubai's incredible rise to the top can be measured by the **Dubai World Trade Centre** (184m), the city's first high-rise landmark. When it opened in 1979, it was the tallest building in the Middle East; now it barely scrapes into *Dubai's* top-100 highest buildings, at a lowly #92.

Named after Sheikh Khalifa bin Zayed al Nahyan, the current ruler of Abu Dhabi, the "Khalifa Tower" was designed by the U.S. architectural firm Skidmore, Owings and Merrill, whose high-rise credits include the Sears Tower in Chicago and the Freedom Tower in New York. Most of the tower is occupied by private apartments, along with the world's first Armani hotel and the stunning At The Top observation deck (see p 12) on the 124th floor. (Despite the name, it's actually only around two-thirds of the way up the building, at 555m.) You can also enjoy the views at leisure by dining at the At.mosphere restaurant (see p 89) on the 122nd floor. ⓘ *45 min. (or 2 hr. if visiting At The Top). Downtown Dubai.*

Catch a taxi from the Dubai Mall to the JW Marriott Marquis hotel (around 15 AED), or the Red Line metro from the Burj Khalifa/Dubai Mall station to the Business Bay station.

❾ ★ **Business Bay.** Immediately south of the Burj Khalifa and Downtown Dubai, the Business Bay development features another dense cluster of high-rises. Pride of place goes to the JW Marriott Marquis, the world's tallest hotel, a pair of towers whose jagged outlines were inspired by date palm trunks.

Turn left out of the hotel and walk down the road past other unusual buildings, such as the striking Iris Bay building, shaped like a vertical eye, and the Prism Tower, a pair of conjoined glass triangles. At the next major road intersection, look left and you'll see the even zanier O-14 Tower, with its white concrete exterior punched with hundreds of circular holes—a design that quickly earned it the nickname "the Swiss Cheese Building."

Dubai downtown and Burj Khalifa.

Visiting the Burj Al Arab

Entrance to the Burj Al Arab is strictly controlled. Unless you're staying or have a reservation at one of the hotel's restaurants or bars, you won't be allowed in. To see the inside is an expensive pleasure. High-rollers head to the hotel's two signature restaurants, either the subterranean fine-dining **Al Mahara** seafood restaurant (complete with huge aquarium) or the vertiginous **Al Muntaha,** perched at the top of the building. There are also less expensive buffets at the Arabian-style **Al Iwan** and Asian-style **Junsui** (lunch and dinner AED 505 and AED 560 at both). The cheapest, most popular, and in many ways the best option is to have a drink or sumptuous afternoon tea either at **Skyview Bar** (p 106), atop the hotel next to Al Muntaha restaurant (drinks minimum AED 350 per person; high tea AED 620) or at the **Sahn Eddar** lounge in the spectacular atrium (drinks minimum AED 290, high/afternoon teas AED 400 and AED 560). For reservations, call ☎ 04-301-7600 or email BAArestaurants@jumeirah.com. www.burjalarab.com.

Take a taxi south (about AED 30) to:

⓾ ★★★ **Burj Al Arab.** Frequently claimed to be the world's

most luxurious hotel, the Burj Al Arab has become as much an icon of Dubai as the Eiffel Tower is to Paris or the Empire State Building is

Burj Al Arab hotel.

to New York. As a symbol of the emirate, it has done more than anything else to stamp Dubai on the global consciousness—at once a contemporary architectural masterpiece, one of the modern world's great PR stunts, and the most beautiful building in the city. Completed in 1999, the Burj's billowing outline, inspired by the shape of a dhow's sail, looms over the coastline south of Downtown Dubai. Burnished white by day, it is magically illuminated like a huge lantern after dark—a huge but consummately graceful edifice that continues to provoke a sense of wonder, however many times you see it. For the best views, head to Umm Suqeim Public Beach, on the north side of the Burj, or the Madinat Jumeirah, to the south.

Whereas the Burj's extraordinary exterior is universally admired, its extravagant interior has earned mixed reviews. Its enormous atrium (big enough to swallow the Statue of Liberty) is decorated in broad swaths of bright primary colors, along with myriad gold-plated columns and a pair of fish tanks so deep that cleaners have to don scuba-diving gear to scrub them out. ⏲ *10 min. to view the outside. www.burjalarab.com. For accommodations, see p 119.*

⓫ ★★ **Jumeirah Beach Hotel.** Opened in 1997, the Jumeirah Beach was Dubai's first world-class five-star hotel. It was built in what purports to suggest the shape of a huge breaking wave (although it really looks more like a giant rollercoaster) in homage to the city's maritime past, thus establishing the nautical theme that would later be echoed by the sail-shaped Burj Al Arab next door. Dwarfed now by

more recent developments (incredibly, just the *spire* of the Burj Al Arab is taller than the entire Jumeirah Beach Hotel), the hotel remains one of Dubai's most original and instantly recognizable buildings. ⏲ *10 min., longer if viewing inside. For accommodations, see p 122.*

Take a taxi (about AED 15) to the Palm Monorail station.

⓬ ★ **The Palm Jumeirah.** Stretching for some 4km off the coast of the southern city, the Palm Jumeirah epitomizes all that's best and worst about modern Dubai's record-breaking mega-projects. The world's largest artificial island, it's constructed (as the name suggests) in the shape of an enormous palm tree, complete with trunk, "fronds," and enclosing breakwater.

A state-of-the-art monorail (daily 10am–10pm; 2–3 departures hourly; AED 25 round-trip) runs the length of the trunk, from Palm Jumeirah station on the mainland to the iconic pink Atlantis resort. The monorail offers superb high-level views of the island and the massed skyscrapers of the nearby Dubai Marina.

The overall concept of the development is breathtaking, although most of the trunk and fronds are occupied by humdrum residential and office developments. The string of huge resorts that dot the breakwater, meanwhile, are notable mainly for their exuberant (if not particularly original) kitsch, ranging from the vast Atlantis resort (see p 119) and the superb Ottoman-Turkish Jumeirah Zabeel Saray (see p 123) through to the bizarre Yemeni-style Kingdom of Sheba, the Indian Mughal Taj Exotica, and the chintzy neoclassical Kempinski Hotel—not so much

Dubai Marina.

back to the future as fast-forward to the Disneyfied past.

Catch the monorail back to the Palm Jumeirah station, then ride the Dubai Tram to the Dubai Marina Mall station.

⓭ ★★ **Dubai Marina.** Largely constructed in just a few years between 2005 and 2010, the huge Dubai Marina is yet another example of the upwardly mobile scale of the city's recent developments. Effectively a new city within a city, the Marina musters more skyscrapers per square meter than any other part of the city—a great concrete forest of skinny high-rises, jostling for elbow room around the Marina itself, a narrow strip of water lined with expensive yachts. It's an incredible sight, and all the more amazing when you consider that as recently as 2005, this entire area was nothing but almost empty desert.

Exit the Marina Mall station and head north along the waterfront walkway, which offers fine views of the towers. At the northern end of the Marina, you can't fail to notice the unique Cayan Tower (aka the Infinity Tower), a huge skyscraper with a distinctive 90-degree twist, looking like a giant piece of twisted rubber. Immediately north rises a further group of supertall (300m+) towers clustered tightly together. It's been dubbed "the tallest block in the world"—although none of the buildings is of any particular architectural merit.

Head left here and walk around to the pleasant beachfront promenade, known as The Walk, lined with shops and restaurants. Rising next to The Walk is the unquestionably ugly Jumeirah Beach Residence development, with 40 towers and living space for 15,000 people—the world's largest single-phase residential development. ⏱ *45 min. www.dubaimarina.ae.* ●

Shopping Best Bets

Best **Mall**
★★★ Dubai Mall (p 67)

Best for **Cheap Diamonds**
★★ Gold and Diamond Park (p 66)

Best for **Gold**
★★★ Gold Souk, *Deira (p 66)*

Best for **Arabian Music**
★★ Virgin Megastore, *Dubai Mall* (p 70)

Best for **Books**
★★★ Kinokuniya, *Dubai Mall (p 62)*

Best for **Glam Partyware**
★★ Aizone, *Mall of the Emirates* (p 63)

Best for **Animals with Humps**
★★ The Camel Company, *Souk Madinat Jumeirah (p 70)*

Best for **Unusual Scents**
★★ Arabian Oud, *Wafi (p 70)*

Best for **Cute Arabian Slippers**
★★ International Aladdin Shoes, *Bur Dubai (p 64)*

Best for **Italian Kitsch**
★★★ Mercato, *Jumeirah (p 68)*

Best for **Kids**
★★ The Toy Store, *Mall of the Emirates (p 70)*

Best for **Arabian Crafts & Souvenirs**
★★★ Khan Murjan, *Wafi (p 62)*

Best for **Mad Decor**
★★ Ibn Battuta Mall, *Dubai Marina* (p 68)

Best for **Spending a Lot of Money Very Quickly**
★★ Fashion Avenue, *Dubai Mall* (p 67)

Best for **Designer Fakes**
★★★ Karama Souk (p 64)

Best for **Big Juicy Dates**
★★ Bateel, *BurJuman Centre (p 65)*

Best for **Rugs**
★★ Deira Tower, *Deira (p 62)*

Best **Views of Dubai**
★★ Gallery One, *Souk Madinat Jumeirah (p 62)*

Best for **Independent Boutiques**
★★ The Village, *Jumeirah (p 65)*

Best for **Delicious Deli Food**
★★ Wafi Gourmet, *Wafi (p 66)*

Best for **Heavily Discounted Designer Clothes & Bags**
★★ Priceless, *Deira (p 64)*

Above: Waterfall in Dubai Mall. Previous page: Ibn Battuta shopping mall.

Dubai **Shopping A to Z**

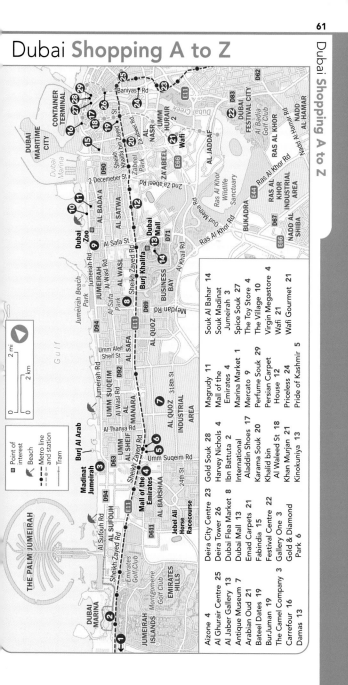

Aizone 4
Al Ghurair Centre 25
Al Jaber Gallery 13
Antique Museum 7
Arabian Oud 21
Bateel Dates 19
BurJuman 19
The Camel Company 3
Carrefour 16
Damas 13

Deira City Centre 23
Deira Tower 26
Dubai Flea Market 8
Dubai Mall 13
Emad Carpets 21
Fabindia 15
Festival Centre 22
Gallery One 3
Gold & Diamond
Park 6

Gold Souk 28
Harvey Nichols 4
Ibn Battuta 2
International
Aladdin Shoes 17
Karama Souk 20
Khalid bin
Al Waleed St 18
Khan Murjan 21
Kinokuniya 13

Magrudy 11
Mall of the
Emirates 4
Marina Market 1
Mercato 9
Perfume Souk 29
Persian Carpet
House 12
Priceless 24
Pride of Kashmir 5

Souk Al Bahar 14
Souk Madinat
Jumeirah 3
Spice Souk 27
The Toy Store 4
The Village 10
Virgin Megastore 4
Wafi 21
Wafi Gourmet 21

Books

★★★ Kinokuniya DOWNTOWN DUBAI Dubai's immense outpost of the famous Japanese bookshop is brilliantly stocked, not just with standard English-language fare but also with a fascinating range of comic books, manga, graphic novels, plus French- and German-language titles. Pure bibliophile heaven. *Dubai Mall (p 67).* ☎ 04-434-0111. www.kinokuniya. com. Map p 61.

★★ Magrudy JUMEIRAH This long-running local bookstore chain was, until not so long ago, the only decent bookseller in the entire UAE. Now with branches countrywide, the original store in Jumeirah is still the best, stocking a good range of English-language fiction and nonfiction, plus local-interest books. *Jumeirah Rd., near the Jumeirah Mosque.* ☎ 04-344-4193. www. magrudy.com. Map p 61.

Carpets, Handicrafts & Souvenirs

★ Al Jaber Gallery DOWNTOWN DUBAI Dubai's main chain of handicraft shops has branches in most malls. Stock is variable, admittedly, and there's usually a lot of junk to wade through, including the inevitable Burj Al Arab paperweights, fluorescent camels, and kitschy coffee pots. Look hard, however, and you might find some nice Arabian- and Indian-style items, including pretty carved wooden boxes. *Dubai Mall (p 67) and other branches citywide.* ☎ 04-339-8566. www.aljabergallery.ae. Map p 61.

★★ Antique Museum AL QUOZ One of Dubai's strangest shopping experiences, this place isn't a museum at all, but a dimly lit, poorly ventilated warehouse in the depths of Al Quoz industrial zone, stuffed to the rafters with a wonderful mish-mash of Arabian and Asian handicrafts and antiques at bargain prices. You could spend hours hunting through the stuff here, turning up collectibles like century-old Bedouin silver jewelry, Thai Buddhas, Moroccan lanterns, or even heirloom-quality wooden furniture, statues, and chandeliers. *Rd. 12B, Al Quoz Industrial Area.* ☎ 04-347-9935. Map p 61.

★★ Deira Tower DEIRA The bottom two floors of this landmark Deira high-rise are the best place in Dubai for serious carpet fanciers, with prices significantly cheaper than you'll find in the more prestigious malls. Dozens of small shops offer a vast range of carpets and *kilims* in all price ranges, from kitsch factory-made rugs to heirloom-quality Persian collectibles. *Baniyas Sq. Map p 61.*

★★ Emad Carpets OUD METHA One of the city's leading rug sellers, Emad offers a range of superior hand- and loom-woven woolen and silk *kilims*, plus carpets of all sizes from Iran, Turkey, Afghanistan, Central Asia, and Pakistan. You'll also find a few superior handicrafts and pashminas. *Wafi (p 69).* ☎ 04-324-2206. Branches also in the Dubai Mall & Souk al Bahar. Map p 61.

★★ Gallery One UMM SUQEIM This is the place to find a visual memory of your trip to take home—beautiful limited-edition photos of Dubai and the Emirates, plus colorful original paintings. It also sells a range of superior postcards for those with shallower pockets. *Souk Madinat Jumeirah (p 63, ⑪).* ☎ 04-368-6055. www.g-1.com. Branches also citywide. Map p 61.

★★★ Khan Murjan GARHOUD This sumptuous Arabian-style souk is the best (if not the cheapest) place in the city to shop for handicrafts, with around 125 shops selling a staggering array of traditional

Rugs for sale in Khan Murjan Souk.

goods and artifacts ranging from *abayas* to *ouds*. *Next to Wafi mall (see p 69). Map p 61.*

★★ Persian Carpet House UMM
SUQEIM   The city's most upscale carpet and handicrafts chain stocks a fabulous array of beautifully crafted wool and silk carpets from Iran and elsewhere in Central Asia, along with wooden furnishings, Moroccan-style hanging lanterns, and so on. *Souk Madinat Jumeirah (p 39, ⑪).* ☎ 04-368-6535. www.pch.ae. *Also at Souk al Bahar (p 39, ⑩) & elsewhere in the city. Map p 61.*

★★ Pride of Kashmir UMM
SUQEIM   Another good place to browse for Indian and Central Asian souvenirs and collectibles, this store has a particularly good selection of Persian, Afghan, and Kashmiri carpets, silk carpets, and *kilims* as well as shawls, pashminas and shahminas, antiques (real and reproduction), and antique-style wooden furniture. *Souk Madinat Jumeirah (p 39, ⑪).* ☎ 04-368-6110. www.prideofkashmir.com. *Also at Souk al Bahar (p 39, ⑩). Map p 61.*

★★★ Souk Madinat Jumeirah
UMM SUQEIM   This atmospheric replica souk in the sensational Madinat Jumeirah development rivals Khan Murjan (p 62) as the best place in the city to shop for

handicrafts. Quality is consistently high, with a superior selection of stores including Gallery One, the Camel Company, Persian Carpet House, Pride of Kashmir, and other outlets selling Arabian and Asian artifacts. *Madinat Jumeirah (see p 39, ⑪). Map p 61.*

Clothes, Shoes & Designer Fakes

★★ Aizone AL SUFOUH   This
flashy outpost of the glam Beirut store is full of international labels with the emphasis on Arabian-style bling: Think tiny sparkly party

Madinat Souk at Madinat Jumeirah Hotel.

frocks, gauzy tops, and lots of fake fur. It's all very Dubai. There's a small menswear section, too, but the shop as a whole is aimed mainly at the ladies. *Mall of the Emirates (p 68).* ☎ *04-347-9333. www.aishti.com. Map p 61.*

★★ **Fabindia** BUR DUBAI This Bur Dubai offshoot of the superb Indian chain sells irresistible sub-continental men's and ladies' cloth-ing—kurtas, shalwar kameez, and so forth—plus home decor items from cushion covers and throws to tablecloths and napkins, all made from the company's signature hand-made, ethically sourced textiles. *Mankhool Rd., near EPPCO petrol station.* ☎ *04-398-9633. www. fabindia.com. Map p 61.*

★★ **Harvey Nichols** AL SUFOUH Oozing minimalist chic, this Dubai branch of the famous London store sports a mix of classic and contem-porary British and international labels, along with other envy-induc-ing products, including designer accessories and fragrances. *Mall of the Emirates (p 68).* ☎ *04-409-8888. www.harveynichols.com. Map p 61.*

★★ **International Aladdin Shoes** BUR DUBAI This famous little stall (there's no sign, although

you can't miss it) is the place to go for beautifully colorful embroidered Arabian slippers, from around AED 50 for a simple pair without decora-tion, up to AED 75 for more highly ornamented examples. *Note:* It doesn't accept credit cards. *Textile Souk (p 37,* ⑥ *), next to the Bur Dubai Old Souk abra station. No phone. Map p 61.*

★ **Karama Souk** KARAMA The down-at-heel Karama Souk is the best place in the city for designer fakes. No one's pretending that all the branded clothing and sports gear on sale here is anything but a creative approximation of the real thing, but it's a fun place to shop for all sorts of knock-off clothing, bags, watches, and the like. There are also a few passable little souve-nir and handicraft shops, where you may find some interesting antiques, such as old coins, Bedouin jewelry, or Omani *khanjars* (daggers). *See p 38,* ⑦ *. Map p 61.*

★★ **Priceless** DEIRA A well-kept secret, this inconspicuous shop is a great source of massively discounted designer gear, selling unsold stock from the city's Harvey Nichols and Bloomingdale's department stores at prices usually around two-thirds off the original. It's pot-luck as to what's available at any particular time, but

International Aladdin Shoes at the Textile Souk.

there's usually a good selection of leading labels, and nice bags too. *Al Maktoum St., Deira (toward the Clocktower, opposite Emirates NBD).* ☎ 04-221-5444. Map p 61.

★★ **The Village** JUMEIRAH One of many small malls dotted along the north end of Jumeirah Beach Road, the Village is particularly good for funky ladieswear, with a chichi selection of small independent boutiques, including the popular S*uce. *Jumeirah Beach Rd. Map p 61.*

Food

★★ **Bateel Dates** BUR DUBAI Dubai's best place for dates purveys around 20 of the finest and fattest varieties, imported from Bateel's own plantations in Saudi Arabia. Dates are sold either on their own, covered in chocolate (much nicer than it might sound), or stuffed with delicate slivers of lemon, almond, and orange. It also sells superb chocolates and beautifully boxed date and chocolate assortments. They make great presents, although you'll probably want to eat them yourself. *BurJuman (p 67).* ☎ 04-355-2853. www.bateel.com. *Branches also citywide, including at Dubai Mall, Deira City Centre, Marina Mall & Souk al Bahar. Map p 61.*

Bateel dates.

★★ **Carrefour** AL SUFOUH This popular French hypermarket isn't exactly the most atmospheric place to shop in Dubai, but it stocks a huge and inexpensive range of good-quality Arabian produce, from dates and honey to saffron and sweets. *Mall of the Emirates (p 68).* ☎ 800-73232. www.carrefouruae.com. *Branches also citywide. Map p 61.*

★★★ **Spice Souk** DEIRA Dubai's most atmospheric souk sells all sorts of spices, including good cheap(ish) saffron, plus other local specialties, as well as frankincense, rose petal tea, dried lemons, *alum* (a crystalline stone used to soothe the skin after shaving), and "natural" Viagra. *See p 34, ❷. Map p 61.*

Tailoring in Dubai

Bur Dubai and Karama are both good places to have tailor-made clothes run up at fairly affordable prices, whether you want to have a copy made of an existing item of clothing or something created from scratch. Bring pictures or magazine cuttings with you if possible. You can pick up good cheap cloth in the shops in and around the Bur Dubai **Textile Souk** (p 37, ❻) and in the larger outlets along nearby Al Fahidi Street as well as in various places in Karama. There are dozens of tailors in the **Meena Bazaar** area of Bur Dubai—**Dream Girl Tailors** (37D St., off Al Hisn St.; ☎ 04-388-0070) is one of the more popular and reliable places, doing gents' and ladies' tailoring in Western and Indian styles.

★★ **Wafi Gourmet** OUD METHA
The city's best deli is full of Middle
Eastern fresh produce, including
big tubs of juicy olives and shelves
full of freshly prepared sweets and
pastries, salads, and dips—a great
place to put together a picnic or
buy packaged foods to take home.
Wafi (p 69). 📞 *04-324-4433. www.
wafigourmet.com. Branches also at
Dubai Mall & Festival City. Map p 61.*

Electronics

★ **Khalid bin Al Waleed Street**
BUR DUBAI   Khalid bin Al Waleed
Street, also known as "Computer
Street," is where you'll find Dubai's
greatest concentration of electronics and computer shops. Most of
the action is concentrated in the
Mussalla Tower Mall and the Al Ain
Centre, on either side of the junction of Khalid bin Al Waleed with Al
Mussalla/Makhool roads. Both
malls are stuffed with shops selling
the latest laptops and other digital
paraphernalia. *Khalid bin Al Waleed
St., Bur Dubai. Map p 61.*

Gold & Jewelry

★ **Damas** DOWNTOWN DUBAI
The city's leading jewelry chain,
with branches in all the major malls,
retails a vast array of offerings in
gold, silver, and precious stones,
from stylish Italian designs to outra-
geous Arabian bling. *Dubai Mall*

(p 67). 📞 *04-339-8846. www.
mydamas.com. Branches also citywide. Map p 61.*

★★ **Gold & Diamond Park** AL
SUFOUH   This unprepossessing
little mall, just north of the Mall of
the Emirates off Sheikh Zayed Road,
is one of the city's best places to
shop for gold and especially diamonds, which are up to 50%
cheaper than overseas. *Sheikh
Zayed Rd., btw. interchanges 3 & 4.*
📞 *04-362-7777. www.goldand
diamondpark.com. Map p 61.*

★★ **Gold Souk** DEIRA   As you'd
expect, Deira's bustling Gold Souk
is a great place to shop for gold
jewelry, sold in all manner of
designs, from suave European-style
pieces to extravagant Arabian
designs. The traditional Emirati
bracelets displayed in many shop
windows are particularly pretty. It's
also good for precious stones, ranging from diamonds to more unusual
gems, such as tanzanite. You can
also hook up here with local touts if
you want to buy designer fakes. *See
p 33,* ❶*. Map p 61.*

Malls

★ **Al Ghurair Centre** DEIRA
One of the oldest malls in the city,
Al Ghurair recently was given a
major makeover and now rivals Bur-
Juman as the shopping destination

Bracelets on display at the Gold Souk.

Al Ghurair Centre.

of choice in the old city. The wide range of shops doesn't particularly dazzle, but it covers most retail bases. There's also a good selection of in-mall restaurants and cafes. *Al Rigga Rd., Deira. www. alghuraircentre.com. Map p 61.*

★★ **BurJuman** BUR DUBAI Old Dubai's premier shopping spot, this huge mall (currently undergoing extensive modernization) pulls in vast crowds thanks to its size and central location. The mall boasts more than 320 outlets spread over three floors; more humdrum shops are in the original section of the mall, while all things designer (including Saks Fifth Avenue department store) are located in the glitzy modern extension. *Junction of Khalid bin al Waleed St. & Sheikh Zayed Rd. www.burjuman.com. Map p 61.*

★ **Deira City Centre** DEIRA One of Dubai's older malls, Deira City Centre is still popular among the city's Indian, Filipino, and other low-income expats, who come to fill their trolleys at the huge Carrefour hypermarket (see p 65). It's not the most exciting retail destination but boasts a fair spread of shops, including a good selection of local clothes shops—it's the place to head for if you want to make like a sheikh and pick up a *dishdasha, abbeya,* or Emirati-style headrobe. *Al Ittihad Rd. www.deira citycentre.com. Map p 61.*

★★★ **Dubai Mall** DOWNTOWN DUBAI The largest shopping complex on the planet, the vast Dubai Mall has more than 1,200 retail outlets spread over three floors and around 6 million square feet of marbled retail splendor. Costing a cool $20 billion, the mall boasts pretty much every shop you could imagine as well as heaps of places to eat and drink—although the sheer size of the place can wear out even the most retail-obsessed. Start at the Bloomingdale's and Galeries Lafayette stores, near the main entrance, then explore the world's largest indoor **gold souk** (where you'll also find the Dubai Dino; see p 12, ⑩). Close by, the uber-chic **Fashion Avenue** is packed with top international brands, as is the gorgeous **Level Shoe District,** perhaps the city's sexiest piece of interior design. Other attractions include a 22-screen multiplex, the **SEGA Republic** theme park (see p 47, ⑥) and **KidZania** edutainment center (p 47, ⑤), an Olympic-size ice rink (p 79), and the **Dubai Aquarium** (p 45, ④), whose huge tank gives the mall a spectacular focal point and attracts steady crowds. *www.thedubaimall.com. Map p 61.*

★ **Festival Centre** FESTIVAL CITY The centerpiece of the new waterside Festival City development, the bright Festival Centre mall offers a good spread of shopping options

Dubai Shopping Festival

Dubai's shopping malls come (even more) alive during the ever-popular Dubai Shopping Festival, a month-long affair running through January (p 162). The festival inspires discounts galore at all sorts of stores, and price cuts of up to 75%—making a whole swath of beautiful designer stuff suddenly tantalizingly affordable.

in all price brackets, featuring most of the big names in Dubai retail. It's also normally a bit less frenetic than other city malls. Its waterfront cafes and promenades are a pleasant bonus. *Festival City. www.festival centre.com. Map p 61.*

★★ **Ibn Battuta** THE GARDENS Far and away Dubai's zaniest shopping destination, Ibn Battuta is also hugely enjoyable—that is, if you don't actually want to buy anything. Almost a mile in length, the mall is divided into six sections, each themed after one of the countries visited by legendary Arab adventurer Ibn Battuta—Morocco, Andalucia, Tunisia, Persia, India, and China—as well as a spectacularly tiled Persian hall (it could be a genuine mosque, if only it didn't have a Starbucks branch in the middle of it). There's also an atmospherically twilit Tunisian

Festival Centre waterfront.

village, a Rajput palace complete with life-size elephant, and an enormous Chinese junk, plus surprisingly interesting exhibits on Ibn Battuta and the history of exploration and navigation in the Islamic world. After all that, unfortunately, the mall's lowbrow shopping options are a letdown. *Off Sheikh Zayed Rd. www.ibnbattutamall.com. Map p 61.*

★★ **Mall of the Emirates** AL SUFOUH   After the Dubai Mall, this is the city's best one-stop shopping destination, with around 500 shops covering all retail essentials. It's not exhaustingly huge, and spacious atriums make it pleasantly bright and sunny. There's an excellent range of restaurants, too, while the surreal snow slopes of Ski Dubai (see p 80) can be seen for free from the west end of the mall. *Sheikh Zayed Rd. www. malloftheemirates.com. Map p 61.*

★★★ **Mercato** JUMEIRAH   The sort of place you either love or hate, this kitsch mall was built in the form of a miniature Italian Renaissance city, with colorful and cartoonish medieval-looking buildings under a big glass roof. The shops here are mainly aimed at the affluent local Jumeirah expat crowd, with a good selection of rather upmarket designer shops, plus a Spinney's supermarket and Virgin Megastore. The downstairs Starbucks is a popular hangout for local Emirati men. *Jumeirah Rd. www.mercato shoppingmall.com. Map p 61.*

China court at Ibn Battuta.

★ **Souk Al Bahar** DOWNTOWN DUBAI   Tucked away behind the Dubai Mall, this small Arabian-styled souk offers a refreshing change of scale from its super-size neighbor. The main draw here are the various restaurants lining the waterfront terrace outside, with superb Burj Dubai views. Shops inside are best for souvenirs, handicrafts, and antiques, with branches of leading stores, such as Pride of Kashmir and Emad Carpets. *Sheikh Mohammed bin Rashid Blvd. www. soukalbahar.ae. Map p 61.*

★★ **Wafi** OUD METHA   This Egyptian-themed mall is one of the most pleasant places to shop in the city. Never too busy or crowded, it has a good range of predominantly upmarket shops—while the quirky statues, hieroglyphics, and stained-glass ceiling make you feel as if you've just wandered into an Asterix cartoon. There are several good food and beverage options, and the next-door Khan Murjan Souk (see p 38, ⑧) is a nice bonus. *Sheikh Rashid Rd. www.wafi.com. Map p 61.*

Markets

Dubai Flea Market SHEIKH ZAYED ROAD   Come here for anything and everything from antiques to mobile phones. *Entrance #5, Safa Park. www.dubai-fleamarket.com. Oct–May 1st Sat of the month 8am–3pm & at other locations elsewhere in the city—see website for details. Map p 61.*

Mall of the Emirates.

Virgin Megastore.

Marina Market DUBAI MARINA
A colorful market set up behind the
Marina Mall in Dubai Marina features
funky clothing, jewelry, homeware,
and other stuff by independent
designers. *Marina Mall.* ☎ *055-
5532-065. www.marinamarket.ae.
Oct–Apr Wed–Sat 10am–10 or 11pm.
Map p 61.*

Music & DVDs

★★ **Virgin Megastore** DOWN-
TOWN DUBAI   This flagship store,
now defunct in the UK, lives on in
the Gulf. Stock includes all the
usual CDs, DVDs, plus books and
electronics, but the real attraction is
its interesting selection of Arabian
and Middle Eastern music (including local Emirati artists). Listening
posts let you sample tracks from
the albums before you buy. *Dubai
Mall (p 67).* ☎ *04-325-3330. www.
virginmegastore.me. Branches also
citywide. Map p 61.*

Perfume

★★ **Arabian Oud** GARHOUD
This upscale Saudi chain is one of
the best places in the city to find traditional Arabian oil-based perfumes
(*attar*), most of them using essences
derived from the fragrant *oud*
(derived from agarwood, or aloe, as
it's known in the West)—although

you might find similar fragrances
at cheaper prices in the Deira Perfume Souk. *Wafi (p 69).* ☎ *04-324-
4117. www.arabianoud.com.
Branches also citywide. Map p 61.*

★ **Perfume Souk** DEIRA   Deira's
Perfume Souk offers a good range
of mainstream Western scents
alongside traditional oil-based Arabian perfumes, or *attar*, often sold
in beautiful little glass bottles. *See
p 35,* ❸. *Map p 61.*

Toys

★★ **The Camel Company** UMM
SUQEIM   The camel is king at this
chain of cute little shops, selling
stuffed toy dromedaries with big
doe eyes and soulful expressions. It
also does a long line of camel-
themed mugs, T-shirts, pens, and
more. *Souk Madinat Jumeirah (p 39,
⓫).* ☎ *04-368-6048. www.camel
company.ae. Branches also at Ibn
Battuta Mall & Dubai Mall. Map
p 61.*

★★ **The Toy Store** AL SUFOUH
Giant stuffed animals welcome you
to Dubai's leading toy store, stocking a vast array of kids' stuff. *Mall of
the Emirates (p 68).* ☎ *04-341-2473.
Also at Ibn Battuta Mall & Dubai
Mall. Map p 61.* ●

Spas

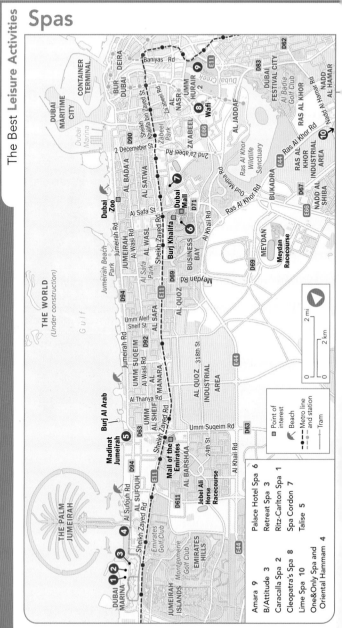

Amara 9

B/Attitude 3

Caracalla Spa 2

Cleopatra's Spa 8

Lime Spa 10

One&Only Spa and
Oriental Hammam 4

Palace Hotel Spa 6

Retreat Spa 3

Ritz-Carlton Spa 1

Spa Cordon 7

Talise 5

Previous page: Yoga at Talise Spa in the Madinat Jumeirah Hotel.

Dubai is a haven for the senses, and not surprisingly the city boasts a fabulous array of top-notch spas, offering heaven-sent levels of luxury and indulgence. You'll find every conceivable style of treatment and therapy here, from mainstream massages, wraps, and facials to arcane procedures, such as color therapy and gem healing.

★★★ Amara GARHOUD
This gorgeously serene spa—one of the best in the city—has eight treatment rooms (including three for couples), all with outdoor rain shower and private walled garden. (You won't have to brave any communal changing rooms here.) The signature "Jewels of Arabia" rituals are based on the ancient healing properties of diamond, emerald, ruby, and sapphire, using exclusive products by Anne Semonin and others. Treatments range from phyto-aromatic facials to chiro deep-body massages—using golf balls. Crash out afterward on one of the loungers around the idyllic tree-shaded pool, which visitors are free to use for the day, assuming they take a minimum 1-hour treatment. *Park Hyatt.* ☎ *04-602-1660. www.dubai.park.hyatt.com.*

★★ B/Attitude DUBAI MARINA
Perhaps the most visually stunning spa in the city, B/Attitude looks like a bespoke Buddhist temple full of Orientalist allure. Mystical massages include a fine Tibetan spa ritual, marma (energy-point) and rebalancing massages, and a special "Bushido Spa," inspired by the Japanese samurai tradition and promising "strength, power, and deep relaxation." *Grosvenor House Hotel, Dubai Marina.* ☎ *04-399-8888. www.grosvenorhouse-dubai.com.*

★★ Caracalla Spa DUBAI MARINA
This over-the-top Roman-themed spa offers a wide array of treatments, including Swedish and Balinese massages, reflexology, wraps, facials and other treatments. Stressed-out travelers might try the

Relax in one of the pools in the Caracalla Spa.

Footloose & Fancy-Free

Buffing up stressed cuticles and having one's nails shaped and polished before heading off to the beach is something of a Dubai institution. Although all the city's spas offer an extensive range of manicures and pedicures, you can also head to the nearest outlet of the **N-Bar** chain (www.nbaruae.com), with branches around the city, including in the Ibn Battuta Mall (☎ 04-366-9828), the Palm Strip Mall in Jumeirah (☎ 04-346-1100), the Emirates Towers Boulevard on Sheikh Zayed Road (☎ 04-330-1001), Al Ghurair City in Deira (☎ 04-228-9009), and the Grosvenor House hotel in Dubai Marina (☎ 04-399-9009).

"Clear Your Mind" aromatherapy massage, while those with cash to burn can indulge in a sumptuous golden caviar facial. *Le Royal Méridien, Dubai Marina.* ☎ 04-399-5555. *www.lemeridien.com/royaldubai.*

★★ Cleopatra's Spa OUD METHA   Located in the chic Egyptian-themed Wafi complex, the ever-popular Cleopatra's Spa offers an excellent and relatively affordable alternative to the sumptuous spas in the five-star hotels. Treatments include Ayurveda, Swedish, and Balinese massages; traditional Arabian *rasul* (using mineral-rich mud and steam); and the signature Cleopatra's Milk Bath. There's also a good range of mainstream facials and other beauty treatments. *Wafi (p 69).* ☎ 04-324-0000. *www. cleopatrasspaandwellness.com.*

★★★ Lime Spa OUTSKIRTS The serene Per Aquum Lime Spa at the laid-back Desert Palm resort is one of the nicest places for an indulgent day out in the city. The emphasis is on personalized and holistic treatments, exemplified by the popular "Intuitive Massage," which combines various techniques—Swedish, Thai, shiatsu, aromatherapy, and Balinese—to suit individual needs. Men are well looked after

with treatments featuring products by London's The Refinery. A full range of grooming and beauty treatments is also available. *Desert Palm, International City.* ☎ 04-323-8888. *www.desertpalm.peraquum.com/lime-spa.*

★★ One&Only Spa and Oriental Hammam DUBAI MARINA   A stunning Ottoman-style hammam (Turkish bath) is the centerpiece of this gorgeous spa, with specialty packages featuring assorted Moorish-inspired massages, wraps, and scrubs—try a vigorous scrub with a traditional loofah for a really authentic hammam experience. Further massages, facials, and other treatments are also available in the adjacent spa. *One&Only Royal Mirage hotel, Dubai Marina.* ☎ 04-399-9999. *www.royalmirage.* oneandonlyresorts.com.

★★ The Palace Hotel Spa DOWNTOWN BURJ DUBAI   This opulent Arabian-themed hotel is home to downtown Dubai's most alluring spa. It's divided into ladies' and men's sections, each offering a huge range of treatments including Oriental hammam rituals, traditional massages (anything from Thai, Singaporean, and Philippine to four-hand and hot-stone), and

Relaxation Room at the Oriental Hammam in the One&Only Royal Mirage.

the lavish queen's and king's rituals—150 minutes of pure sensory indulgence. *The Palace Hotel, Downtown Dubai.* ☎ *04-428-7888. www. theaddress.com.*

★★ Retreat Spa DUBAI
MARINA   B/Attitude's sister spa at the very cool Grosvenor Hotel, Retreat Spa specializes in marine-based Phytomer treatments, with a range of facials, wraps, and massages, not to mention the signature *rasul* skin ceremony using specially harvested natural mud. *Grosvenor House Hotel, Dubai Marina.* ☎ *04-399-8888. www.grosvenor house-dubai.com.*

★★ Ritz-Carlton Spa DUBAI
MARINA   Located in the sumptuous Ritz-Carlton hotel, this luxurious and pleasantly old-school spa has treatments including a rejuvenating array of traditional massages (Balinese, Swedish, aromatherapy, and hot stone) along with oxygen facials, detox treatments, and body scrubs. *Ritz-Carlton Hotel, Dubai Marina.* ☎ *04-399-4000. www. ritzcarlton.com.*

★★ Spa Cordon DIFC   Serving
the overworked executives of the adjacent Dubai International Financial Centre, this award-winning spa offers excellent facials, massages, and Oriental baths alongside manicures, pedicures, and other beauty treatments, all delivered by exceptionally attentive and highly professional staff. *Sky Gardens, Park Avenue, DIFC, off Sheikh Zayed Rd.* ☎ *04-421-3424. www.spacordon. com.*

★★★ Talise MADINAT JUMEIRAH
Arguably the city's best all-round spa experience, the rambling Talise spa is like a miniature private health resort, with almost 30 treatment rooms in individual villas (some with their own hammams) buried in the depths of the Madinat Jumeirah (p 15, ❸). There's a reasonable range of treatments, including an indulgent day-retreat package that includes 3 hours of treatments, plus yoga, tai-chi, meditation, and body therapies, including lymphatic drainage massages, cavitation, and velasmooth. *Madinat Jumeirah.* ☎ *04-366-6818. www.jumeirah.com/talise.*

The Best of **Active Dubai**

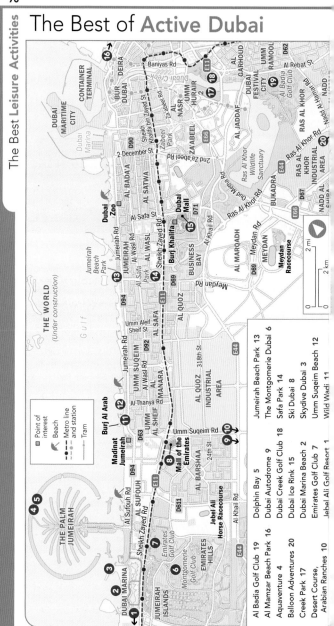

Al Badia Golf Club 19
Al Mamzar Beach Park 16
Aquaventure 4
Balloon Adventures 20
Creek Park 17
Desert Course,
Arabian Ranches 10

Dolphin Bay 5
Dubai Autodrome 9
Dubai Creek Golf Club 18
Dubai Ice Rink 15
Dubai Marina Beach 2
Emirates Golf Club 7
Jebel Ali Golf Resort 1

Jumeirah Beach Park 13
The Montgomerie Dubai 6
Safa Park 14
Ski Dubai 8
Skydive Dubai 3
Umm Suqeim Beach 12
Wild Wadi 11

Many people come to Dubai just for the beach—and who can blame them? But there are plenty of other active pursuits here. Watersports and other marine attractions may top the list, but you'll find several more unexpected diversions, including the Middle East's only ski slope and its finest collection of golf courses.

Beaches

★ kids Al Mamzar Beach Park.
Often blissfully quiet (except at weekends), Sharjah's Al Mamzar Beach offers a string of shady cove-beaches, big swaths of lawn, and fine views of distant skyscrapers. Facilities include a pool, simple cafe, and children's play areas. *Al Mamzar. AED 5.*

★★ Dubai Marina Beach.
Dubai's premier public beach seems to get better every year as new amenities open. The huge swath of golden sand is idyllic (although busy most days), and there's a good range of watersports (see p 80). You'll also find a jogging track, lounge chairs for hire, changing facilities, restrooms, and plenty of cafes, restaurants, and bars. *The Walk, Jumeirah Beach Residences. Open access 24 hr. Free admission.*

★★ kids Jumeirah Beach Park.
The ever-popular Jumeirah Beach Park boasts a generous arc of soft, palm-shaded white-gold sand and a decent selection of facilities. Currently closed for renovations, it's due to reopen in late 2016. *Jumeirah Rd.*

★★ Umm Suqeim Beach.
Also known as "Sunset Beach," this fine strip of crumbly white sand has stunning views of the nearby Burj Al Arab, one of the world's most exclusive hotels. The beach can get busy, and there are virtually no facilities, so take everything you need. Nearby **Kite Beach,** slightly farther north, offers a similar strip of fine sand, although the views aren't quite as dramatic. *Jumeirah Rd. Open access 24 hr. Free admission.*

Enjoying Dubai Marina Beach.

Hotel & Private Beaches

Don't fancy mingling with the crowds on the public beaches? You can always pay to use the beaches and pools at these oceanside hotels or clubs. Note that some hotels close their beaches to nonguests during times of high occupancy (always phone in advance to check). Facilities include use of towels, showers, and lounge chairs on the beach. Part of the cost may be redeemable against food and drink. Most places offer discounts for children under age 12.

Al Qasr: ☎ 04-366-8888. Daily AED 595 (AED 150 redeemable against food & drink).

Hilton Jumeirah Resort: ☎ 04-399-1111. Sun–Wed AED 220, Thurs–Sat AED 250.

Jumeirah Beach Hotel: ☎ 04-348-0000. Daily AED 550 (including AED 150 food & drink). See p 57, ⓫.

Méridien Mina Seyahi & Westin: ☎ 04-399-3333. Sun–Wed AED 225, Thurs–Sat AED 350.

Mina A'Salam: ☎ 04-366-8888. Daily AED 500 (including AED 150 food & drink).

One&Only Royal Mirage: ☎ 04-399-9999. Daily AED 350.

Ritz-Carlton: ☎ 04-399-4000. Daily AED 500.

Le Royal Méridien : ☎ 04-399-4000. Sun–Thurs AED 250, Fri–Sat AED 300.

Sheraton Jumeirah Beach: ☎ 04-399-5533. Sun–Thurs AED 200, Fri, Sat & public holidays AED 300.

Zero Gravity Beach Club: ☎ 04-399-0009. Sun–Thurs AED 150 (including AED 50 food & drink), Fri–Sat AED 250 (including AED 100 food & drink). Discounts for couples.

Driving

★ **Dubai Autodrome.** Speedsters enjoy Dubai's state-of-the-art autodrome, offering all sorts of racecar and go-karting experiences for everyone from first-time kids to adult petrolheads. *Dubailand.* ☎ *04-367-8700. www.dubaiautodrome.com.*

Flying High

★★ **Balloon Adventures.** See the UAE as you've never seen it before, with hypnotic early-morning 1-hour balloon flights over the desert near Al Ain. *Al Ain.* ☎ *04-285-4949. www.ballooning.ae.*

★★ **Skydive Dubai.** For the ultimate adrenaline kick, fall out of the sky above either southern Dubai (the Palm Jumeirah has never looked so good) or out in the desert. Tandem dives and training are available for beginners, while experienced divers can go solo. *Dubai Marina.* ☎ *04-377 8888. www.skydivedubai.ae.*

Golf

★★ **Al Badia Golf Club.** This 18-hole championship course was designed by Robert Trent Jones. *Festival City Garhoud.* ☎ *04-601-0101. www.albadiagolfclub.ae.*

★★ **Desert Course, Arabian Ranches.** A stunning course designed by Ian Baker-Finch features immaculate fairways and greens surrounded by unspoiled desert scenery. *Arabian Ranches, Dubailand.* ☎ 04-366-4700. www. arabianranchesgolfdubai.com.

★★ **Dubai Creek Golf Club.** Dubai's most famous course is centered on its landmark club building (p 51, ❸), with lessons offered at its innovative Golf Academy and floodlit play after dark. *Garhoud.* ☎ 04-380-1234. www.dubaigolf.com.

★★★ **Emirates Golf Club.** Arguably the top club in the city, Emirates Golf Club is currently home to the prestigious Dubai Desert Classic golf tournament, attracting many of the world's leading players. *Dubai Marina.* ☎ 04-380-1234. www.dubaigolf.com.

★ **Jebel Ali Golf Resort & Spa.** This long-established golf resort has a 9-hole course in the far south of the city. *Off Sheikh Zayed Rd., Jebel Ali.* ☎ 04-883-5555. www. jaresortshotels.com.

★★ **The Montgomerie, Dubai.** Designed by Colin Montgomerie,

Aerial view of Emirates Golf Club.

this championship course's unusual features include the par-3 13th, designed in the shape of the UAE, with a 360-degree teeing area around an island fairway and green. *Dubai Marina.* ☎ 04-390-5600. www.themontgomerie.com.

Parks

★★ **Creek Park.** The city's top park offers a beautiful waterside location, with fine views of the quirky Dubai Creek Golf and Yacht Clubs and the serene Park Hyatt hotel. The park and its immediate surroundings are particularly good for kids, home to Children's City (p 45, ❶) and the Dubai Dolphinarium (p 45, ❷); the Wonderland theme park (p 45, ❸) is just around the corner. An old-fashioned cable car (AED 25, AED 10 for kids 14 and under) ferries visitors slowly down the middle of the park, offering bird's-eye views. *Oud Metha.* ☎ 04-336-7633. AED 5. Daily 8am–11pm.

★ **Safa Park.** Spacious Safa Park is one of the few places in Dubai where walkers and joggers can really get up a head of steam without risking being run over or bumping into pedestrians. Dotted among wide swaths of open grass are a small children's funfair, boating lake, and several children's play areas, while the high-rises of Sheikh Zayed Road provide an impressive backdrop. *Al Wasl Rd., Jumeirah.* ☎ 071-800-900. AED 5, free for children 2 & under. Daily 8am–10pm.

Skiing & Skating

★ **Dubai Ice Rink.** Another of the many attractions in the vast Dubai Mall (p 12, ❿), the Olympic-size Dubai Ice Rink is extremely popular and can get crowded at peak hours—visit early in the day if you're a serious skater. Entrance is in 1-hr.-and-45-min. slots during public sessions. Skating lessons and special disco sessions are also

Ski Dubai.

available. *Dubai Mall.* ☎ 800-38224-6255. www.dubaiicerink.com. AED 60 per 1 hr. 45 min. session (includes skate hire), AED 25 for kids under 1m. Daily 10am–10:45pm.

★★ **Ski Dubai.** Only in Dubai would the idea of skiing in the desert seem sensible. The quintessentially weird Ski Dubai is an 85m-high (279 ft.) snow-covered artificial ski slope complete with chairlifts, fir trees, and Alpine rock effects—all of it visible through observation windows from the adjacent Mall of the Emirates. Five runs for skiers and snowboarders (the longest is 400m) range from gentle beginners' courses to the world's first indoor black run (although serious skiers find it a bit tame). You must meet the center's "minimum skill requirements" before you're allowed on the main slope. Novices can sign up for lessons. Alternatively, just buy a pass to the snow gallery to make snowmen, throw snowballs, or ride the Snow Bullet zipline. *Mall of the Emirates.* ☎ 071-800-386. www.skidxb.com. Ski slope (2 hr.) AED 200 adults, AED 170 kids 11 & under. No children under 2. Prices include clothing, boots & equipment (but not gloves or hats). Daily 10am–11pm (Thurs–Sat until midnight).

Watersports

★★ **Aquaventure.** At the huge Atlantis resort (p 18, ❷), this top-notch waterpark is centered on the imposing "Tower of Neptune," equipped with seven epic water slides, including the stomach-churning Leap of Faith, which drops you down a near-vertical 27.5m (90-ft.) slide into an underwater acrylic tunnel inside the shark lagoon below. You can also ride Aquaconda, the world's largest waterslide; experience watery weightlessness on the Zoomerango; or simply drift along the river, which stretches for 2.3km (1.5 miles) around the edge of the park. Younger kids enjoy Splashers, an enormous play structure with slides and water jets. The park also has a beach where you can crash on the sand between forays into the park. *Atlantis, The Palm.* ☎ 04-426-0000.

Watersports & Boat Trips

Watersports can be arranged through several beach resorts, or at Dubai Marina Beach through either **Sky & Sea** (www.water sportsdubai.com) or **Water Adventure Dubai** (www.wateradventure.ae). Both are located on the beach behind the Sheraton hotel and offer a similar range of activities, including kayaking, windsurfing, sailing, wake- and kneeboarding, parasailing, banana-boat rides, water-skiing, and jet-skiing. Sky & Sea also runs fishing trips around the UAE. Surfing can be arranged through **Surf House Dubai** (www.surfingdubai.com), and kitesurfing is available through the **Kitesurf School Dubai** (www.kitesurf.ae).

Numerous boat trips are available around the Marina. As well as public ferry services (see p 166), highly rated sightseeing trips can be arranged through the **Yellow Boats** (www.theyellowboats.com), while Captain Jack offers sedate 1-hr. cruises around the Marina on a traditional wooden dhow. Yachts and other boats can be chartered from various places around the Marina, such as **Bristol Charter** (www.bristolcharter.net) and **First Yacht** (www.first yacht-me.com).

www.atlantisthepalm.com. (Rates if booked online) AED 250 adults, AED 205 children under 1.2m, free for kids under age 2; locker rental AED 40/75, towel rental AED 30. Free

admission for guests staying at Atlantis, The Palm. Daily 10am–sunset.

★★ **Dolphin Bay.** Also in the Atlantis resort (p 18, ❷), Dolphin

Waterskiing is offered from Talise Sports Club at the Jumeirah Beach Hotel.

Diving

The waters around Dubai aren't great for diving due to limited visibility and a relative lack of marine life. Serious divers will want to head over to the UAE's east coast around Fujairah or up to the Musandam peninsula in Oman, whose clear waters and abundant marine life provide some of the Gulf's most memorable underwater experiences. Diving trips to these places (as well as the full range of PADI courses) can be arranged through various operators, including **Pavilion Dive Centre,** at the Jumeirah Beach Hotel (p 57, ⑪; www.jumeirah.com; follow links to the Jumeirah Beach Hotel); **Al Boom** diving center (www.alboomdiving.com); **ProDive Middle East** (www.prodiveme.com); and **Sky & Sea** (www.water sportsdubai.com).

Bay consists of three spacious lagoons with their own troupe of resident bottlenose dolphins. You can swim with the dolphins here: A 90-minute package includes a half-hour in the water with the dolphins (maximum 10 visitors per dolphin). As with most things at Atlantis, prices are steep (nearly twice the price of similar programs at the Dubai Dolphinarium), but at least entrance into the Aquaventure waterpark (see p 80) is also included. *Atlantis, The Palm.* ☎ *04-426-0000. www.atlantisthe palm.com. Shallow-water interactions from AED 795, deep-water interactions from AED 960, observer AED 300. Atlantis guests get a roughly 20% discount. Daily 10am–sunset.*

★★ **Wild Wadi.** Next to the Jumeirah Beach Hotel, this enduringly popular rival to **Aquaventure** (p 80), and Abu Dhabi's **Yas Waterworld** (p 151, ⑬) provides watery thrills and spills for everyone from young kids to hard-core adrenalin junkies. Younger or more sedate visitors can ride a tube down Lazy River or bob around in the artificial waves of Juha's lagoon. Thrill-seekers can try the Masterblaster whitewater rides, tackle the surfing waves of the Wipeout and Riptide Flowriders, or—the ultimate challenge—plummet down the Jumeirah Sceirah, the world's eighth-tallest waterslide. *Jumeirah Rd.* ☎ *04-348-4444. www.wildwadi. com. AED 295, AED 250 children below 1.1m, free for kids under 2. Free admission if staying at Jumeirah Beach Hotel (p 57, ⑪) or Madinat Jumeirah Hotel (p 15, ❸). Daily 10am to 6 or 7pm or later, depending on time of year. Ladies' night Thurs.* ●

5 The Best **Dining**

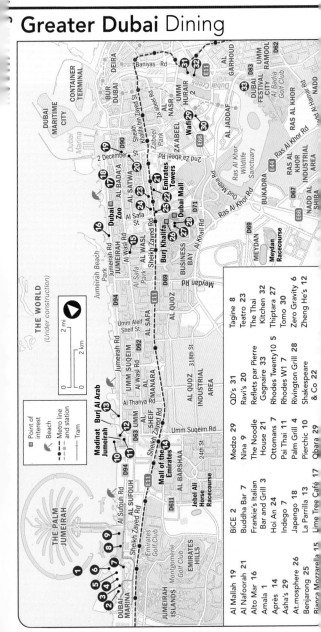

THE WORLD
(Under construction)

- Point of interest
- Beach
- Metro line and station
- Tram

Al Mallah 19
Al Nafoorah 21
Alto Mar 16
Amala 1
Après 14
Asha's 29
At.mosphere 26
Benjarong 25
Bianca Mozzarella 15
BiCE 2
Buddha Bar 7
Frankie's Italian Bar and Grill 3
Hoi An 24
Indego 4
Japengo 18
La Parrilla 13
Lime Tree Café 17
Medzo 29
Nina 9
The Noodle House 21
Ottomans 7
Pai Thai 11
Palm Grill 4
Pierchic 10
Obara 29
QD's 31
Ravi's 20
Reflets par Pierre Gagnaire 33
Rhodes Twenty10 5
Rhodes W1 7
Rivington Grill 28
Shakespeare & Co 22
Tagine 8
Teatro 23
The Thai Kitchen 32
Thiptara 27
Tomo 30
Zero Gravity 6
Zheng He's 12

Previous page: Tagine Moroccan Restaurant at One&Only.

City Center Dining

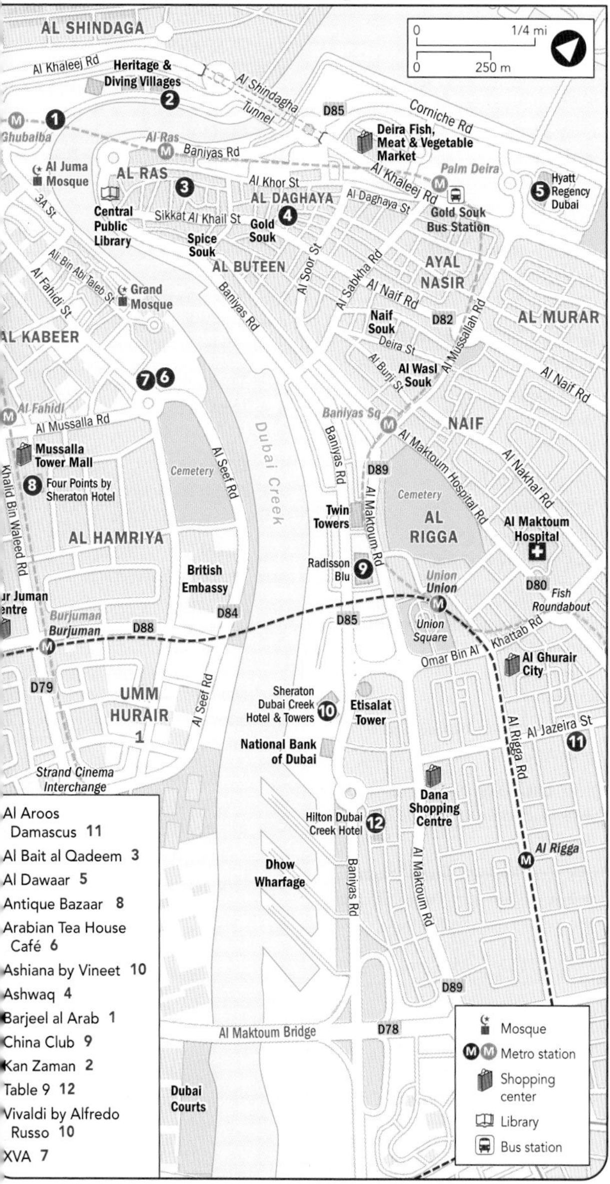
AL SHINDAGA
0 1/4 mi
0 250 m
Al Khaleej Rd
Heritage & Diving Villages
Al Shindagha Tunnel
D85
Corniche Rd
Ghubaiba
Al Ras
Baniyas Rd
Deira Fish, Meat & Vegetable Market
Al Juma Mosque
AL RAS
Al Khor St
Palm Deira
Hyatt Regency Dubai
AL DAGHAYA
Al Khaleej Rd
Al Daghaya St
Gold Souk Bus Station
3A St
Central Public Library
Sikkat Al Khail St
Gold Souk
Spice Souk
AL BUTEEN
Al Soor St
Al Sabkha Rd
AYAL NASIR
Ali Bin Abi Taleb St
Al Fahidi St
Grand Mosque
Baniyas Rd
Al Naif Rd
Naif Souk
D82
Al Mussallah Rd
AL MURAR
AL KABEER
Deira St
Al Buri St
Al Wasl Souk
Al Naif Rd
Al Fahidi
Al Mussalla Rd
Baniyas Sq
NAIF
Mussalla Tower Mall
Four Points by Sheraton Hotel
Cemetery
Al Seef Rd
Dubai Creek
Baniyas Rd
D89
Al Maktoum Hospital Rd
Al Nakhal Rd
Khalid Bin Waleed Rd
Cemetery
Twin Towers
Al Maktoum Rd
AL RIGGA
Al Maktoum Hospital
AL HAMRIYA
British Embassy
Radisson Blu
Union
D80
Fish Roundabout
Burjuman Centre
D84
D85
Union Square
Khattab Rd
Burjuman
D88
Omar Bin Al
Al Ghurair City
D79
UMM HURAIR 1
Al Seef Rd
Sheraton Dubai Creek Hotel & Towers
Etisalat Tower
Al Rigga Rd
Al Jazeira St
National Bank of Dubai
Strand Cinema Interchange
Dana Shopping Centre
Hilton Dubai Creek Hotel
Al Rigga
Dhow Wharfage
Baniyas Rd
Al Maktoum Rd
D89
Al Maktoum Bridge
D78
Dubai Courts
Al Aroos Damascus 11
Al Bait al Qadeem 3
Al Dawaar 5
Antique Bazaar 8
Arabian Tea House Café 6
Ashiana by Vineet 10
Ashwaq 4
Barjeel al Arab 1
China Club 9
Kan Zaman 2
Table 9 12
Vivaldi by Alfredo Russo 10
XVA 7
Mosque
Metro station
Shopping center
Library
Bus station

Dining **Best Bets**

Best **Panoramic Views**
★★ At.mosphere, *Burj Khalifa* (p 89)

Best **Waterside Views**
★★ Pierchic, *Al Qasr* (p 93)

Best for the **Beach**
★★ Palm Grill, *Ritz-Carlton* (p 92)

Best for **Romance**
★★★ Pai Thai, *Dar Al Masyaf* (p 92)

Best for **Mixing with the Locals**
★★ Kan Zaman, *Shindagha* (p 91)

Best **Cafe**
★★ Lime Tree Café, *Jumeirah Road* (p 92)

Best **Cheap Eats**
★★ Ravi's, *Satwa* (p 93)

Best **Arabian Cuisine**
★★ Al Nafoorah, *The Boulevard* (p 87)

Best for **Traditional Arabian Atmosphere**
★★ Al Bait al Qadeem, *Deira* (p 87)

Best for **Fresh Seafood**
★★ Alto Mar, *Jumeirah* (p 88)

Best **Latino-Style Steakhouse**
★★ La Parrilla, *Jumeirah Beach Hotel* (p 91)

Best **for French Fine Dining**
★★★ Reflets par Pierre Gagnaire, *Intercontinental, Festival City* (p 93)

Best of **British**
★★★ Rhodes W1, *Grosvenor House Hotel* (p 94)

Best **Italian**
★★ BiCE, *Hilton Jumeirah Beach* (p 90)

Best **Italian Bistro**
★★ Bianca Mozzarella, *Jumeirah* (p 90)

Best for **Oriental Style**
★★★ Buddha Bar, *Grosvenor House Dubai* (p 90)

Best **Thai with Views**
★★ Thiptara, *The Palace Hotel* (p 95)

Best **Chinese**
★★ Zheng He's, *Mina A'Salam* (p 96)

Best **Sushi**
★★ Tomo, *Raffles Hotel* (p 95)

Best **Noodles**
★★ The Noodle House, *The Boulevard* (p 92)

Best **Modern Indian**
★★★ Indego, *Grosvenor House Dubai* (p 91)

Best for **Shawarma on the Go**
★ Ashwaq, *Junction of Sikkat Al Khail and Al Soor roads* (p 89)

Best for **Multicuisine Madness**
★★ Japengo, *Jumeirah* (p 91)

Dubai **Dining A to Z**

★★ Al Aroos Damascus DEIRA *ARABIAN* Big, bustling, and deservedly popular, this local restaurant serves up massive portions of excellent Lebanese fare at bargain prices—tasty mezze, sandwiches, wraps, and juices, plus succulent grills and kebabs. Unlicensed. *Al Muraqqabat Rd.* ☎ *04-221-9825. www.aroosdamascus.com. Entrees AED 20–50. MC, V. Map p 85.*

★★ Al Bait Al Qadeem DEIRA *ARABIAN* "The Old House" is exactly what the name says, attractively located in a fine traditional property right next to Al Ahmadiya School. Food comprises a good range of inexpensive and well-prepared Middle Eastern dishes (including a few local specialties, such as *machboos* and *goboli*). There's seating either in the photogenic little dining room or in the rustic courtyard out the back. Unlicensed. *Old Baladiya Rd.* ☎ *04-225-6111. www.albaitalqadeem.com. Entrees AED 30–45. MC, V. Daily 8am–10pm. Map p 85.*

★ Al Dawaar DEIRA *INTERNATIONAL* Dubai's only revolving restaurant, Al Dawaar is a great place from which to take in the old city skyline over one of the restaurant's daily lunch and dinner buffets—not the most memorable culinary experience you'll have in Dubai, but worth it for the views. *Hyatt Regency, Deira.* ☎ *04-209-1234. www.dubai.regency.hyatt.com. Daily 12:30–3:30pm & 7pm–midnight. Lunch AED 185, dinner AED 235. AE, DC, MC, V. Map p 85.*

★★ Al Mallah SATWA *ARABIAN* At this classic Lebanese cafe, the menu offers a good range of *shawarmas* and grills at bargain prices. You can sit inside, although it's much more fun to grab a seat on the spacious patio and watch the crowds—and fancy cars—roll past. Unlicensed. *Al Diyafah St.* ☎ *04-398-4723. www.almallah-rest.com. Mezze AED 12–20, entrees AED 30–60. V, MC. Sat–Thurs 7am–11am. Map p 84.*

★★ Al Nafoorah SHEIKH ZAYED ROAD *ARABIAN* Easily overlooked, this sedate and understated restaurant is one of the best places for Arabian food in the entire city. The hot and cold mezze are exemplary, the *shawarma* succulent, and the seafood and charcoal-grilled kabobs perfectly prepared, while there's also a good wine list including Lebanese vintages by the glass or bottle. *The Boulevard at Jumeirah Emirates Towers.* ☎ *04-432-3232. www.facebook.com/AlNafoorahDubai. Entrees AED 60–AED 135. AE, DC, MC, V. Daily*

Friday Brunch

Friday Brunch is something of an institution in Dubai, equivalent to the UK's Sunday lunch, except with a decided party atmosphere and a lot more booze. Bars and restaurants all over the city offer all-you-can-eat (and drink) deals during which stressed-out expats let off considerable amounts of steam. Check *Time Out Dubai* magazine for the best deals, and note that for the more popular locations, it is a good idea to book well in advance.

Antique Bazaar at Four Points.

noon–3:30pm & 6:30–midnight. Map p 84.

★★ Alto Mar JUMEIRAH *MEDITERRANEAN SEAFOOD* One of the city's real hidden gems is tucked away close to the Jumeirah fishing harbor in a simple little ocher-colored building. Freshly caught seafood is the main draw. Either choose from the a la carte menu or select your choice of fish or crustacean fresh from the restaurant aquariums and have it prepared in a style of your choice. There's also a decent meat and vegetarian selection, plus salads, but it's the seafood that calls loudest. *180 4c St.* ☎ *04-343-5225. www.alto-mar.com. Entrees AED 100–AED 190. AE, MC, V. Tues–Sun noon–midnight (Fri from 2pm). Map p 84.*

★★ Amala PALM JUMEIRAH *INDIAN* One of several excellent restaurants in the spectacular Jumeirah Zabeel Saray hotel, Amala is a genuine feast for the senses, from the extravagant decor to the excellent (and quite reasonably priced) Mughlai-style food, with richly flavored curries, kabobs, and biryanis. *Jumeirah Zabeel Saray Hotel.* ☎ *04-453-0444. http://bit.ly/AmalaDubai. Entrees AED 75–AED 175. AE, DC, MC, V. Daily 6pm–1am, Fri–Sat also 1–4pm. Map p 84.*

★★ Antique Bazaar BUR DUBAI *NORTH INDIAN* This exquisitely decorated restaurant looks like the inside of a Rajput palace and serves up a fair range of competitively priced north Indian meat, fish, and veg standards. A good Indian band and dancers perform nightly from 9pm. *Four Points by Sheraton.* ☎ *04-397-7444. www.antiquebazaar-dubai.com. Entrees AED 46–AED 130. AE, DC, MC, V. Daily 24 hr. Map p 85.*

★★ Après MALL OF THE EMIRATES *EUROPEAN* A good place for some après-ski rest and recuperation, this lively bar-restaurant serves up great views of the snow slopes of Ski Dubai (see p 80) framed through a big picture window, along with a good selection of European-style cafe food and kick-ass cocktails to put some warmth back into frosty extremities. *Mall of the Emirates.* ☎ *04-341-2575. http://bit.ly/ApresDubai. Entrees AED 65–AED 195. MC, V. Daily noon–1am (Fri–Sat from 10am, Thurs–Fri until 2am). Map p 84.*

★★ Arabian Tea House Cafe BUR DUBAI *CAFE* This serene little courtyard cafe in a traditional Emirati building dishes up a reliable array of mainly Arabian-style breakfasts, snacks, and more substantial grills and kabobs, plus good juices, smoothies, and specialty coffees. *Bastakiya (next to the main entrance).* ☎ *04-353-5071. www.arabianteahouse.co. Entrees AED 50–AED 60. MC, V. Daily 8am–10pm. Map p 85.*

★★ Asha's OUD METHA *INDIAN*
A colorful modern Indian restaurant
owned by legendary Bollywood
singer Asha Bhosle, Asha's has an
inventive menu mixing mainstream
north Indian classics along with
more unusual regional dishes,
including some favorite recipes from
Bhosle's own family recipe book.
Wafi. 📞 *04-324-4100. www.ashas
restaurants.com. Entrees AED 60–
AED 175. AE, DC, MC, V. Daily 12:30–
3pm & 7pm–midnight. Map p 84.*

★★ Ashiana by Vineet DEIRA
INDIAN Now overseen by subcontinental master chef Vineet Bhatia, this long-running, pleasantly
old-fashioned restaurant offers
above-average north Indian fare,
with old-school classics alongside
more innovative contemporary-style
dishes. Live music most evenings.
Sheraton Dubai Creek. 📞 *04-221-
3468. www.ashianadubai.com.
Entrees AED 75–AED 150. AE, DC,
MC, V. Sun–Thurs noon–3pm; daily
7–11pm. Map p 85.*

★ Ashwaq DEIRA *SHAWARMA*
Near the entrance to the Gold Souk,
this streetside cafe and kabob stand
dishes up flavorsome *shawarmas* and
juices, providing a perfect pit stop
during a tour of the Deira souks.

Outdoor dining at Asha's Wafi.

Unlicensed. *Junction of Sikkat Al Khail
& Al Soor roads, Deira. No phone.
Shawarmas AED 4–AED 25. No credit
cards. Sat–Thurs 10am–midnight; Fri
3pm–midnight. Map p 85.*

★★ At.mosphere DOWNTOWN
DUBAI *INTERNATIONAL*
At.mosphere's principal selling
point is pretty clear: This is the
world's highest restaurant, located
on the 122nd floor of the world's
tallest building at a height of 442m
(1,450 ft.)—the only way you'll dine
higher than this is by getting on a
plane. International fine dining is
the order of the day. Choose
between the upscale restaurant (set
lunch AED 450/AED 600 for two/
three courses; dinner a la carte main
courses AED 200–AED 450) and the
more casual lounge (sandwiches
and salads AED 80–AED 150, main
courses AED 200–AED 250). A minimum spend of AED 200 to AED 500
per person is applicable for some
tables, although menu prices aren't
as horrendously sky-high as you
might fear, especially if you eat
modestly in the lounge. *Burj Khalifa.*
📞 *04-888-3828. www.atmosphere
burjkhalifa.com. Lounge daily noon–
2am. Restaurant daily 12:30–3pm &
6:30–11:30pm. Map p 84.*

★ Barjeel Al Arab SHINDAGHA
ARABIAN This appealing restaurant in the lovely Barjeel Heritage
Guest House (see p 119) serves
tasty Arabian fare, including local
Emirati specialties and good camel
burgers and steaks (tasting a lot
like beef). Sit either in the cute dining room or on the lovely waterfront terrace outside. Unlicensed.
*Barjeel Heritage Guest House,
Shindagha.* 📞 *04-354-4424. www.
heritagedubaihotels.com. Entrees
AED 40–AED 70. AE, DC, MC, V.
Daily noon–midnight. Map p 85.*

★★ Benjarong SHEIKH ZAYED
ROAD *THAI* At the top of the
landmark Dusit Thani, this quality

restaurant serves up delicately spiced meat, seafood, and vegetarian Thai classics. There are also great views over the city, offering a surreal contrast with the restaurant's beautiful traditional wooden decor. *Dusit Thani.* ☎ *04-343-3333. www.facebook.com/BenjarongDTDU. Entrees AED 72–AED 145. AE, DC, MC, V. Sat–Thurs noon–3pm & 7–11:30pm; Fri brunch 12:30–4pm & dinner 7–11:30pm. Map p 84.*

★★ **Bianca Mozzarella** JUMEIRAH *ITALIAN* One of a string of new cafes in the quaint Box Park development, Bianca Mozzarella does a great line in fresh Italian cafe cuisine, using authentic ingredients (including locally produced mozzarella) in its selection of salads, pastas, and meat and fish main courses. Unlicensed. *Box Park, Al Wasl Rd.* ☎ *04-345-5300. www.be-bianca.com. Entrees AED 48–AED 117. MC, V. Daily 10am–midnight. Map p 84.*

★★ **BiCE** DUBAI MARINA *ITALIAN* Arguably the best Italian in town, this suave modern restaurant uses only the freshest and most authentic ingredients, serving up an inventive range of pastas and pizzas alongside traditional meat and seafood courses, including signature dishes like lobster carpaccio and milk-fed veal tenderloin. *Hilton* *Jumeirah Resort.* ☎ *04-399-1111. www.facebook.com/bicedubai. Entrees AED 75–AED 215. AE, DC, MC, V. Daily 12:30–4pm & 7–11:30pm. Map p 84.*

★★★ **Buddha Bar** DUBAI MARINA *PAN-ASIAN* One of the city's most spectacular restaurants, this is a huge and atmospheric culinary temple presided over by a giant Buddha statue, serenely regarding the hordes of diners below like a rather supercilious maitre d'. There's a fine array of Japanese, Chinese, and Thai food on the menu, plus bespoke Asian-style cocktails. Wildly popular, so make a reservation. *Grosvenor House Hotel.* ☎ *04-399-8888. www.buddhabar.com. Entrees AED 180–AED 295. AE, DC, MC, V. Daily 7am–midnight (drinks until 2am). Map p 84.*

★★ **China Club** DEIRA *CHINESE* The best Chinese restaurant in the old city center offers well-executed Cantonese and Beijing-style dishes, plus dim sum and good *yum cha* set lunches and dinners (AED 99/AED 139). *Radisson Blu Dubai Creek.* ☎ *04-222-7171. http://bit.ly/BluDubaiEating. Entrees AED 62–AED 168. AE, DC, MC, V. Daily noon–3pm & 7:30–11pm. Map p 85.*

★★ **Frankie's Italian Bar and Grill** DUBAI MARINA *ITALIAN* A lively and enjoyable Italian restaurant

BiCE restaurant.

Outdoor patio of Indego by Vineet in the Grosvenor House.

created by champion jockey Frankie Dettori and UK celebrity-chef Marco Pierre White, Frankie's features a wide-ranging menu stretching from fairly inexpensive pizza and pasta to elaborate (and quite pricey) meat and seafood creations. *The Walk, Jumeirah Beach Residences.* ☎ 04-399-4311. www. frankiesdubai.com. *Entrees AED 60–AED 245. Daily 12:30–3:30pm & 5:30pm–12:30am. Map p 84.*

★★ **Hoi An** SHEIKH ZAYED ROAD *VIETNAMESE* This superb Vietnamese restaurant has smooth decor styled after the interiors of colonial Indochina and a menu of top-notch Vietnamese cuisine given a fine-dining twist. The signature oven-baked sea bass in lotus leaf with galangal and kumquat compote is a guaranteed hit. *Shangri-La Hotel.* ☎ 04-343-8888. http://bit.ly/HoiAn Dubai. *Entrees AED 138–AED 172. AE, DC, MC, V. Dinner daily. Map p 84.*

★★★ **Indego** DUBAI MARINA *MODERN INDIAN* Dubai's finest Indian restaurant, overseen by Michelin-starred chef Vineet Bhatia, features such traditional offerings as Goan fish curry and butter chicken alongside inventive modern creations, such as uttupam lasagna and lamb chop biryani, all exquisitely prepared and presented. *Grosvenor House Hotel.* ☎ 04-317-6000. www.indegobyvineet.com. *Entrees AED 125–AED 320. AE, DC, MC, V. Daily 7pm–midnight. Map p 84.*

★★ **Japengo** JUMEIRAH *MULTI-CUISINE* This funky cafe's madly eclectic menu features a mix of tasty salads, sushi, sashimi, and other Japanese dishes along with sandwiches, pasta, stir-fries, and assorted Asian, Lebanese, and European dishes. Unlicensed. *Jumeirah Rd. (plus other branches citywide).* ☎ 04-345-4979. *Entrees AED 58–AED 68. AE, MC, V. Sun–Wed 7am–1am; Thurs–Sat 8am–2am. Map p 84.*

★★ **Kan Zaman** BUR DUBAI *ARABIAN* This sociable restaurant is one of the best places in town for a traditional and relatively untouristy Arabian night out, busy most evenings with local Emiratis and expat Arabs puffing on *shisha*s. The menu offers an excellent and inexpensive range of mezze, grills, and seafood, and there's seating either in the attractive dining room or on the even more appealing Creekside terrace outside. Unlicensed. *Shindagha (next to Heritage Village).* ☎ 04-393-9913. http://bit.ly/Kan ZamanDubai. *Mezze AED 20–AED 28, entrees AED 40–AED 65. AE, MC, V. Daily 1pm–4am. Map p 85.*

★★ **La Parrilla** UMM SUQEIM *ARGENTINIAN* The Argentinian-themed La Parrilla steakhouse offers at least three reasons to visit: spectacular views of the adjacent Burj Al Arab; succulent Argentinian, Australian, and Wagyu steaks; and a rip-roaring Latin atmosphere, complete with tango dancers and musicians. Reservations essential.

25th floor, Jumeirah Beach Hotel. ☎ 04-432-3232. http://bit.ly/LaParrillaDubai. Entrees AED 180–AED 310. AE, DC, MC, V. Daily 6:30–11:30pm. Map p 84.

★★ **Lime Tree Café** JUMEIRAH *CAFE* This classic Jumeirah cafe is eternally popular with local expat ladies-who-lunch, thanks to its super-fresh rolls, wraps, and salads, plus superb cakes and other classy cafe fare, all very inexpensively priced. Unlicensed. *Jumeirah Rd.* ☎ 04-325-6325. www.thelimetreecafe.com. *Main courses AED 26–AED 30. AE, MC, V. Daily 8am–6pm. Map p 84.*

★★ **Medzo** OUD METHA *ITALIAN/MEDITERRANEAN* This stylish contemporary bistro does equally well for a business lunch or a romantic supper, with a top-notch range of Mediterranean pasta, pizza, meat, and seafood dishes. *Wafi Pyramids.* ☎ 04-324-4100. www.wafi.com. *Entrees AED 82–AED 195. AE, DC, MC, V. Daily 12:30–3pm & 7–11:30pm. Map p 84.*

★★ **Nina** DUBAI MARINA *MODERN INDIAN* One of the best modern Indian restaurants in town, Nina mixes the traditional flavors of the subcontinent with lighter, more Western-influenced textures and ingredients. *One&Only Royal Mirage.* ☎ 04-399-9999. http://bit.ly/NinaDubai. *Entrees AED 70–AED 95. AE, DC, MC, V. Mon–Sat 7–11:30pm. Map p 84.*

★★ **The Noodle House** SHEIKH ZAYED ROAD *PAN-ASIAN* A long-running city institution, the Noodle House scores highly for its lively atmosphere and delicious and affordable Thai, Malaysian, and Chinese food served up at long communal tables—a great place for a brisk lunch or evening meal, if not for a quiet romantic tête-à-tête. *Emirates Towers Blvd. (and other branches citywide).* ☎ 04-319-8757. www.thenoodlehouse.com. *Entrees AED 50–AED 90. AE, DC, MC, V. Daily noon–11:30pm. Map p 84.*

★★ **Ottomans** DUBAI MARINA *TURKISH* This sumptuous Turkish restaurant specializes in historic Ottoman palace recipes given a modern makeover, with meaty masterpieces like *kuzu tandir* (slow-cooked lamb's leg) alongside a few seafood and vegetarian options, including a good *sebze güve* (vegetable stew). *Grosvenor House Hotel.* ☎ 04-317-6000. www.ottomans-dubai.com. *Entrees AED 130–AED 220. AE, DC, MC, V. Tues–Sun 7:30pm–1am. Map p 84.*

★★★ **Pai Thai** MADINAT JUMEIRAH *THAI* Quite possibly the most romantic restaurant in Dubai, beginning with the journey to the restaurant by *abra* along the waterways of Madinat Jumeirah. Gorgeous decor and fine Thai food await, with delicious curries and stir-fries—not the most original menu in town, but well prepared and not too shockingly expensive, given the setting. *Dar Al Masyaf Hotel.* ☎ 04-432-3232. http://bit.ly/PaiThaiDubai. *Entrees AED 80–AED 195. AE, DC, MC, V. Daily 6:30–11:30pm; Fri–Sat 12:30–3pm. Map p 84.*

★★ **Palm Grill** DUBAI MARINA *INTERNATIONAL* Beachside informality meets bespoke dining at this enjoyable seafront grill, with

Nina dining room in the Arabian Court.

Singaporean Curry Laksa at the Noodle House.

tables right on the sand. The mix of meat and seafood dishes features top-notch international ingredients—Atlantic lobster and Scottish salmon alongside fine American and Australian steaks (although no vegetarian options)—and there's a live band Thursday through Saturday from 6pm. *Ritz-Carlton Hotel.* ☎ 04-318-6150. http://bit.ly/PalmGrillDubai. Entrees AED 160–AED 260. AE, DC, MC, V. Wed–Mon noon–11pm. Map p 84.

★★ **Pierchic** MADINAT JUMEIRAH *SEAFOOD* Arguably Dubai's most spectacularly situated restaurant, Pierchic sits at the end of a pier jutting out from the beach at Al Qasr Hotel and commands sublime views of the Burj Al Arab and the coastline. Try to get a seat on the terrace outside, because views from inside are disappointing. The predominantly seafood menu is wildly expensive and a little pedestrian, although when the setting's this good, you might not care. *Al Qasr, Madinat Jumeirah.* ☎ 04-432-3232. http://bit.ly/Pierchic. Entrees AED 195–AED 250. AE, DC, MC, V. Daily noon–3:30pm & 7–11:30pm. Map p 84.

★★ **Qbara** OUD METHA *MODERN ARABIAN* This is one of Dubai's sexiest restaurants—moody, opulent, and with dozens of tiny lights overhead twinkling like stars in the night sky. The food matches the setting, with inventive and seductive modern Arabian cuisine

loaded with flavors and ingredients—Syrian lamb with sour cherry kofta and barberries, for example, or grilled peaches, halloumi, and spiced dates. *Al Razi St. (next to Raffles Hotel).* ☎ 04-709-2500. www.qbara.ae. Entrees AED 100–AED 170. AE, MC, V. Map p 84.

★★ **QD's** GARHOUD *INTERNATIONAL* The big draw at this lively al fresco restaurant-cum-bar-cum-shisha cafe is the superb Creekside setting backed up by a lively party atmosphere, especially at weekends, when the resident DJ (Thurs–Fri from 9am) turns up the volume. Food includes a good and inexpensive range of food from pizzas to kabobs, plus lots of shisha. *Dubai Creek Yacht Club.* ☎ 04-295-6000. www.facebook.com/QdsDubai. Entrees AED 50–AED 110. AE, DC, MC, V. Daily 5pm–2am. Map p 84.

★ **Ravi's** SATWA *PAKISTANI* This famous, no-nonsense curry house pulls in crowds of subcontinental expats and Western tourists alike thanks to its spicy north Indian food, with all sorts of mutton and chicken dishes and a few vegetarian options, all at giveaway prices. Unlicensed. *Satwa Roundabout.* ☎ 04-331 5353. http://bit.ly/PalmGrillDubai. Entrees AED 16–AED 25. No credit cards. Daily 5am–3am. No reservations. Map p 84.

★★★ **Reflets par Pierre Gagnaire** FESTIVAL CITY *FRENCH* Often claimed to be Dubai's top

Outdoor deck of Pierchic.

fine-dining destination, under the direction of Michelin-starred chef Pierre Gagnaire, Reflets par Pierre serves sublime, seasonally changing modern French dishes backed up by a superb wine list and perhaps the smoothest service in the city. *InterContinental Hotel.* ☎ *04-701-1199. www.facebook. com/refletsparpierregagnaire. Entrees AED 225–AED 280. AE, DC, MC, V. Daily 7–11pm. Map p 84.*

★★★ Rhodes Twenty10
DUBAI MARINA *MODERN INTERNATIONAL* This wildly popular restaurant by Britain's Gary Rhodes showcases his distinctive brand of modern British cuisine alongside more international creations, some with an Arabian twist. Very affordably priced, given the quality. *Le Royal Méridien Hotel.* ☎ *04-316-5550. www.rhodestwenty10.com. Entrees AED 95–AED 195. AE, DC, MC, V. Daily 7pm–midnight. Map p 84.*

★★ Rhodes W1 DUBAI MARINA
MODERN EUROPEAN Formerly the Rhodes Mezzanine, this is the original Dubai outpost of UK celeb chef Gary Rhodes, recently renamed and revamped with cool white decor and a slightly more relaxed (and less expensive) feel. The seasonally changing menu features Rhodes's signature remakes of such British and European classics as chicken Kiev, shepherd's pie, and Welsh rarebit. There are good set menus

(AED 300–AED 425) and a fine afternoon tea (AED 195) served daily from 2:30pm. *Grosvenor House Hotel.* ☎ *04-317-6000. www.rw1-dubai.com. Entrees AED 110–AED 195. AE, DC, MC, V. Daily 7pm–midnight. Map p 84.*

★★ Rivington Grill DOWNTOWN DUBAI *BRITISH* One of the nicest of the many restaurants around the Burj Khalifa Lake, the Rivington Grill serves such British dishes as slow-cooked rabbit leg, beef Wellington (order ahead), and sticky toffee pudding. The interior offers a good-looking slice of pseudo-London, although you'll probably prefer to sit out on the spacious terrace, with fine views of the Burj Khalifa opposite. *Souk al Bahar.* ☎ *04-423-0903. www. rivingtondubai.ae. Entrees AED 95–AED 265. AE, DC, MC, V. Daily noon–11pm. Map p 84.*

★★ Shakespeare & Co.
SHEIKH ZAYED ROAD *CAFE* Decorated with plentiful chintz cushions and wicker furniture, this charming cafe is a great place for English and Arabian breakfasts, light lunchtime sandwiches, salads, and crepes as well as more filling pizza, pasta, meat, and fish grills, while locals flock here for *shisha*. Unlicensed. There are other branches across the city and the rest of the UAE. *Al Saqr Business Tower, Sheikh Zayed Rd. (& branches citywide).* ☎ *04-331-1757.*

Overlooking the Dubai fountain show from Thiptara.

Shakespeare & Co. in the Al Saqr Business Tower.

www.shakespeare-and-co.com.
Entrees AED 35–AED 75. AE, MC, V.
Daily 7am–1am. Map p 84.

★★ **Table 9** DEIRA *MODERN EUROPEAN* In the venue formerly occupied by Gordon Ramsay's Verre, Table 9 continues the fine-dining traditions of its predecessor, and at a very affordable price. The seasonally changing menu features a short but interestingly eclectic selection—anything from Welsh lamb rack to harissa tiger prawns—all superbly executed by head chef Darren Velvick and team. *Hilton Dubai Creek.* ☎ 04-227-1111. www. facebook.com/table9dubai. Entrees AED 75–AED 110. AE, DC, MC, V. Daily 6:30–11pm; Fri 12:30–3:30pm. Map p 85.

★★ **Tagine** DUBAI MARINA *MOROCCAN* Tagine dishes up a well-prepared range of kebabs, tagines, and couscous dishes, along with such Moroccan classics as *bastilla d'jaj* (traditional chicken pie) and Marrakech-style *tangia*. The menu is mainly lamb and chicken, plus a bit of seafood, although not much for vegetarians. *One&Only Royal Mirage.* ☎ 04-399-9999. http://bit.ly/TagineDubai. Entrees AED 105–AED 148. AE, DC, MC, V. Tues–Sun 7–11:30pm. Map p 84.

★★ **Teatro** SHEIKH ZAYED ROAD *INTERNATIONAL* Theatrically themed restaurant serving up a mishmash of Italian, Indian, and Asian dishes, plus sushi and sashimi—anything from lobster linguini to Goan fish curry. It sounds like a recipe for disaster, but somehow it all works, with good food, big portions, and a buzzing atmosphere. *Towers Rotana Hotel.* ☎ 04-343 8000. http://bit.ly/TeatroDubai. Entrees AED 80–AED 185. AE, DC, MC, V. Daily 6pm–midnight. Map p 84.

★★ **The Thai Kitchen** GARHOUD *THAI* This attractive restaurant set on the Park Hyatt's beautiful Creekside terrace offers quality Thai cuisine, served in tapas-size portions designed for sharing, allowing you to try a range of dishes in one sitting. *Park Hyatt Dubai.* ☎ 04-602-1814. http://bit.ly/ThaiKitchenDubai. Dishes AED 42–AED 70. AE, DC, MC, V. Daily 7:30pm–midnight. Map p 84.

★★ **Thiptara** DOWNTOWN DUBAI *THAI* Downtown Dubai's most eye-catching restaurant has gorgeous Southeast Asian decor and a stunning terrace location overlooking the Dubai Fountain. Sumptuous Bangkok-style seafood is the main draw, and there's also a good selection of meat dishes (although few vegetarian options). *The Palace Hotel.* ☎ 04-428-7961. http://bit.ly/ThiptaraDubai. Entrees AED 120–AED 200. AE, DC, MC, V. Dinner daily. Map p 84.

★★ **Tomo** OUD METHA *JAPANESE* In a privileged location almost at the top of the landmark

Views of downtown from QD's at Dubai Creek Yacht Club.

Raffles hotel, Tomo's trio of Japanese chefs cook up a fine selection of food to match the views, ranging from sushi and sashimi to shabu-shabu and Japanese and Australian wagyu. Surprisingly affordable, unless you start trying the big list of fine sakes (from AED 95) that are also available. *Raffles Hotel.* ☎ *04-357-7888. www.tomo.ae. Entrees AED 70–AED 90. AE, DC, MC, V. Daily noon–1am. Map p 84.*

★★ Vivaldi by Alfredo Russo

DEIRA *ITALIAN* One of the oldest Italian restaurants in the city, Vivaldi recently got a major face-lift and now boasts bright modern decor and gorgeous Creek views through big picture windows. Michelin-starred Alfredo Russo, meanwhile, has revamped the menu, concocting a good, very reasonably priced selection of pasta and pizza along with more elaborate meat and seafood dishes, such as slow-cooked amberjack and Piedmont braised veal in red wine. DJ plays Tuesday through Thursday from 8pm and Friday from 2 to 4pm. *Sheraton Dubai Creek Hotel.* ☎ *04-221-3468. www.vivaldidubai. com. Entrees AED 60–AED 140. AE, DC, MC, V. Sat–Thurs noon–3am (Fri 2–4pm) & 7–11pm. Map p 85.*

★★ XVA Cafe BUR DUBAI

CAFE In a traditional Arabian house in deepest Bastakiya, this lovely little courtyard cafe has lots of atmosphere. Food comprises a tasty and unusual range of Arabian-style meat-free mezze and light meals, plus teas, coffees, and fresh juices. Unlicensed. *Bastakiya.* ☎ *04-353-5383. www.xvahotel.com/ cafe. Entrees AED 48–AED 60. AE, MC, V. Daily 7am–10pm. Map p 85.*

★★ Zero Gravity DUBAI

MARINA *INTERNATIONAL* This beach club-cum-bar-cum-restaurant is one of the marina's most enjoyable hang-outs, with food served in the funky dining room, on the upstairs terrace, or in the attractive sea-facing gardens. The tasty, reasonably priced fare includes assorted breakfasts plus sandwiches, salads, pizzas, and more substantial meat and seafood grills. There's a good drinks list too. *Sky Dive Dubai Drop Zone.* ☎ *04-399-0009. www.0-gravity.ae. Entrees AED 75–AED 110. AE, MC, V. Sun–Thurs 10am until late; Fri–Sat 8am until even later. Map p 84.*

★★ Zheng He's MADINAT

JUMEIRAH *CHINESE* Dubai's top Chinese restaurant showcases classic dishes (mainly Cantonese, plus a few Szechuan offerings), given the full fine-dining treatment. Sit inside in the colorful dining room or outside on the terrace by the waterway. *Mina A'Salam Hotel.* ☎ *04-432-3232. http://bit.ly/ZhengHe Dubai. Entrees AED 90–AED 220. AE, DC, MC, V. Sat–Thurs noon–3pm & 6:30pm–midnight; Fri 12:30–4pm & 7pm–midnight. Map p 84.* ●

Dubai **Nightlife**

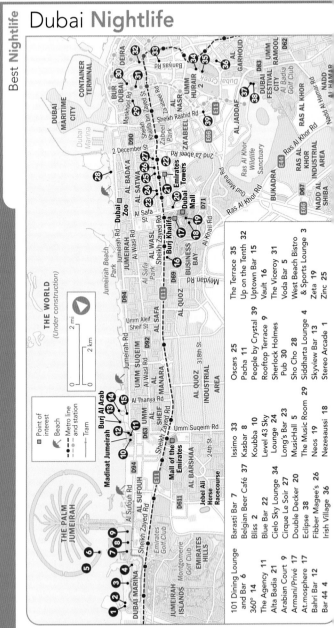

THE WORLD
(Under construction)

■ Point of interest
🏖 Beach
●–●– Metro line and station
→ Tram

101 Dining Lounge and Bar **6**	Issimo **33**	Oscars **25**
360° **14**	Kasbar **8**	Pacha **11**
The Agency **11**	Koubba **10**	People by Crystal **39**
Alta Badia **21**	Level 43 Sky Lounge **24**	Rooftop Terrace **9**
Arabian Court **9**	Long's Bar **23**	Sherlock Holmes Pub **30**
Armani/Privé **17**	MusicHall **5**	Sho Cho **28**
At.mosphere **17**	The Music Room **29**	Siddharta Lounge **4**
Bahri Bar **12**	Neos **19**	Skyview Bar **13**
Bar 44 **4**	Nezesaussi **18**	Stereo Arcade **1**
Barasti Bar **7**		The Terrace **35**
Belgian Beer Café **37**		Up on the Tenth **32**
Bliss **2**		Uptown Bar **15**
Blue Bar **22**		Vault **16**
Cielo Sky Lounge **34**		The Viceroy **31**
Cirque Le Soir **27**		Voda Bar **5**
Double Decker **20**		West Beach Bistro & Sports Lounge **3**
Eclipse **38**		Zeta **19**
Fibber Magee's **26**		Zinc **25**
Irish Village **36**		

Previous page: Koubba Bar at Jumeirah Al Qasr.

Dubai Arts & Entertainment

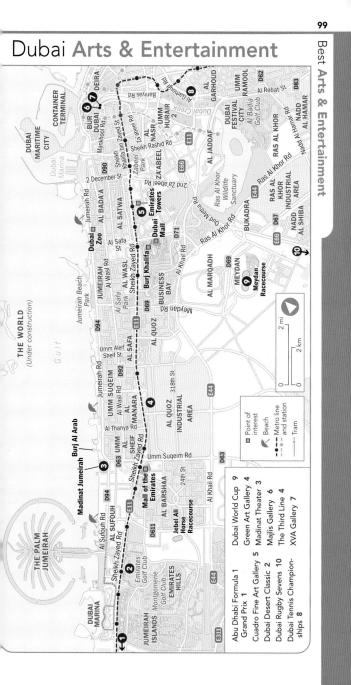

THE WORLD
(Under construction)

Gulf

THE PALM JUMEIRAH

DUBAI MARINA

CONTAINER TERMINAL

DUBAI MARITIME CITY

Dubai Marina

Burj Al Arab

Madinat Jumeirah

Juméirah Beach Park

Jumeirah Islands
Montgomerie Golf Club
EMIRATES HILLS

Emirates Golf Club

JUMEIRAH

Mall of the Emirates

AL BARSHAA

AL SUFOUH

AL QUOZ INDUSTRIAL AREA

AL QUOZ

AL SAFA

AL MANARA

UMM AL SHEIF

UMM SUQEIM

Jebel Ali Horse Racecourse

Dubai Zoo

Dubai Mall

Burj Khalifa

Emirates Towers

BUSINESS BAY

ZA'ABEEL
Za'abeel Park

AL SATWA

AL BADA'A

AL WASL

Al Safa Park

AL HUDAIBA

BUR DUBAI

DEIRA

Dubai Creek

UMM HURAIR

AL NASR

AL KARAMA

DUBAI FESTIVAL CITY

AL JADDAF

UMM RAMOOL

AL GARHOUD

Al Badia Golf Club

RAS AL KHOR

RAS AL KHOR INDUSTRIAL AREA

BUKADRA

NADD AL SHIBA

NADD AL HAMAR

MEYDAN

AL MARQADH

AL KHAIL

Ras Al Khor Wildlife Sanctuary

Meydan Racecourse

- Point of interest
- Metro line and station
- Beach
- Tram

2 mi
2 km

Abu Dhabi Formula 1 Grand Prix **1**
Cuadro Fine Art Gallery **5**
Dubai Desert Classic **2**
Dubai Rugby Sevens **10**
Dubai Tennis Championships **8**
Dubai World Cup **9**
Green Art Gallery **4**
Madinat Theater **3**
Majlis Gallery **6**
The Third Line **4**
XVA Gallery **7**

Nightlife, Arts & Entertainment
Best Bets

Best **Bar**
★★★ Bahri Bar, *Mina A'Salam, Madinat Jumeirah (p 105)*

Best **Chill-Out Venue**
★★★ 360°, *Jumeirah Beach Hotel, Umm Suqeim (p 109)*

Best for **Quirky Decor**
★★ Double Decker, *Al Murooj Rotana, Sheikh Zayed Road (p 110)*

Best **Cocktails**
★★ Skyview Bar, *Burj Al Arab, Umm Suqeim (p 106)*

Best **British Pub**
★★ Fibber Magee's, *Sheikh Zayed Road (p 111)*

Best **Wine Bar**
★★ The Agency, *Souk Madinat Jumeirah, Umm Suqeim (p 112)*

Best for **High-Rise Chic**
★★ Bar 44, *Grosvenor House Hotel, Dubai Marina (p 105)*

Best for **Beachside Partying**
★★ Barasti, *Mina A'Seyahi, Dubai Marina (p 105)*

Best **Belgian Beer**
★★ Belgian Beer Café, *Crowne Plaza, Festival City (p 105)*

Best **Old City Views**
★★ Up on the Tenth, *Radisson Blue Deira Creek, Deira (p 108)*

Best **Arabian Atmosphere**
★★ Rooftop Terrace, *One&Only Royal Mirage, Dubai Marina (p 106)*

Best for **Shameless Posing**
★★ Armani/Privé, *Armani Hotel, Downtown Dubai (p 108)*

Best **Creekside Views**
★★ Cielo Sky Lounge, *Dubai Yacht Club, Garhoud (p 110)*

Best for **Blues**
★★ Blue Bar, *Novotel, Sheikh Zayed Road (p 107)*

Best **Live Music**
★★ The Music Room, *Majestic Hotel, Bur Dubai (p 107)*

Best **Burlesque**
★★ MusicHall, *Jumeirah Zabeel Saray hotel, Palm Jumeirah (p 104)*

Best for **Sports**
★★ West Beach Bistro & Sports Lounge, *Mövenpick Hotel, Dubai Marina (p 111)*

Best **Mega-Club**
★★ Pacha, *Souk Madinat Jumeirah, Umm Suqeim (p 108)*

Best for **Unpretentious Drinking & Dancing**
★★ Zinc, *Crowne Plaza, Sheikh Zayed Road (p 109)*

Best for **A Quiet Shisha**
★★ Arabian Court, *One&Only Mirage, Dubai Marina (p 111)*

Best **Art Gallery**
★★ Majlis Gallery, *Bastakiya, Bur Dubai (p 103)*

Best **Excuse for Spending Money**
★★ Dubai Shopping Festival, *Citywide (p 101)*

Best **Excuse for a Party**
★★ Dubai Rugby Sevens, *outskirts (p 103)*

Dubai Nightlife, Arts & Entertainment A to Z

Annual Festivals & Events

★ **Dubai International Film Festival** First held in 2004, DIFF showcases art-house films from around the world, including the work of promising home-grown directors, and attracts a range of local and international silver-screen celebs. *Held annually over a week in Dec. www.dubaifilmfest.com.*

★★ **Dubai Shopping Festival** Dubai's shopping malls come (even more) alive during the ever-popular Dubai Shopping Festival, a month-long affair running throughout January. There are discounts galore over all sorts of stores, and price cuts of up to 75%—making a whole level of beautiful designer stuff tantalizingly affordable. *Every year from early Jan to early Feb.*

★ **Dubai Summer Surprises** An offshoot of the Dubai Shopping Festival, Dubai Summer Surprises is another mainly mall-based event, designed to pull in punters during the hot summer months. Shops citywide offer various discounts and promotions, and there's a good program of kids' events, presided over by the festival mascot, Modesh, Dubai's (bright yellow) answer to the Michelin man. *Annually late July to early Sept.*

Abu Dhabi Grand Prix F1.

Annual Sporting Events

★★★ **Abu Dhabi Formula 1 Grand Prix** ABU DHABI   First held in 2010, this is now the UAE's premier sporting event, and the world's only twilight F1 Grand Prix, held at the stunning Yas Marina Circuit on Yas Island (see p 151). Previous winners include Lewis Hamilton and Sebastian Vettel. *Yas Marina Circuit, Abu Dhabi. 3 days in late Nov or early Dec. www.yasmarina circuit.com.*

★★ **Dubai Desert Classic** DUBAI MARINA   The Gulf's premier golf tournament attracts some of the

Hot Tickets

Tickets for smaller gigs are usually sold on the door on the night. For big concerts and club nights, tickets are often available through the *Time Out* ticket office, either online at https://www.itp.net/tickets or by phone (☎ 800-4669, or 971-4-444-3459 if calling from abroad).

Ramadan Customs

The holiest month in the Islamic calendar, Ramadan occurs in the early summer. During Ramadan, practicing Muslims are required to fast from dawn until dusk, to pray regularly, and to abstain from sexual relations during daylight hours. Non-Muslim visitors are advised not to eat, drink, smoke, or chew gum in public (although you're free to do so in the privacy of your hotel). Loud music, singing, dancing, cursing, or any sign of physical contact between members of the opposite sex are also severely frowned upon. Live music is banned for the month, so many nightclubs close for the duration. Alcohol is still served, although only after dark, and discreetly.

At dusk, after its long day of abstinence, the entire city sits down to supper, known as Iftar ("The Breaking of the Fast"). Many hotels lay on extravagant Iftar buffets, sometimes in specially designed tents. The festival of Eid Al Fitr, the day signaling the end of Ramadan, is marked by exuberant citywide celebrations.

The exact dates of Ramadan are calculated according to the Islamic lunar calendar and can change according to when the new moon is sighted. Estimated dates for the next few years are as follows: **2016,** June 6–July 5; **2017,** May 27–June 25; **2018,** May 16–June 14; **2019,** May 6–June 4.

Practicing Muslims are required to pray through the month of Ramadan.

biggest names in the game. Former champions include Tiger Woods, Ernie Els, Seve Ballesteros, and Rory McIlroy. *Held over 1 week in Feb. Emirates Golf Club, near Dubai Marina. www.dubaidesertclassic.com.*

Dubai World Cup horse race.

★★ Dubai Rugby Sevens OUT-SKIRTS One of the city's most popular sporting events, this rugby tournament draws crack teams from around the world, with matches usually followed by wild bouts of drinking and partying. *Held over 3 days in early Dec. The Sevens (on the E66 Al Ain Hwy. on the edge of Dubai). www.dubairugby7s.com.*

★★ Dubai Tennis Championships GARHOUD Recent winners of this prestigious ATP/WTA international men's and ladies' singles' and doubles' tournament include Roger Federer, Novak Djokovic, Petra Kvitová, and Venus Williams. *Held over 2 weeks in late Feb. Dubai Tennis Stadium, Garhoud. www.dubaitennischampionships.com.*

★★ Dubai World Cup NAD AL SHEBA The world's richest horse race offers $10 million in prize money. *Held annually in Mar at the Nad Al Sheba Racetrack. www.dubaiworldcup.com.*

Art Galleries

★ Cuadro Fine Art Gallery DIFC One of a cluster of upmarket galleries in the Gate Village area (part of the Dubai International Financial Centre development), Cuadro features a wide spectrum of works in various media. *The Gate Village.* ☎ *04-425-0400. www.cuadroart.com. Sun–Thurs 10am–8pm; Sat noon–6pm. Map p 99.*

★ Green Art Gallery Al QUOZ This long-established gallery is now based (along with numerous other galleries) in the burgeoning arts quarter that has grown up in the low-rent Al Quoz industrial district. Temporary exhibitions focus on works in a range of media by a select group of artists from the Middle East, north Africa, and beyond. *Al Serkal Ave., Al Quoz.* ☎ *04-346-9305. www.gagallery.com. Sat–Thurs 10am–7pm. Map p 99.*

★★ Majlis Gallery BUR DUBAI The oldest and still one of the best galleries in Dubai, the Majlis Gallery is set in a beautiful old traditional house in Bastakiya. It showcases artworks by Western and Middle Eastern artists—usually figurative, and often with an Arabian theme. *Al Fahidi Roundation, by main entrance to Bastakiya.* ☎ *04-353-6233. www.themajlisgallery.com. Sat–Thurs 10am–6pm. Map p 99.*

★ The Third Line AL QUOZ This leading Al Quoz gallery presents the work of a wide range of Middle Eastern artists. *St. 6, Al Quoz.* ☎ *04-341-1367.*

Art installation at the Third Line Gallery.

www.thethirdline.com. Sat–Thurs 10am–7pm. Map p 99.

★★ **XVA Gallery** BUR DUBAI Cafe-cum-hotel-cum-art gallery (see also p 96), XVA mounts regularly changing exhibitions of painting and sculpture by mainly Middle Eastern artists. *Bastakiya.* ☎ 04-353-5383. www.xvagallery.com. Daily 10am–6pm. Map p 99.

Arts & Entertainment— Performing Arts

★ **Madinat Theater** MADINAT JUMEIRAH   In a city of 100 shopping malls, this is Dubai's only dedicated theater. It's an attractive, state-of-the-art venue, although the program of events is threadbare and pretty dull, with hackneyed musicals, commercial theater shows, and light Muzak (Western and Arabian). *Souk Madinat Jumeirah (p 39, ⑪).* ☎ 04-366-6546. www.madinat theatre.com. Map p 99.

★★ **MusicHall** PALM JUMEIRAH A novel take on the traditional

State-of-the-art Madinat Theater.

dinner-and-dance concept, the MusicHall presents twice-weekly shows that feature a medley of 10 or so musicians performing in a range of styles—anything from rock to gypsy—while guests listen over dinner and drinks. *Jumeirah Zabeel Saray Hotel, Palm Jumeirah.* ☎ 056-270-8670. www.themusichall.com. Thurs–Fri 9pm–3am. Map p 98.

Nightlife—Bars

★★ **Alta Badia** SHEIKH ZAYED ROAD   One of Dubai's highest bars, the long-running Alta Badia (formerly Vu's Bar) has been rather overtaken by newer and more spectacular venues but is still a fun spot for a drink, with huge steel girders framing bird's-eye views over the city. The extensive, Italian-inspired drinks list features all sort of cocktails, wines, spirits, and champagnes—a bargain (given the setting) during the daily 6–9pm happy hour. *51st floor, Jumeirah Emirates Tower, Sheikh Zayed Rd.*

☎ 04-330-0000. www.jumeirah
emiratestowers.com. Daily 6pm–3am.
Map p 98.

★★ **At.mosphere** DOWNTOWN
DUBAI On the 122nd floor of the
Burj Khalifa, at a height of 442m, the
world's highest bar smashes records
almost for fun. You can come either
for a meal (see p 89) or just for a
drink and snack in the lounge.
Advance reservations are essential,
and there's a minimum spend of
AED 250 (or AED 200 for a non-
window table after dark), although
drinks are not extravagantly priced.
Burj Khalifa. ☎ 04-888-3828. www.
atmosphereburjkhalifa.com. Daily
noon–2am. Map p 98.

★★★ **Bahri Bar** MADINAT JUMEI-
RAH This sublime Moroccan-style
bar has picture-perfect little outdoor terraces overlooking the
Madinat Jumeirah and Burj Al Arab—
beautiful at any time of the day or
night, but particularly gorgeous at
sunset. Cocktails, wines, and beers
are served, plus a small range of light
bar meals and snacks. Mina A'Salam
Hotel, Madinat Jumeirah. ☎ 04-366-
8888. www.jumeirah.com. Daily 4pm–
2am (Thurs–Fri until 3am). Map p 98.

★★★ **Bar 44** DUBAI MARINA
Situated on the 44th floor of tower
1 of the suave Grosvenor House
Hotel, this very chic cocktail bar
offers the perfect perch to enjoy a
long, slow drink while gazing out at
the illuminated towers of the
Marina. Grosvenor House Hotel,
Dubai Marina. ☎ 04-399-8888. www.
grosvenorhouse-dubai.com. Daily
6pm–2am (Thurs–Fri 3am). Map p 98.

★★ **Barasti Bar** DUBAI MARINA
This huge beachside bar complex
has a bit of everything. A lot of folks
head down to the chilled-out beach
area (although live DJs at weekends
raise the temperature). Others prefer the livelier Middle Deck upstairs,
with a large bar, live music most
nights, sports on big-screen TVs,

and a spacious pool. Le Méridien
Mina Seyahi Hotel, Dubai Marina.
☎ 04-399-3333. www.barastibeach.
com. Daily 11am–1am. Map p 98.

★★ **Belgian Beer Café** FESTIVAL
CITY Refreshingly different and
surprisingly authentic, this Belgian
bar-cafe has a convivial atmosphere
and a good range of draft and bottled Belgian beers, plus cheery
Flemish food, including the inevitable mussels. There's another branch
in the Madinat Jumeirah. Crowne
Plaza, Festival City. ☎ 04-701-1127.
www.facebook.com/belgianbeer
cafedubai. Daily noon–2am (Thurs–Fri
until 3am). Map p 98.

★★ **Eclipse** FESTIVAL CITY Wonderful city views from the top of the
InterContinental are the main draw at
this swanky bar; the champagne and
cocktail list isn't bad either. 26th floor,
InterContinental, Festival City. ☎ 04-
701-1128. Daily 6pm–2pm. Map p 98.

★ **Issimo** DEIRA Suave and
sedate, this cocktail bar in the Hilton
Dubai Creek has a distinctive boat-
shaped bar. It's an excellent spot for
an aperitif (or nightcap) before a visit
to the excellent Table 9 restaurant
upstairs. Hilton Dubai Creek, Deira.
☎ 04-227-1111. www.hilton.com/
dubai. Daily 3pm–1am. Map p 98.

★★ **Koubba** MADINAT JUMEIRAH
Very similar to the superb Bahri Bar
nearby, the Arabian-styled Koubha
offers superb Burj Al Arab views.
The decor and ambience are perhaps a fraction less memorable,
although it often has space when
Bahri Bar is full. The excellent
house band Heart & Soul plays
nightly from around 8pm. Al Qasr
Hotel, Madinat Jumeirah. ☎ 04-432-
3232. www.jumeirah.com/as-qasr.
Daily 5pm–2am. Map p 98.

★★ **Level 43 Sky Lounge**
SHEIKH ZAYED ROAD There's a
surprising lack of high-level bars
along Sheikh Zayed Road, making

this the go-to option for bird's-eye views of the strip. On the outdoor rooftop terrace of the Sheraton, it's small and not particularly atmospheric, but the views down the road are stunning, and prices aren't too sky-high. *Four Points Sheraton.* ☎ *04-316-9888. www.facebook. com/Level43SkyLounge. Daily 4:30pm–2:30am. Map p 98.*

★★ **Neos** DOWNTOWN DUBAI One of Dubai's most spectacular high-rise drinking venues, situated at the top of the Address Downtown Hotel (p 117), Neos boasts stunning views across to the Burj Dubai and over the rest of the city. Kitsch decor adds to the surreal, head-in-the-clouds experience. Check ahead to make sure the bar has reopened after the hotel's New Year's Eve 2015 fire. *63rd floor, The Address Downtown Hotel.* ☎ *04-888-3444. www.theaddress.com. Daily 6pm–2:30am. Map p 98.*

★★ **Rooftop Terrace** DUBAI MARINA This atmospheric Moroccan-looking bar is set in the beautiful One&Only Mirage hotel. The upstairs rooftop area is the nicest part, with lounge seating amid a quirky design of domes and tiny pavilions (and a live DJ most nights playing "arabesque chill-out" music).

Rooftop at One&Only Mirage.

The indoor sports lounge downstairs is less exciting, although it has a fine ocean-facing terrace outside. Reservations are recommended. *One&Only Royal Mirage.* ☎ *04-399-9999. www.oneandonlyresorts.com. Daily 5pm–2am. Map p 98.*

★ **Skyview Bar** UMM SUQEIM Poised atop the Burj Al Arab, the Skyview Bar offers one of Dubai's ultimate views—although you'll need to book in advance and agree to a minimum spend of AED 350 per person. The expert mixologists and bespoke cocktail list do their best to please, and there's a good jazz trio Tuesday to Sunday from 10pm. You can also visit for afternoon tea (see "Visiting the Burj al Arab," p 56). *Burj Al Arab.* ☎ *04-301-7600. www.burjalarab. com. Daily 7pm–2am. Map p 98.*

★★ **The Terrace** GARHOUD Fashionable but not too pretentious, this gorgeous al fresco bar affords dreamy views over the Creek and the flashy millionaires' toys moored in the adjacent yacht club. A discreet chill-out soundtrack, good cocktail list, and superior bar food help things along nicely. *Park Hyatt, Garhoud.* ☎ *04-602-1814. www.dubai.park. hyatt.com. Noon–2am (food until midnight). Map p 98.*

★ **Uptown Bar** UMM SUQEIM Near the top of the Jumeirah Beach Hotel, this bar isn't much to look at, but it scores highly for its location and brilliant views of the Burj Al Arab and Marina. There's seating indoors or on the breezy terrace outside and a good selection of cocktails and wines. *24th floor, Jumeirah Beach Hotel.* ☎ *04-432-3232. www.jumeirahbeachhotel.com. Daily 6pm–2am. Map p 98.*

★★ **Vault** BUSINESS BAY If you want to have a drink at the top of the world's tallest hotel, this is the

Voda Bar.

place. Perched on the 72nd floor of the JW Marriott Marquis, the Vault offers 360-degree views through floor-to-ceiling windows. The menu of fancy cocktails, premium spirits, and cigars is predictably ostentatious, although the 5 to 7pm happy hour and DJ Nicole (Tues–Sat from 9pm) help lighten the mood. *JW Marriott Marquis Hotel.* ☎ *04-414 3000. www.jwmarriottmarquisdubai life.com. Daily 5pm–3am. Map p 98.*

★★ **Voda Bar** PALM JUMEIRAH Resembling the inside of a giant ice cave—all frosty whites and blues— this is arguably the coolest-looking bar in Dubai. A fancy drinks list (visit during the daily 6–8pm happy hour for less financial pain) and fine Japanese food complete the package, while shisha is served on the panoramic terrace outside. *Jumeirah Zabeel Saray Hotel.* ☎ *04-453 0444. www.jumeirah.com. Daily 6pm– 3am. Map p 98.*

★★ **Zeta** DOWNTOWN DUBAI Directly opposite the Burj Khalifa and overlooking the Dubai Fountain, this pan-Asian restaurant-lounge occupies one of the city's most prized and spectacular locations. Most people come to eat, although you can also just rock up for a drink, with a decent spread of wine, cocktails, and beer. Pricey, but

worth it for the view. If there's no room at Zeta, the adjacent Calabar bar is another option, although the views aren't so good. *The Address Hotel.* ☎ *04-436-8888. www.the address.com. Daily noon–midnight; closed during summer. Map p 98.*

Bars with Live Music

★★ **Blue Bar** SHEIKH ZAYED ROAD A good selection of Belgian beers (draft and bottled) and regular live blues and soul are the twin draws at this stylish little place. Things can get surprisingly lively when there's music on, but it's usually pleasantly mellow at other times. *Novotel Hotel.* ☎ *04-310-8150. www.facebook.com/BlueBar NovotelWTC. Sat–Wed noon–1am; Thurs–Fri noon–3am. Map p 98.*

★★ **The Music Room** BUR DUBAI A classic slice of Bur Dubai nightlife, this big and busy pub stages regular live music performances (daily except Fri 9pm–2am) by the resident cover band, with big amps and plenty of va-va-voom. Regular drinks promotions, lots of pool tables, and the usual sports matches on TV keep things busy at other times. *Majestic Hotel, Mankhool Rd.* ☎ *04-359-8888. www.facebook. com/MusicRoomDubai/. Daily 6pm– 3am. Map p 98.*

Ladies Nights

Ladies Nights are a big feature of Dubai's nightlife, with venues attempting to pull in members of the fairer sex with offers that usually include generous (and sometimes unlimited) quantities of free booze. Just be aware that where the ladies lead, large groups of would-be amorous blokes frequently follow.

Ladies Nights crop up at various venues around the city from Sunday through Thursday. Tuesdays are particularly popular, in an attempt to drum up customers in the middle of the week. Check *Time Out Dubai* magazine for the latest happenings.

★ Up on the Tenth DEIRA
Perched high above the Creek, Up on the Tenth has arguably the best view of any old city bar and is also a cozy and relaxing place to hunker down over a glass of wine or a cocktail while listening to the regular live jazz singer (nightly except Tues from 10pm). *Radisson Blu, Deira.* ☎ *04-222-7171. www.radissonblu. com/hotel-dubaideiracreek. Daily 6:30pm–3am. Map p 98.*

Clubs

★★ Armani/Privé DOWNTOWN DUBAI
The cool club at the Armani Hotel is virtually a work of art in its own right—and a good place to watch Dubai's wealthy, beautiful, and expensively dressed at play. Regular House nights and big-name visiting DJs mean the dance floor is rarely empty. *Armani Hotel, Burj Khalifa. www.dubai.armanihotels.com. Tues–Sat 10pm–3am. Map p 98.*

★★ Cirque Le Soir SHEIKH ZAYED ROAD
Dubai's kookiest club, this "circus nightclub" features an outlandish and colorful cast of burlesque-style circus performers—stilt-walkers, midgets, jugglers, magicians, and sword-swallowers, plus international DJs and plenty of on-tour celebs in the crowd. *Fairmont Hotel. www.cirque lesoir.com/dubai. Mon–Tues & Thurs– Fri 10:30pm–3am. Map p 98.*

★★ Kasbar DUBAI MARINA
This Arabian-themed hotel nightclub isn't exactly cutting-edge, but it does boast opulent Moroccan-inspired decor, an enjoyably eclectic music policy, and a relatively pretension-free atmosphere compared to more fashionable venues around the city. Some nights there's more happening at the nearby Rooftop Terrace (see p 106). *One&Only, Royal Mirage.* ☎ *04-399-9999. www.oneandonly resorts.com. Mon–Sat 9:30pm–3am. Over 25s only. Map p 98.*

★★ Pacha UMM SUQEIM
Dubai's burgeoning club scene has been pushed to a new level with the arrival in 2014 of a Gulf outpost of

Dancing at Kasbar in the One&Only Royal Mirage.

The 360° bar at Jumeirah Beach Hotel.

Ibiza's famous Pacha club. The opulent, multilevel, Arabian-styled venue (formerly home to the Trilogy club) is one of the biggest and best in town, with an up-for-it crowd and all the big-name acts this nightclub franchise is famous for. *Madinat Jumeirah.* ☎ *04-567-0000. www.pacha.ae or www.facebook.com/pachaibizadubai. Tues–Sun 8pm–3am. Map p 98.*

★★ **People by Crystal** OUD METHA   In a very sexy setting at the summit of the glass-topped, pyramidal Raffles hotel, this is one of the most glam clubbing destinations in town. Dress to impress. *Raffles Hotel.* ☎ *050-297-2097. www. peoplebycrystal.com. Thurs–Sat 11pm–3am. Map p 98.*

★★ **Zinc** SHEIKH ZAYED ROAD One of Dubai's most down-to-earth and enjoyable clubs, Zinc delivers more drinking and dancing than pouting and posing, with mainstream, pretension-free music supplied by resident house DJs. *Crowne Plaza, Sheikh Zayed Rd.* ☎ *050-151-5609. www.facebook.com/zincnight club. Daily 9pm–3am. Map p 98.*

DJ Bars

★★ **101 Dining Lounge and Bar** PALM JUMEIRAH   Spectacular views across the water to Dubai Marina and beyond are the main draw at this very smooth venue on a pier at the One&Only's private marina (with indoor and outdoor seating). Full meals are available in the restaurant, or just come for a drink and snack on some tapas. DJs spin a mainly chill-out soundtrack nightly from 8pm (weekdays) or 5pm (weekends). *One&Only, The Palm Hotel.* ☎ *04-440-1030. www. thepalm.oneandonlyresorts.com. Daily 11:30am–2am. Map p 98.*

★★★ **360°** UMM SUQEIM   One of the city's finest after-dark drinking spots, 360° is set at the end of a long breakwater poking out into the Arabian Gulf, with sublime views of the Burj Al Arab and Jumeirah Beach Hotel and a mainly chic young crowd. Chilled-out earlier in the evening, things liven up later on, with regular appearances by leading local and international DJs and a mainly house soundtrack. *Jumeirah Beach Hotel.* ☎ *04-432-3232. www.jumeirahbeachhotel.com. Daily 5pm–2am; Fri from 4pm. Map p 98.*

★★ **Bliss** AREA   If you want to drink and relax on the beach, this is as good a place as any (although daytime views are somewhat blighted for the time being by construction work on the new Dubai Eye opposite). Choose between a lounge chair on the sands or a seat on the boardwalk-style terrace, while the resident DJs spin a mix of chill-out and deep house, growing increasingly upbeat as the night wears on. *Sheraton Jumeirah Beach Resort.* ☎ *04-399-5577. www.bliss loungedubai.com. Daily 4pm–3am. Map p 98.*

★★ **Cielo Sky Lounge** GAR-HOUD In a superb location on a rooftop terrace high above the Creek, Cielo is about as cool as it gets in the older part of the city. Fine food and fancy cocktails come standard, and the bar takes its music quite seriously, with one of the city's better line-ups of local and international DJs. *Dubai Creek Yacht Club.* ☎ *04-416-1800. www.cielodubai. com. Daily 5pm–2am (Fri–Sat from 4pm); closed Apr–Sept. Map p 98.*

★★ **Sho Cho** JUMEIRAH This chichi little bar isn't as ultra-fashionable as it used to be but is still a pleasant spot for a cocktail and a bit of idle people-watching and fashion-scouting. There's a live DJ most nights; passable sushi is served in the restaurant. *Dubai Marine Beach Resort, Jumeirah Rd.*

☎ *04-346-1111. www.sho-cho.com. Daily 7pm–3am. Map p 98.*

★★ **Siddharta Lounge** DUBAI MARINA This seductive little lounge-bar is tucked away in Tower 2 of the Grosvenor House Hotel. Choose between terrace seating around the small pool outside or the very cool interior—snow-white with gold trimmings. A DJ plays nightly except Sunday from 9pm, and there's also good Mediterranean and Asian bites and meals. *Grosvenor House Hotel.* ☎ *04-317-6000. www. siddhartalounge.com. Daily 10am– 1am (Thurs–Fri until 2am). Map p 98.*

Pubs

★★ **Double Decker** SHEIKH ZAYED ROAD A quirky British-style pub, Double Decker has fun decor themed after the old London Routemaster buses. Things can get surprisingly lively some evenings, helped along by regular DJ and/or live music acts most nights. *Al Murooj Rotana Hotel, off Sheikh Zayed Rd.* ☎ *04-321-1111. www.facebook. com/DoubleDeckerDubai. Daily noon–3am. Map p 98.*

Siddharta Lounge at the Grosvenor House Hotel.

★★ Fibber Magee's SHEIKH ZAYED ROAD Perhaps the most authentic British-cum-Irish-style pub in Dubai, Fibber Magee's has a cozy wood-paneled interior, a borderline raucous atmosphere, cheap beer, and good pub grub. Tricky to find (check the website for directions) but worth the effort. *Saeed Tower One.* ☎ 04-332-2400. www.fibbersdubai. com. Daily 8am–3am. Map p 98.

★★ Irish Village GARHOUD This ever-popular Irish pub near the airport provides good food, cheap beer, and occasional live music—best in the cool winter months, when you can sit out on the spacious outdoor terrace. *The Aviation Club, Garhoud.* ☎ 04-282-4750. www. theirishvillage.com. Daily 11am–1am (Wed–Thurs until 2am). Map p 98.

★★ Long's Bar SHEIKH ZAYED ROAD More pub than bar, Long's does a fair impression of a traditional British boozer, boasting a loyal following of old-time expats and sozzled tourists, with cheap beer, plenty of sports on the myriad TV screens, and the longest bar in the Middle East—just like it says on the packet. *Towers Rotana Hotel.* ☎ 04-312-2202. http://bit.ly/Longs Dubai. Daily noon–3am. Map p 98.

★★ Nezesaussi DOWNTOWN DUBAI This convivial sports pub and grill features sports on myriad TV screens as well as a good range of South African, Australian, and New Zealand food—hence the bizarre name. (Say "Nezzasozzy," although people might just think you've spent too long at the bar.) *Manzil Hotel, Downtown Dubai.* ☎ 04-428-5933. www.facebook. com/NezesaussiGrill/. Daily 5pm–2am (Fri–Sat from noon). Map p 98.

★★ Sherlock Holmes Pub BUR DUBAI The most sociable pub in this part of town, the Sherlock Holmes has cozy English decor, assorted Holmes-related bric-a-brac, and reliable bar food, including camel burgers. *Arabian Court Hotel, Al Fahidi St., Bur Dubai.* ☎ 04-351-9111. www.sherlockholmespub.net. Daily noon–2am. Map p 98.

★★ Stereo Arcade DUBAI MARINA This good-looking pub is probably the nicest in the Marina, with an above-average selection of draft beers, live music most evenings, and, best of all, an attached room full of classic old arcade video games (Mario Bros, Asteroids, and so on), all free to play when you buy a drink. *DoubleTree by Hilton Hotel, The Walk, Dubai Marina.* ☎ 052-618-2424. www.facebook. com/StereoArcade. Daily 6pm–2am. Map p 98.

★★ The Viceroy BUR DUBAI Sedate and pleasantly atmospheric, this English pub is rather like supping inside a dimly lit and cozy wooden box, with lots of dark oak paneling and leather armchairs. There's a reasonable beer and wine selection, and decent bar food, too. *Four Points by Sheraton, Khalid Bin Al Waleed St.* ☎ 04-397-7444. www.theviceroypub. com. Daily noon–2am. Map p 98.

★★ West Beach Bistro & Sports Lounge DUBAI MARINA This spacious, good-looking modern pub has TVs on every wall for sports fans. It's also one of the least expensive places in the Marina for a drink, especially during what's claimed to be "Dubai's longest happy hour" (daily noon–9pm). *Mövenpick Hotel, Jumeirah Beach Residences.* ☎ 04-449-8888. http:// bit.ly/WestBeachDubai. Map p 98.

Shisha

★★ Arabian Court DUBAI MARINA Recline with a shisha amid the illuminated palm trees in one of the One&Only's magical Moroccan-themed courtyards. You won't find a prettier place for a

Good Places for Shisha

As well as Arabian Court (p 111), the following are just a few of the many other places around the city serving shisha, the bubbling waterpipes that come in a range of flavors:

360° (p 109): Jumeirah Beach Hotel.
Kan Zaman (p 91): Bur Dubai.
QD's (p 93): Garhoud.
Shakespeare & Co. (p 94): Sheikh Zayed Road.
Voda (p 107): Palm Jumeirah.

waterpipe, and there's also a reasonable drinks list, plus meze and Arabian-style mains. (There's a second, almost identical, venue—but with less food—called The Palace Courtyard, in the One&Only's The Palace wing.) *Arabian Court, One&Only Royal Mirage.* ☎ *04-399-9999. http://bit.ly/OOCourtyards. Daily 7pm–1am. Map p 98.*

Wine Bars
★★ **The Agency** UMM SUQEIM
Chic and convivial, this modern wine bar (plus small attached terrace) serves up a huge range of international vintages, although most are only available by the (rather expensive) bottle. Prices do

tumble a bit during the daily happy hour. *Madinat Jumeirah.* ☎ *04-432-3232. www.jumeirah.com. Sat–Thurs noon–1am; Fri 4pm–2am. Map p 98.*

★★ **Oscars** SHEIKH ZAYED ROAD
A rustic little wine bar with bare brick walls and tables made out of barrels—you'd hardly expect to find such a slice of rural France halfway up a high-rise in Sheikh Zayed Road. There are more than 50 wines by the glass to sample, plus assorted French-style food. *Crowne Plaza Hotel, Sheikh Zayed Rd.* ☎ *04-331-1111. www.facebook. com/oscarsdubai. Daily 6pm–midnight. Map p 98.* ●

Enjoying a glass of wine and a cheese plate at the Agency.

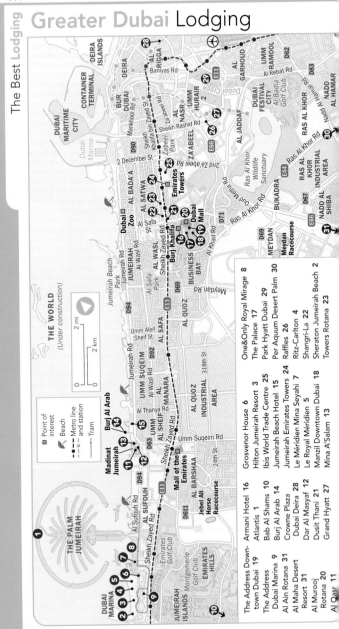

THE WORLD
(Under construction)

- Point of interest
- Beach
- Metro line and station
- Tram

2 mi

2 km

THE PALM JUMEIRAH

THE WORLD (Under construction)

Burj Al Arab

Madinat Jumeirah

Mall of the Emirates

DUBAI MARINA

JUMEIRAH ISLANDS

EMIRATES HILLS

Jebel Ali Horse Racecourse

Montgomerie Golf Club

Emirates Golf Club

Jumeirah Beach

AL SUFOUH

AL BARSHAA

AL QUOZ INDUSTRIAL AREA

AL QUOZ

UMM SUQEIM

AL MANARA

AL SHEIF

AL SAFA

AL WASL

JUMEIRAH

AL WASL

AL SATWA

AL BADA'A

Burj Al Arab

Dubai Zoo

Emirates Towers

Dubai Mall

Burj Khalifa

BUSINESS BAY

Meydan Racecourse

MEYDAN

CONTAINER TERMINAL

DEIRA ISLANDS

DUBAI MARITIME CITY

BUR DUBAI

DEIRA

AL RIGGA

Baniyas Rd

Dubai Creek

AL GARHOUD

UMM RAMOOL

DUBAI FESTIVAL CITY

Al Badia Golf Club

RAS AL KHOR

RAS AL KHOR INDUSTRIAL AREA

NADD AL SHIBA

NADD AL HAMAR

BUKADRA

Ras Al Khor Wildlife Sanctuary

AL JADDAF

UMM HURAIR 2

ZAABEEL

Zabeel Park

AL NASR

Previous page: Pool and private cabanas at the Park Hyatt Dubai.

The Address Down-town Dubai 19
The Address Dubai Marina 9
Al Ain Rotana 31
Al Maha Desert Resort 31
Al Murooj Rotana 20
Al Qasr 11
Armani Hotel 16
Atlantis 1
Bab Al Shams 10
Burj Al Arab 14
Crowne Plaza Dubai Deira 28
Dar Al Masyaf 12
Dusit Thani 27
Grand Hyatt 21
Grosvenor House 6
Hilton Jumeirah Resort 3
Ibis World Trade Centre 25
Jumeirah Beach Hotel 15
Jumeirah Emirates Towers 24
Le Méridien Mina Seyahi 7
Le Royal Méridien 5
Manzil Downtown Dubai 18
Mina A'Salam 13
One&Only Royal Mirage 8
The Palace 17
Park Hyatt Dubai 29
Per Aquum Desert Palm 30
Raffles 26
Ritz-Carlton 4
Shangri-La 22
Sheraton Jumeirah Beach 2
Towers Rotana 23

City Center Lodging

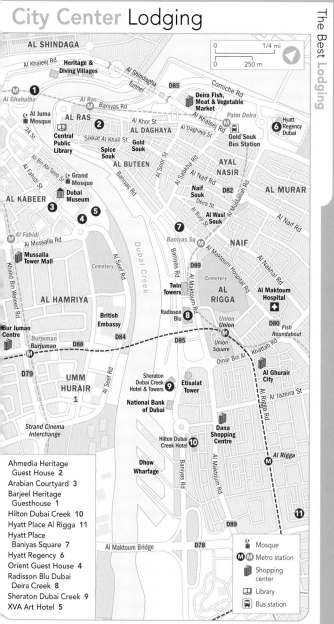

ALSHINDAGA

Al Khaleej Rd

Heritage & Diving Villages

Al Shindagha Tunnel

D85

Corniche Rd

Deira Fish, Meat & Vegetable Market

Palm Deira

Al Ghubaiba

Al Ras

Baniyas Rd

Al Khor St

AL RAS

AL DAGHAYA

Al Daghaya St

Al Khaleej Rd

Gold Souk Bus Station

Hyatt Regency Dubai

Al Juma Mosque

Central Public Library

Sikkat Al Khail St

Spice Souk

Gold Souk

AL BUTEEN

Al Spor St

Al Sabkha Rd

AYAL NASIR

Al Naif St

AL MURAR

3A St

Ali Bin Abi Taleb St

Al Fahidi St

Grand Mosque

Baniyas Rd

Naif Souk

Deira St

D82

Al Naif Rd

AL KABEER

Dubai Museum

Al Bun St

Al Wasl Souk

Al Fahidi

Al Mussalla Rd

Baniyas Sq

Al Maktoum Hospital Rd

NAIF

Al Nakhal Rd

Mussalla Tower Mall

Cemetery

Dubai Creek

Al Seef Rd

Baniyas Rd

D89

Cemetery

AL RIGGA

Al Maktoum Hospital

Khalid Bin Waleed Rd

AL HAMRIYA

Twin Towers

Al Maktoum Rd

D80

Fish Roundabout

British Embassy

Radisson Blu

Union Union

Bur Juman Centre

Burjuman

Burjuman

D88

D84

D85

Union Square

Omar Bin Al Khattab Rd

Al Ghurair City

D79

UMM HURAIR

Al Seef Rd

Sheraton Dubai Creek Hotel & Towers

Etisalat Tower

Al Rigga Rd

Al Jazeira St

1

National Bank of Dubai

Dana Shopping Centre

Al Rigga

Strand Cinema Interchange

Hilton Dubai Creek Hotel

Dhow Wharfage

Baniyas Rd

Al Maktoum Rd

Al Maktoum Bridge

Al Maktoum Rd

D89

D78

11

0   1/4 mi
0   250 m

Mosque
M Metro station
Shopping center
Library
Bus station

Lodging Best Bets

Best of the Best
★★ Burj Al Arab $$$$$ (p 119)

Best City Center Hotel
★★★ Park Hyatt Dubai $$$$
(p 125)

Best in Old Dubai
★★ Arabian Courtyard $$ (p 118)

Best for Business
★★ Jumeirah Emirates Towers
$$$$ (p 123)

Best Over-the-Top Beach
Resort
★★ Jumeirah Zabeel Saray $$$$
(p 123)

Best for Contemporary Style
★★★ Raffles Dubai $$$$ (p 125)

Best for Urban Chic
★★★ Grosvenor House $$$
(p 120)

Best for Kids
★★★ Jumeirah Beach Hotel $$$$
(p 122)

Best for Family Fun
★★ Atlantis $$$$$ (p 119)

Best Retreat from the City
★★ Per Aquum Desert Palm $$$
(p 125)

Best Value for Money
★★ Hyatt Place Baniyas Square
$$ (p 121)

Best for Local Ambience
★★ XVA Hotel $$ (p 115)

Best Arabian Nights Ambience
★★★ One&Only Royal Mirage
$$$$ (p 124)

Best Desert Resort
★★★ Al Maha Desert Resort
$$$$$ (p 117)

Room Rates

Trying to give a realistic idea of room prices in Dubai is difficult. All the big hotels vary their prices on a daily basis, according to demand, and rates can fluctuate wildly from excellent value to horribly expensive.

Quoted prices are based on rates for the **most inexpensive double room in high season** (roughly Nov–Feb, highest in Jan–Feb, excluding peak periods over Christmas and New Year). Prices often fall by a third or even more during the hot summer **low season** (Apr–Sept). The best advice is to shop around online, checking the hotels' own websites, looking for special offers, having a look at online agents such as Expedia.com, and scouting for discounted flight-plus-hotel packages. Note that rates quoted below include all taxes, including the customary 20% tax (10% service charge plus 10% VAT levied by all the larger hotels).

Dubai Lodging A to Z

★★ The Address Downtown Dubai

DOWNTOWN DUBA This luxurious high-rise directly opposite the Burj Khalifa sits at the very heart of the Downtown Dubai action. Rooms are stylish with every amenity; facilities include a spa, fitness center, restaurants aplenty, and a stunning infinity pool overlooking the Burj Khalifa Lake. A massive fire on New Year's Eve 2015 damaged much of the hotel—check on its current status. ☎ 04-436-8888. *www.theaddress.com. 196 units. Doubles AED 2,100. AE, DC, MC, V. Map p 114.*

★★ The Address Dubai Marina

DUBAI MARINA The best of the various hotels clustered around the Dubai Marina, the Address is directly connected to the swanky Marina Mall. Service is super-sharp, rooms are beautifully furnished and superbly equipped (those on higher floors also have good views), and the pool is the biggest in the area. *Dubai Marina.* ☎ 04-436-7403. *www.theaddress. com. 200 units. Doubles AED 1,500. AE, DC, MC, V. Map p 114.*

★ Ahmedia Heritage Guest House

DEIRA This atmospheric little heritage hotel is set in a traditional house in the backstreets of Deira right next to Al Ahmadiya School. Rooms are attractively decorated with Arabian-style wooden furniture and fabrics, and there's a nice little courtyard cafe. Rates are often superb values. *Al Ras.* ☎ 04-225-0085. *www.heritagedubaihotels. com. 15 units. Doubles AED 350 w/ breakfast. AE, DC, MC, V. Map p 115.*

★★ Al Ain Rotana

AL AIN If you want to overnight in Al Ain, this landmark five-star is easily the nicest place to stay, with spacious and stylish rooms and a conveniently central location (it's the only decent hotel close to the city center). The excellent facilities include a fine selection of restaurants, idyllic grounds with a pair of lovely pools, and the award-winning Zen spa, plus fitness club. *Sheikh Zayed Rd.* ☎ 03-754 5111. *www.rotana.com. 242 units. Doubles AED 600. AE, DC, MC, V. Map p 114.*

★★★ Al Maha Desert Resort

DESERT Dubai's ultimate desert

Falaj pool at Al Ain Rotana.

Room at the Arabian Courtyard.

retreat is set in the depths of the beautiful Dubai Desert Conservation Reserve, teeming with oryx, gazelle, and other rare wildlife. It's wonderfully laid-back and luxurious (and wonderfully expensive too), with beautiful rooms, a gorgeous spa, and pleasant public areas. The main draw, however, is the chance to sit back and take in the views of the superb sands stretching around as far as the eye can see. *Dubai Desert Conservation Reserve.* ☎ *04-832-9900. www.al-maha.com. 42 units. Doubles AED 5,000–7,000 w/breakfast. Map p 114.*

★★ **Al Murooj Rotana** SHEIKH ZAYED ROAD Well placed for the Dubai Mall and Downtown Dubai, this place looks and feels more like a resort than a hotel just 5 minutes' walk from one of the modern world's biggest urban developments. The spacious terraced gardens, with a larger-than-average pool and stacks of sunloungers, are a real winner, and the smart modern rooms and facilities don't disappoint either. *Al Saffa St.* ☎ *04-321-1111. www. rotana.com. 247 units. Doubles from around AED 750–AED 1,000. AE, DC, MC, V. Map p 114.*

★★ **Al Qasr** MADINAT JUMEIRAH One of Dubai's ultimate Arabian-themed hotels, Al Qasr marries traditional Middle Eastern design with a distinct touch of Hollywood bling, complete with cascading fountains, acres of marble, and gargantuan chandeliers. Rooms are gorgeously furnished with Arabian fabrics and artifacts, and there's an incredible array of places to eat, drink, and shop, both in house and at the attached Souk Madinat Jumeirah. ☎ *04-366-8888. www.madinatjumeirah.com. 294 units. Doubles AED 1,900–AED 2,100. Map p 114.*

★★ **Arabian Courtyard** BUR DUBAI The most appealing hotel in Bur Dubai occupies a brilliantly central location overlooking the Dubai Museum. Amenities include fetching Arabian-themed rooms, a spa, a good in-house pub, and a trio of restaurants, although the pool is disappointingly small. Excellent value. *Al Fahidi St., opposite Dubai Museum.* ☎ *04-351-9111. www.arabiancourtyard.com. 173 units. Doubles AED 425–AED 625. AE, DC, MC, V. Map p 115.*

★ **Armani Hotel** DOWNTOWN DUBAI The world's first Armani hotel in the world's tallest building more or less sells itself (even at this price), especially if you're a fan of

Giorgio's super-cool, understated chic, which is very much to the fore in the design of the hotel. Not surprisingly, it's proved a massive hit with Dubai's label-conscious elite, and rooms and facilities (including several top-notch restaurants) are of the highest standard. What it won't give you, however, is any particular sense of being in Dubai (as opposed to being in Milan, or Paris, or wherever), and you can get a lot more atmosphere elsewhere for a lot less cash. *Burj Khalifa.* ☎ *04-888-3888. www.armanihotels.com. Doubles AED 2,400–AED 2,900. AE, DC, MC, V. Map p 114.*

★★ **kids Atlantis** THE PALM, JUMEIRAH   The vast Atlantis complex (p 18, **2**) is not so much a conventional hotel as a self-contained leisure and entertainment mega-resort, with attractions including the Lost Chambers (p 19, **3**), a dolphinarium (p 45, **2**) and the spectacular Aquaventure water park (p 80)—and guests get free or discounted admission to all these otherwise-expensive attractions. It's all thoroughly over the top and shamelessly kitschy, although there's a huge array of in-house facilities, including plenty for families and kids, plus a great stretch of (artificial) beach. *Palm Jumeirah.* ☎ *04-426-2000. www.atlantisthepalm.com. 1,539 units. Doubles AED 1,500–AED 2,750. AE, DC, MC, V. Map p 114.*

★★ **Bab Al Shams Desert Resort** DESERT   This superb desert resort is still within easy striking distance of the city, in a gorgeous Arabian-themed complex with views over the dunes. It offers beautifully furnished rooms, the fairy-tale Al Hadheerah restaurant, and a range of outdoor activities, including camel- and horse-riding and desert safaris. ☎ *04-809-6100.*

www.meydanhotels.com/babalshams. 113 units. Doubles AED 1,500. AE, DC, MC, V. Map p 114.

★★ **Barjeel Heritage Guesthouse** BUR DUBAI   In a plum location on the Shindagha waterfront, this attractive guesthouse occupies a traditional building. Rooms don't quite live up to the setting—they're a bit gloomy and equipped with slightly tacky Arabian-style furnishings—but it's still a decent choice, and usually at bargain rates. It's also home to the above-average Barjeel al Arab restaurant (see p 89). *Shindagha.* ☎ *04-354 4424. www. heritagedubaihotels.com. 9 units. Doubles AED 350–AED 450. AE, DC, MC, V. Map p 115.*

★★ **Burj Al Arab** UMM SUQEIM   Dubai's famous "seven-star" hotel (p 56, **10**) offers the last word in luxury—with a predictably extravagant price tag. Suites (there are no rooms) are huge, sumptuous, and equipped with luxuries ranging from gold-rimmed TV screens and remote-control curtains to 24-hour butler service and a special "pillow menu" as well as fabulous views through huge picture windows. There's also a superb stretch of private beach, the opulent Talise Spa, plus nine very fancy eating and drinking venues (see the box on p 56). It's perfect for image-conscious celebrities on vacation, although mere mortals may find the relentless extravagance slightly overpowering—and there are far more peaceful and intimate places for those in search of a romantic break. ☎ *04-301-7777. www.burj-al-arab.com. 202 units. Doubles AED 5,000–AED 8,000 w/breakfast. Map p 114.*

★★ **Crowne Plaza Dubai Deira** DEIRA   An old Dubai landmark (formerly the Renaissance

Hotel) has been renovated and reinvigorated under new ownership. It's not the most fashionable area in town, but it's very convenient for both airport and metro as well as the lively Al Rigga Road. Very spacious, attractively furnished rooms and vast public areas (plus pool terrace) give the whole place a sense of unusual roominess—and often at highly competitive rates. *Salahuddin Rd.* ☎ *04-262-5555. www.crowneplaza.com. 300 units. Doubles AED 600–AED 850. AE, DC, MC, V. Map p 114.*

★★ **Dar Al Masyaf** MADINAT JUMEIRAH   The most upmarket of the Madinat Jumeirah's accommodations options boasts all the dreamy Arabian style of the neighboring Al Qasr and Mina A'Salam Hotels, but with an added level of privacy and intimacy, set in a string of sumptuous private villas dotted around luxurious palm-studded grounds and waterways. ☎ *04-366-8888. www.madinatjumeirah.com. 283 units. Doubles AED 1,600–AED 2,600. Map p 114.*

★★ **Dusit Thani** SHEIKH ZAYED ROAD   In a famous wai-shaped landmark building (see p 52), this slick hotel offers plenty of style at a relatively affordable price. Facilities include a good modern gym, a rooftop pool, and the excellent Benjarong restaurant (see p 89). ☎ *04-343-3333. www.dusit.com. 321 units. Doubles AED 775–AED 1000. AE, DC, MC, V. Map p 114.*

★ **Grand Hyatt** OUD METHA   The second-biggest hotel in Dubai (after Atlantis), the Grand Hyatt stands in solitary splendor in a strategic position between the old and new cities. Functional rather than inspiring, it does offer a huge range of in-house facilities, including no fewer than 13 restaurants, plus lush gardens and a huge pool. *Al Qataiyat Rd.* ☎ *04-317-1234. www.dubai. grand.hyatt.com. 674 units. Doubles from around AED 1,100. AE, DC, MC, V. Map p 114.*

★★★ **Grosvenor House** DUBAI MARINA   This is the most alluring of the many hotels jostling for elbow room amid the upwardly

King room at Dusit Thani.

The pool at Hilton Dubai Creek.

mobile skyscrapers of the Dubai Marina, with exceptionally polished service and plenty of suave contemporary chic. Spread over two identical towers, the elegant rooms and sleek public areas are complemented by a superb array of in-house restaurants and bars, plus two gorgeous spas. The only bad news is that it's not actually on the beach—although it's very close, and guests can use the excellent beachside facilities at the neighboring Le Royal Méridien. ☎ 04-399-8888. *www.grosvenorhouse-dubai.com. 749 units. Doubles AED 1,000–AED 1,300. AE, DC, MC, V. Map p 114.*

★ **Hilton Dubai Creek** DEIRA Here is one of the few hotels in the old city with any pretensions to style. The interior was designed by Carlos Ott (creator of the Bastille Opera House in Paris) and features vast expanses of shiny chrome fittings in the public areas alongside suave, white-and-cream rooms. In-house amenities include the excellent Table 9 restaurant (see p 95) and a spectacular rooftop pool.

Baniyas Rd. ☎ *04-227-1111. www. placeshilton.com/dubai-creek. 150 units. Doubles from around AED 750– AED 900. AE, DC, MC, V. Map p 115.*

★ **Hilton Jumeirah Resort** DUBAI MARINA One of the smaller beachside hotels, this rather flash establishment is better for poolside posing than an authentic beach holiday (and the beach is rather small). Facilities include a spa and a couple of good restaurants (including BiCE; see p 90), plus a large pool and attractive terraced gardens. *Dubai Marina.* ☎ *04-399-1111. www.hilton.com. 389 units. Doubles AED 1,100–AED 1,400. AE, DC, MC, V. Map p 114.*

★★ **Hyatt Place Baniyas Square** DEIRA A new idea in Dubai, the Hyatt Place Baniyas offers quality lodgings closer to the center of the old city than anyone else has yet attempted, combining upscale creature comforts with cut-throat rates. The simple facilities (including small pool) tick all the necessary boxes, while the five-star standard rooms are a pleasant surprise, with an almost loft-style sense of airiness, cool modern artwork, and spacious sofas. Some also have great views through big picture windows over Baniyas Square. *Baniyas Sq.* ☎ *04-404-1234. www.dubaibaniyassquare.place.hyatt.com. 126 units. Doubles AED 550. AE, DC, MC, V. Map p 115.*

★ **Hyatt Place Al Rigga** DEIRA Very similar to the Hyatt Place in Baniyas Square, this hotel has a slightly more out-of-the-way location (although very handy for the metro). The bright and airy rooms with chic furnishings and big picture windows are superb values at this price, and the basic facilities include a small pool plus gym, 24-hour restaurant, and coffee lounge-cum-bar. *Al Rigga Rd.* ☎ *04-608-1234. www.dubaialrigga.place.hyatt.com. 210 units. Doubles AED 550. AE, DC, MC, V. Map p 114.*

★★ **Hyatt Regency** DEIRA Looming above the northern side of Deira, this huge city-center landmark is one of the oldest—and most central—five-star hotels in the city, though it's been well looked after

The beach at Jumeirah Beach Hotel.

The Avenue of Indulgence at Jumeirah Zabeel Saray.

and hardly looks its age. Proximity to the old city is the main draw, and there's also a good array of facilities and attractive rooms (many with stunning views), all at very competitive prices. *Al Khaleej Rd.* ☎ *04-209-1234. www.dubai.regency.hyatt.com. 421 units. Doubles AED 700–AED 800. AE, DC, MC, V. Map p 115.*

★ **Ibis World Trade Centre** SHEIKH ZAYED ROAD One of the cheapest hotels south of Bur Dubai (although it's still no bargain), the Ibis has smallish but perfectly comfortable rooms. Although there are no in-house facilities, guests can use those at the adjacent Novotel for a small fee. *World Trade Centre.* ☎ *04-332-4444. www.ibishotel.com. 210 units. Doubles AED 500–AED 700. AE, DC, MC, V. Map p 114.*

★★★ **kids Jumeirah Beach Hotel** UMM SUQEIM This landmark hotel (p 57, ⓫) remains one of the city's most appealing places to stay, thanks to its wonderful beachside location and host of

amenities, including a vast spread of places to eat and drink. It's great for families too, with some of the city's best children's facilities, including a huge pool and beach and excellent kids' club, and there's also an in-house diving and watersports center. Rates fluctuate wildly. ☎ 04-348-0000. www.jumeirah beachhotel.com. 600 units. Doubles AED 1,500–AED 3,000. AE, DC, MC, V. Map p 114.

★★ Jumeirah Emirates Towers SHEIKH ZAYED ROAD Regularly voted the best business hotel in the Middle East, the Jumeirah Emirates Tower occupies the smaller of the two landmark Emirates Towers at the heart of the city's business quarter. Rooms are stylishly but soothingly decorated in sober wood finishes and come with all the amenities you could think of, while there are wonderful views from higher floors. Sheikh Zayed Rd. ☎ 04-330-0000. www.jumeirah emiratestowers.com. 400 units. Doubles AED 1,200–AED 1,400. AE, DC, MC, V. Map p 114.

★★★ Jumeirah Zabeel Saray PALM JUMEIRAH The most spectacular hotel to have opened in Dubai in recent years, the Jumeirah Zabeel Saray is a picture-perfect study in flamboyant excess. Designed to resemble a kind of enormous Ottoman-Turkish-style palace, the hotel's interior is a riot of overcooked opulence, with a string of fanciful restaurants and bars—including Amala (see p 88), Voda (see p 107) and the MusicHall (see p 104)—each showcasing a different style of no-expense-spared interior design a la Dubai. Spacious grounds and a beautiful beach round out the package and offer some respite from the Bollywood extravaganza within. Crescent Rd. ☎ 04-453-0000. www.jumeirah.com.

The One&Only Royal Mirage reflection pool.

Doubles AED 1,400–AED 2,400. AE, DC, MC, V.

★★ kids Le Méridien Mina Seyahi DUBAI MARINA Large, dated, and generally uninspiring, this beachside resort is worth a look for families, thanks to its huge grounds (home to the excellent Barasti Bar; see p 105), big beach, and excellent kids' facilities. Rates are pretty competitive too, given the seafront location. Al Sufouh Rd. ☎ 04-399-3333. www.lemeridien-minaseyahi. com. 220 units. Doubles AED 1,000–1,200. AE, DC, MC, V. Map p 114.

★★ kids Le Royal Méridien DUBAI MARINA Spread over three buildings, this rambling resort is a bit dated and run-of-the-mill compared to some other nearby places, but it benefits from enormous and very peaceful beachside gardens, plus its own kids' club, watersports center, and three pools. There's also a superb selection of restaurants and bars, including the excellent Rhodes Twenty10 (see p 94). ☎ 04-399-5555. www.leroyal meridien-dubai.com. 504 units.

The Palace.

Doubles AED 900–AED 1,200. AE, MC, V. Map p 114.

★★ Manzil Downtown Dubai

DOWNTOWN DUBAI Tucked away in the Downtown Dubai "old town" area, Manzil is a genuinely soothing urban retreat, with plenty of old- and new-school charm. Public areas are designed in appealing faux-Arabian fashion, while rooms are done in a smooth and more contemporary "Arab-esque" style. Facilities include a basic gym and medium-size pool. Very nice, although it's no bargain. ☎ 04-428-5888. www.vida-hotels.com. 197 units. Doubles AED 1,000–AED 1,500. AE, DC, MC, V. Map p 114.

★★ Mina A'Salam

MADINAT JUMEIRAH This lovely Arabian-themed beachside hotel is not quite as opulent as the nearby Al Qasr (see p 118), but it has plenty of Arabian-Nights style and all the myriad facilities of the Madinat Jumeirah on the doorstep. ☎ 04-366-8888. www.madinatjumeirah.com. 292 units. Doubles AED 1,700–AED 2,500. Map p 114.

★★★ One&Only Royal Mirage

DUBAI MARINA Dubai's ultimate Arabian fantasy, a stay at the magical and utterly romantic One&Only is like dipping into some dreamy

Scheherazade-like fantasy. The hotel occupies a long sprawl of low, ocher-colored and rather Moorish-looking buildings, enveloped in thousands of palm trees, while inside, labyrinthine corridors open up unexpectedly into sumptuously tiled and decorated courtyards and hallways, offering magical views of the adjacent beach and sea beyond. Facilities include a superb spa, watersports center, kids' club, and some excellent places to eat and drink. ☎ 04-399-9999. www.oneandonlyresorts.com. 475 units. Doubles AED 2,000–AED 2,500. AE, DC, MC, V. Map p 114.

★ Orient Guest House

BASTAKIYA This traditional Arabian-style guesthouse is set in a sensitively restored traditional building around a pretty courtyard—slightly less atmospheric than the similar XVA Art Hotel nearby, although rooms are larger and more comfortable. The location is brilliantly central, and rates are very competitive. Al Fahidi St., Bastakiya. ☎ 04-353-4448. www.orientguesthouse.com. 11 units. Doubles AED 350–AED 400. AE, MC, V. Map p 115.

★★ The Palace

DOWNTOWN DUBAI This sumptuous Arabian-themed hotel sits at the heart of the pleasantly kitsch Downtown

Dubai Old Town development. Facilities include a gorgeous pool running almost directly into Burj Khalifa Lake as well as good in-house restaurants and a spa and gym. There are superb views of the Burj Khalifa throughout. ☎ 04-428-7888. www.theaddress.com. 242 units. Doubles AED 1,700–AED 2,800. AE, DC, MC, V. Map p 114.

★★★ Park Hyatt Dubai GARHOUD

The most appealing hotel in central Dubai, the Park Hyatt has a gorgeous location—next to the Creek and the very expensive boats tethered up at the adjacent Dubai Yacht Club, and backed by the rolling fairways and greens of the Dubai Creek Golf Club. The hotel has loads of style and a seductively peaceful atmosphere, set in a rambling sequence of white-walled and blue-tiled Moroccan-style buildings, with beautifully decorated rooms. An attractive range of in-house facilities includes Amara, one of the city's best spas (see p 73). ☎ 04-602-1234. www.dubai.park.hyatt.com. 225 units. Doubles AED 1,800. Map p 114.

★★ Per Aquum Desert Palm INTERNATIONAL CITY

This peaceful suburban retreat is 20 minutes' drive from the city center, set next to wide-open polo fields. The spacious and serenely decorated rooms and villas come with fully equipped kitchen, dining room, and miniature pools, and there's also the beautiful Lime Spa (see p 74) and good in-house restaurants. Horse-riding excursions can also be arranged. ☎ 04-323-8888. www.desertpalm.peraquum.com. 26 units. Doubles AED 900. AE, DC, MC, V. Map p 114.

★★ Radisson Blu Dubai Deira Creek DEIRA

The oldest five-star hotel in Dubai, the Radisson Blu still boasts a pleasantly swanky air of old-fashioned opulence. Rooms are cozy enough, although the main draw is the brilliantly central Creekside location and the excellent range of in-house drinking and dining options—all at brilliantly competitive rates. Baniyas Rd. ☎ 04-222-7171. www.radissonblu.com/hotel-dubaideiracreek. 276 units. Doubles AED 550–AED 850. AE, DC, MC, V. Map p 115.

★★★ Raffles OUD METHA

This landmark hotel—built in the form of a huge pyramid—is one of the most stylish places to stay in Dubai. The entire hotel is a masterpiece of opulent but tasteful interior design, mixing Egyptian, Arabian, and Oriental influences to memorable effect, backed up by immaculate service, a good of selection of places to eat and drink, and the gorgeous Amrita spa. The hotel's proximity to the adjacent Wafi mall and Khan Murjan souk is another bonus. The only thing missing is a beach. ☎ 04-324-8888. www.raffles.com/dubai. 248 units. Doubles AED 1,900. AE, DC, MC, V. Map p 114.

★★ Ritz-Carlton DUBAI MARINA

This beautiful, European-style, Old-World hotel could be a villa in the Tuscan countryside, apart from the forest of skyscrapers around it. The interior oozes tasteful luxury, while facilities include a fine spa, a huge (and relatively empty) beach, three pools, and a batch of top restaurants. Gorgeous, although at a serious price. ☎ 04-399-4000. www.ritzcarlton.com. 138 units. Doubles AED 2,000–AED 3,000. AE, MC, V. Map p 114.

★★ Shangri-La SHEIKH ZAYED ROAD

The most alluring place to stay on Sheikh Zayed Road, the Shangri-La's rooms are gorgeous little studies in contemporary minimalist style. Facilities include an excellent spread of restaurants and a lovely fourth-floor pool.

The pool at the Ritz-Carlton Dubai.

☎ *04-343-8888. www.shangri-la. com. 250 units. Doubles AED 1,000– AED 1,500. AE, DC, MC, V. Map p 114.*

★★ Sheraton Dubai Creek

DEIRA   This old city-center hotel has a fine Creekside setting and a good central location. The recently renovated rooms are on the small side but quite stylish, with superb Creek views. Facilities include a nice spa, smallish pool, and a couple of excellent restaurants. *Baniyas Rd.* ☎ *04-228-1111. www.sheraton. com/dubai. 268 units. Doubles AED 700–AED 950. AE, DC, MC, V. Map p 115.*

★★ kids Sheraton Jumeirah Beach

DUBAI MARINA   The oldest hotel in the marina, this low-key and very old-fashioned beachside resort feels pleasantly cozy and fuss-free compared to all the surrounding mega-hotels. Facilities include a nice spa and spacious gardens, plus a good kids' club. Rates are usually the cheapest in the marina and can be decent value (at least by Dubai standards) in periods of low demand. ☎ *04-399-5533. www.sheraton.com/jumeirahbeach.*

250 units. Doubles AED 850–AED 1,500 w/breakfast. AE, DC, MC, V. Map p 114.

★★ Towers Rotana

SHEIKH ZAYED ROAD   One of the cheapest places hereabouts, this functional modern four-star hotel doesn't have the frills of other places along the road but is very comfortable and competitively priced, with a gym, (small) spa, and the fun in-house Long's Bar (see p 111) and Teatro restaurant (see p 95). ☎ *04-343-8000. www.rotana. com. 376 units. Doubles AED 625– AED 775. AE, DC, MC, V. Map p 114.*

★★ XVA Art Hotel

BASTAKIYA   If you're looking for traditional Arabian atmosphere, this is the best place in Dubai, with 13 rooms in a lovely old wind-towered house (which also hosts an excellent cafe and art gallery). All rooms are individually styled, although standard rooms are on the small side, making the larger deluxe rooms well worth the extra cash. Book well in advance. ☎ *04-353-5383. www.xvahotel.com. 13 units. Doubles AED 370–AED 430. AE, DC, MC, V. Map p 115.* ●

Sharjah

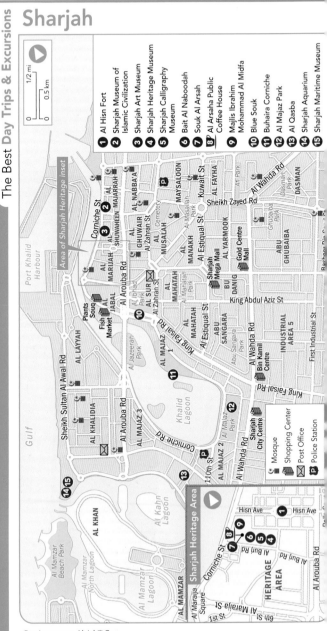

1 Al Hisn Fort
2 Sharjah Museum of Islamic Civilization
3 Sharjah Art Museum
4 Sharjah Heritage Museum
5 Sharjah Calligraphy Museum
6 Bait Al Naboodah
7 Souk Al Arsah
8 Al Arsaha Public Coffee House
9 Majlis Ibrahim Mohammad Al Midfa
10 Blue Souk
11 Buhaira Corniche
12 Al Majaz Park
13 Al Qasba
14 Sharjah Aquarium
15 Sharjah Maritime Museum

Previous page: Al Jahili Fort.

A mere 10km (6¼ miles) from Dubai, the emirate of Sharjah looks at first sight simply like a sprawling extension of its neighbor. Culturally, however, the two emirates couldn't be further apart. Compared to cosmopolitan Dubai, Sharjah is staunchly Islamic—there's no alcohol for sale, for example. It's not exactly Sin City, but Sharjah does have some excellent museums and attractions. START: **Al Hisn Fort.**

❶ ★★ Al Hisn Fort. At the dead center of the city sits the venerable Al Hisn Fort, an impressively impregnable-looking edifice that was formerly home to Sharjah's ruling Al Qassimi family. Once the focal point of the old city, it's now hemmed in by ugly apartment blocks. The original fort was almost completely demolished in 1969, much to the disgust of the emirate's current ruler, Sultan Bin Mohammad Al Qassimi, who promptly had it rebuilt from scratch. Reconstruction work was carried out with great care, and further restoration work in 2013–14 has left the fort looking as good as ever, if not better. The inside of the fort houses a series of displays and refurbished rooms, including a traditional *majlis*, bedroom, and *medbasa* (in which dates were pressed to make molasses), along with the usual weapons and rifles and some interesting photographs of the fort in former years. ⏱ *30 min. Al Burj Ave.* ☎ *06-568-5500. www.sharjah museums.ae. Admission AED 5, free for children 12 & under. Sat–Thurs 8am–8pm; Fri 4–8pm.*

Al Hisn Fort in Sharjah.

Getting to Sharjah

Buses for Sharjah (AED 10) leave regularly from Bur Dubai's Al Ghubaiba bus station and Al Sabkha bus station in the middle of Deira, taking anywhere from 45 to 90 minutes, depending on the traffic. If you choose to take a taxi instead, you'll pay an additional AED 20 on top of the normal fare for any trips into Sharjah. If you're driving yourself, there's plenty of street parking around the city center, although you might have to scout around for an open spot—hunt in the back streets around the Heritage Area.

❷ ★★★ Sharjah Museum of Islamic Civilization. The biggest single reason to journey to Sharjah is to visit the city's superb Islamic museum, set in a spacious custom-built waterfront building. Its galleries offer a wide-ranging overview of the Islamic world, with world-class exhibits and superb (albeit slightly self-congratulatory) explanatory displays. The first part of the museum is

Sharjah Museum of Islamic Civilization.

devoted to Islam itself, including an intriguing description of the sacred pilgrimage (*haj*) to Mecca. Complete with stunning photographs and detailed descriptions of the elaborate rituals involved, it's probably the nearest a non-Muslim can get to experiencing this spiritual event firsthand. Other galleries explore Islamic scientists' many notable contributions to astronomy, chemistry, mathematics, medicine, and navigation. Displays feature touch screens and working models of medieval gadgets, such as astrolabes, armillary spheres, and equatoriums—all essential gear for the early Arabian seafarer. Upstairs galleries are devoted to Islamic arts and crafts, from fine glassware and ceramics to exquisitely decorated weapons, woodwork, textiles, and jewelry. ⏱ *1 hr., 30 min.* ☎ *06-565-5455. www.sharjahmuseums.ae. Admission AED 5, free for children 12 & under. Sat–Thurs 8am–8pm; Fri 4–8pm.*

❸ ★★ Sharjah Art Museum. Close to the Islamic museum is the imposing Sharjah Art Museum (follow the brown sign from the waterfront). Downstairs galleries host temporary displays, including some impressive international touring exhibitions; upstairs, the permanent collection includes modern paintings and sculptures by artists from across the Arab world—worth a quick look, although none of the pieces on display is especially compelling. ⏱ 30 min. ☎ 06-568-8222. www.sharjahmuseums.ae. Free admission. Sat–Thurs 8am–8pm; Fri 4–8pm.

④ ★ Sharjah Heritage Museum. Sharjah's answer to the Dubai Museum serves up a comprehensive survey of the traditional customs and culture of the Sharjah Emirate. Housed in the fine old Bait Saeed al Taweel ("House of Saeed the Tall"), the wide-ranging exhibits cover all the main aspects of traditional Emirati life, including cultural customs, traditional dress, architecture, Islam, the history of the pearling trade, and so on, with many interesting insights into lesser-known aspects of local culture.

⏱ 30 min. ☎ 06-568-0006. www.sharjahmuseums.ae. Admission AED 5, free for children 12 & under. Sat–Thurs 8am–8pm; Fri 4–8pm.

⑤ ★★ Sharjah Calligraphy Museum. This unique museum (closed at the time of writing for renovations) showcases the tradition of Arabic calligraphy—one of the most highly prized of the Islamic arts, thanks to its role in preserving and disseminating the words of the Quran. It draws artistic inspiration from the uniquely beautiful character of Arabic script itself, with its elegant curvilinear lines and flourishes. There's a treasure trove of calligraphic artworks on display here, most of them based on Quranic quotations, such as the *Bismillah* ("In the name of God, most gracious, most merciful") and executed in styles ranging from blocky Kufic script to the incredibly elaborate and cursive diwani script developed

Heart of Sharjah

After many years stuck in the tourist doldrums, Sharjah is finally making a concerted effort to unleash its potential with the ambitious new "Heart of Sharjah" project (www.heartofsharjah.ae). The city already boasts an impressive collection of museums and traditional buildings, although their overall effect is diminished by haphazard infrastructure and the eyesore 1970s' architecture that fills the city center. The Heart of Sharjah project aims to change all this, razing intrusive modern buildings, restoring and opening vintage houses as new museums and galleries, constructing new developments in traditional style, and landscaping the area into a seamless whole. Phase 1 is already nearly complete, with several museums currently under renovation and inner-city rejuvenation in progress—most notably the recently reopened Al Hisn Fort, now restored to its full glory.

in Ottoman Turkey. You'll also find numerous *calligrams*, in which Arabic characters are twisted to form abstract patterns, such as rosettes, discs, and vases, as well as a few striking contemporary pop-art canvases using vivid acrylics and eye-catching abstract designs. ⏱ *20 min.* ☎ *06-568-1738, www. sharjahmuseums.ae. Admission AED 5, free for children 12 & under. Sat–Thurs 8am–8pm; Fri 4–8pm.*

6 ★★ Bait Al Naboodah. The Bait Al Naboodah (temporarily closed for renovations) is easily the prettiest traditional building in Sharjah, sporting coral-and-gypsum walls, chunky timber doors, and a spacious central courtyard, flanked by incongruous wooden Corinthian columns. The house has been left exactly as the Naboodah family left it and now serves as a museum of traditional life in the Gulf. In the usual *majlis* and bedrooms, note the rifles strung up on the walls, an old-fashioned wireless, and a wind-up gramophone. Don't miss the traditional games room, with cute old-fashioned toys, including a funny doll's house and a toy truck made out of tin cans and oil containers. There's also an excellent display on the construction techniques used in making the traditional Emirati house. ⏱ *20 min.* ☎ *06-556-6002. www.sharjah museums.ae. Admission AED 5, free for children 12 & under. Sat–Thurs 8am–8pm; Fri 4–8pm.*

7 ★★ Souk Al Arsah. A tangle of narrow alleyways in the middle of the Heritage Area, the quaint Souk Al Arsah is one of the prettiest spots in Sharjah. The old-fashioned shops here are a fun source of Arabian collectibles, including old

Bedouin jewelry, prayer beads, and *khanjars* (daggers), along with quirkier offerings, from Saddam Husseinera Iraqi banknotes to old British colonial bric-a-brac. ⏱ *20 min. Daily 10am–10pm, although most shops close from around 1–4pm & some remain closed Fri until around 2pm.*

8 Al Arsaha Public Coffee House. This picturesque cafe on the main courtyard of the Souk al Arsah attracts a crowd of local Emiratis and expat Arabs. There's no menu, because the cafe does only a handful of dishes: Choose from fish, lamb, or chicken biryani (AED 15), served in generous portions with a fair amount of spice. *By the entrance to the Souk Al Arsah. Daily 10am–10pm, although it sometimes closes from around 1–5pm. $.*

9 Majlis Ibrahim Mohammad Al Midfa. Immediately behind the Souk Al Arsah, the quaint Majlis Al Midfa is a charming traditional building topped by what is claimed to be the only round wind tower in the UAE. Notice also the wooden door on the house opposite, crowned by a fine pair of galumphing elephants. ⏱ *10 min.*

Now walk (around 20 min) or take a taxi (around AED 10) to:

10 ★★ Blue Souk. Sharjah's most eye-catching landmark, the Central Souk—or Blue Souk, as it's popularly known—is an oddly loveable behemoth of a building. Consisting of two long wings, covered in blue tile work and topped with wind towers, it looks like a cross between an enormous mosque and an Arabian-themed railway station. The interior holds a couple hundred small

Blue Souk.

shops, with a particularly fine collection of carpet sellers (mainly from Iran). The selection is excellent, and prices are generally lower than in Dubai. Other shops sell assorted handicrafts, souvenirs, clothes, and other collectables. ⏱ *30 min. Most shops daily 10am–10pm.*

⑪ ★ **Buhaira Corniche.** Around 1km (½ mile) south of the Blue Souk, an attractive waterfront promenade runs along the handsome Buhaira Corniche, offering fine views of the tranquil Khalid Lagoon, ringed with glass-fronted highrises—particularly attractive late afternoon and after dark.

⑫ ★ **Al Majaz Park.** Stroll south down the Corniche to the palm- and flower-filled Al Majaz Park, home to a pleasant cluster of

lagoon-side restaurants, a jogging track, minigolf, and the small Mini Splash Park (daily 9am–midnight; AED 30), complete with waterfalls, water tunnels, and various other aquatic attractions.

⑬ ★ **kids** **Al Qasba.** Connecting with the western end of Al Majaz Park, the Al Qasba development is Sharjah's best stab at a mega-leisure development. The complex consists of two lines of vaguely Arabian-looking buildings flanking a wide canal and housing a low-key range of cafes and shops. Kids will enjoy the Eye of the Emirates observation wheel (AED 30, AED 15 children), a boat ride along the canal (AED 15, AED 10 children ages 4–10), or the Kids Fun Zone (AED 5 per child). ⏱ *1 hr. www. alqasba.ae. Daily 4:30pm–midnight (Thurs–Sat until 1am).*

Eye of the Emirates in Al Qasba.

Now take a taxi (around AED 10). from Al Qasba to:

⑭ ★★ kids Sharjah Aquarium.
On the far western edge of Sharjah, the state-of-the-art Sharjah

Aquarium offers a good diversion for kids and an interesting glimpse into the marine life of the Gulf. Some 250 species of fish, from tiny clown fish to browsing reef sharks,

Sharjah Aquarium.

Sharjah Maritime Museum.

are displayed in the aquarium's 20-odd tanks plus walk-through underwater tunnel. ⏱ *45 min.* ☎ *06-528-5288. www.sharjah aquarium.ae. Admission AED 25, AED 15 children ages 2–12, free for kids 1 & under. Sat & Mon–Thurs 8am–8pm; Fri 4–10pm.*

⓯ ★★ **Sharjah Maritime Museum.** While you're visiting the aquarium, pop over the road to the nearby Maritime Museum. Sharjah, like Dubai, depended on the sea rather than the desert for its livelihood, and the exhibits here paint a lively picture of its former maritime traditions. Displays include an impressive selection of hand-crafted wooden dhows in the museum's courtyard and one of the world's oldest pearls. ⏱ *30 min.* ☎ *06-522-2002, www.sharjah museums.ae. Admission AED 10, AED 5 children ages 2–12, free for kids 1 & under. Sat–Thurs 8am–8pm; Fri 4–8pm.*

Al Ain

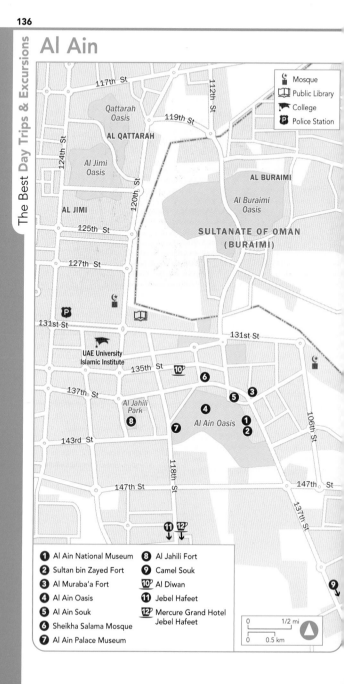

Legend:
- 🕌 Mosque
- 📖 Public Library
- 🎓 College
- 🅿 Police Station

117th St
Qattarah Oasis
119th St
112th St
AL QATTARAH
124th St
Al Jimi Oasis
120th St
AL BURAIMI
Al Buraimi Oasis
AL JIMI
125th St
SULTANATE OF OMAN (BURAIMI)
127th St
131st St
131st St
UAE University Islamic Institute
135th St
10 Al Diwan
6
137th St
5
3
Al Jahili Park
4
8
Al Ain Oasis
1
7
2
106th St
143rd St
147th St
118th St
147th St
137th St
11 12
9

1 Al Ain National Museum
2 Sultan bin Zayed Fort
3 Al Muraba'a Fort
4 Al Ain Oasis
5 Al Ain Souk
6 Sheikha Salama Mosque
7 Al Ain Palace Museum
8 Al Jahili Fort
9 Camel Souk
10 Al Diwan
11 Jebel Hafeet
12 Mercure Grand Hotel Jebel Hafeet

0   1/2 mi
0   0.5 km

The country's only major inland settlement, Al Ain is often described as the UAE's "Garden City" on account of the lush date-palm oases that still swathe many parts of the city (Al Ain means, literally, "The Spring"). Much of modern Al Ain is an uninspiring concrete sprawl, but the city as a whole offers a rewarding glimpse of traditional Emirati life, including the oases themselves, several traditional mudbrick forts, and a camel souk. START: **Al Ain National Museum.**

❶ ★★ Al Ain National Museum.

The old-fashioned National Museum makes a good first point of call, offering an engaging introduction to the culture and history of the oasis city and to the wider history of Abu Dhabi emirate, in which Al Ain is located. The collection is divided into two parts. The opening ethnographic section features colorful and entertaining displays showcasing life in Abu Dhabi in the old days—giant coffee pots, mannequins in traditional dress, antique Qurans, and so on— as well as some wonderful old photographs of Abu Dhabi emirate back in the 1960s, looking not so much 50 years old as 500. The second section covers the archeological history of the emirate—less obviously entertaining but painting an interesting picture of the

Sultan bin Zayed Fort.

prehistory of the Gulf and its surprisingly extensive trading and cultural links. ⓘ 30 min. ☎ 03-711-8331. http://bit.ly/AlAinNatlMus.

Getting to Al Ain

Regular minibuses leave for Al Ain every 40 minutes throughout the day from Bur Dubai's Al Ghubaiba bus station. The journey takes around 90 minutes to 2 hours, depending on traffic. Buses arrive in Al Ain directly behind the Food Souk (and in front of the oasis). If you're driving yourself, be forewarned that Al Ain is an incredibly disorienting place to navigate, with innumerable identical city blocks and roundabouts spread out over a considerable area. The map on p 136 provides a good guide to the city, but if you get lost, look out for the numerous brown signs pointing to places of tourist interest. The good news is that parking isn't usually a problem, with plenty of street parking; you can park at the Al Ain Museum if you follow the itinerary below.

AED 3, AED 1 children 9 & under. *Tues–Thurs & Sat–Sun 8am–7:30pm; Fri 3–7:30pm.*

❷ ★★ Sultan bin Zayed Fort. Next door to the National Museum, the quaint Sultan bin Zayed Fort (also known as the Eastern, or Sultan, Fort) is one of the prettiest of Al Ain's various old mud-brick forts. Dating from 1910, it has a trio of slender towers and a small interior courtyard dotted with a couple of trees and a small well. ⏱ *10 min. Same hours & admission as the National Museum.*

❸ ★ Al Muraba'a Fort. Another of Al Ain's many mud-brick forts, the small but eye-catching Al Muraba'a Fort looks as ancient as the desert but actually dates from the 1940s. It's one of the city's last traditional landmarks predating the oil boom that changed it forever. High walls enclose the usual large courtyard, with a quaint three-story keep inside, its walls dotted with small loopholes just large enough to fire a rifle through. ⏱ *10 min. Free admission. No official visiting hours, although it's often open during daylight hours.*

❹ ★★★ Al Ain Oasis. The enormous Al Ain Oasis is easily the most captivating place in town: a sprawling forest of densely packed date palms that envelops the southern edge of the city center, creating a magical retreat from the modern concrete outside. This is the largest of the seven oases scattered across the city, planted with an estimated 147,000 date palms interspersed with mango, fig, orange, banana, and jujube trees, their roots watered with the traditional stone irrigation channels

Al Ain Oasis.

(*falaj*) that keep the plantations supplied with water during the hot summer months.

It's easy, and very enjoyable, to get lost here, wandering in increasingly disoriented circles for miles through the palms. Head through any of the numerous entrances to the oasis (all open 24 hr.), from which narrow stone-walled roads thread their way among the trees, wonderfully shaded and peaceful even in the heat of the day. Entrance is restricted to foreign tourists and those who own land within the oasis; although a few cars pass through now and then, there's very little to disturb the peace. ⏱ *30 min.*

❺ ★ Al Ain Souk. Between the bus station and the town, Al Ain's food souk follows the pattern of its Dubai cousin, housed in a large, warehouselike structure, with different areas devoted to fish (best early in the day), meat (the usual gory carcasses dangling from hooks), and vegetables (with mainly Indian tradesmen enthroned between huge piles of produce). It's an interesting place for a quick stroll and attracts a colorful crowd of Emiratis in flowing white robes, Omanis in oversized turbans, and occasional Bedouin women in their distinctive black robes and face masks, all searching for bargains among the myriad stalls. ⏱ *10 min. Daily 10am–10pm; some closed 1–4pm.*

❻ ★ **Sheikha Salama Mosque.** A real head-turner amid the humdrum architecture of downtown Al Ain, the Sheikha Salama Mosque is far and away the city's most striking modern landmark. Opened in 2011, the huge mosque has space for some 5,000 worshippers, with a distinctive design blending traditional and modern aesthetics to memorable effect. The mosque isn't open to non-Muslims, but you can get a good view of the open-sided entrance courtyard from any of the surrounding streets. ⏱ *10 min.*

❼ ★ **Al Ain Palace Museum.** On the western side of the oasis, the Al Ain Palace Museum occupies a traditional fort formerly occupied by the revered Sheikh Zayed, the former ruler of Al Ain and Abu Dhabi and the first president of the UAE. The palace consists of a rambling sequence of orangey-pink traditional buildings arranged around a sequence of small courtyards and gardens. You can peek into many of the palace's 30-odd rooms, including the bedrooms of the sheikh, his wife, and their children, along with the ladies' *majlis,* private *majlis,* and large "People's *Majlis*" in which locals would gather to meet their ruler. It's a pleasant spot and a

Sheikha Salama Mosque.

Al Jahili Fort.

good complement to the National Museum (see p 137, ❶) and Al Jahili Fort (see p 140, ❽), the two other main sites associated with the Al Nahyan family. Still, the buildings themselves are relatively bland and modern, and there's very little in the way of exhibits apart from hagiographic portraits of Zayed and his relatives and other self-serving displays relating to the life and family of the great sheikh. ⏱ *20 min. http://bit.ly/AlAinPalaceMus. Free admission. Tues–Thurs & Sat–Sun 8:30am–7:30pm; Fri 3–7:30pm.*

❽ ★★ **Al Jahili Fort.** A block west of the Palace Museum lies the more interesting Al Jahili Fort. Like the Al Ain Palace, this imposing fort, built between 1891 and 1898—the largest traditional mud-brick structure in Al Ain—formerly belonged to the ruling Al Nahyan family. Long crenellated walls surround an enormous central courtyard with an eye-catching four-story

watchtower (probably predating the rest of the fort) on its northern side, each concentric level topped by a ring of spiky battlements. Inside, the main attraction is the brilliant "Mubarak bin London" exhibition, dedicated to the extraordinary British Arabist and explorer **Wilfred Thesiger,** who stayed in the fort in the late 1940s at the end of one of his grueling traverses of the Arabian desert. The exhibition features some of Thesiger's wonderful photographs, replicas of a few personal effects, and a fascinating short film. The information desk here is also an excellent source of information about other lesser-known forts and tourist attractions around the city. ⏱ *30 min. http://bit.ly/AlJahili. Free admission. Tues–Thurs & Sat–Sun 9am–5pm; Fri 3–5pm.*

Drive (or take a taxi) about 5km (3 miles) south of the city center to the Oman border post at Mazyad. Take the road running south from

Camel Souk in Al Ain.

the Hilton hotel, continuing for about 3km (1¾ miles) until you reach the Bawadi Mall. The souk is just behind the mall. You'll need to drive past it and then double back on the other side of the road.

❾ ★★ Camel Souk. Al Ain's celebrated Camel Souk, the last of its kind in the UAE, offers a memorable taste of old-style Arabia. Hundreds of dromedaries (plus sheep, goats, and cows) can be seen here most days, attracting dozens of traders from across the UAE haggling remorselessly over their pounds of camel flesh.

Note before visiting that tourists sometimes are exposed to a certain amount of hassle and high-pressure salesmanship. You may be offered a tour of the souk, which you're by no means obliged to accept. If you do, be sure to agree to a price up front. Ditto with baby camel–petting opportunities. Yes, the souk is also highly photogenic, but be aware that some traders might demand

money if you point your camera at their animals—best to ask first. The souk is open all day, although most of the action usually takes place earlier in the morning. ⏱ *45 min. 5km/3 miles south of city center en route to the Oman border post at Mazyad. AED 30. Daily 6am–7pm, but best in the mornings.*

🔟 Al Diwan. The nicest of the many cafes, restaurants, and fast-food joints along this road, this cheery Middle Eastern joint dishes up a good spread of cheap sandwiches, salads, and juices along with more substantial Lebanese, Iranian, and Western dishes. *Sheikh Khalifa bin Zayed St., a block south of the landmark Globe Roundabout.* ☎ *03-764-4445. $.*

⓫ ★★ Jebel Hafeet. If you have your own transportation, it's well worth driving out of town up the UAE's second-highest

Driving up Jebal Hafeet, UAE's second-largest mountain.

mountain, Jebel Hafeet (1,180m/3,870 ft.), whose craggy outline dominates the town—a dramatic series of rocky, switchback pinnacles looking from some angles like the tail of an enormous dragon. There's an excellent road all the way to the top, easily negotiable in even the smallest vehicle. It's noticeably cooler at the summit (in fact, it's often quite chilly), with sweeping views over Al Ain and the surrounding desert, at their best toward sunset. It's also a haven for local wildlife, home to feral cats, red foxes, and other mammals as well as a rich variety of bird life. ⏱ *90 min. Al Ain. Best at sunset.*

12 **Mercure Grand Jebel Hafeet Al Ain Hotel.** Sitting almost at the top of the mountain, this dramatically situated hotel is a good place for a coffee or drink before heading back down to town. *Jebel Hafeet.* ☎ *03-788-8888. $.* ●

9 Abu Dhabi

The Best of **Abu Dhabi**

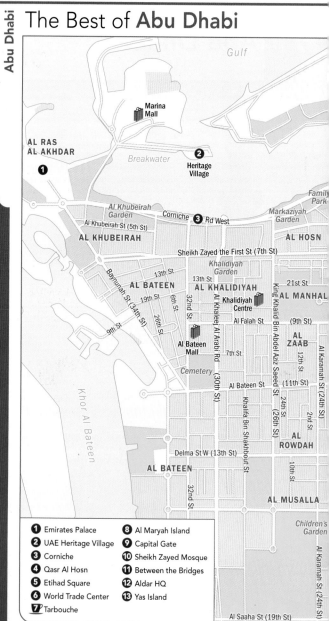

Gulf

Marina
Mall

**AL RAS
AL AKHDAR**

Breakwater

2
Heritage
Village

1

Al Khubeirah
Garden

Corniche **3** Rd West

Family
Park

Markaziyah
Garden

Al Khubeirah St (5th St)

AL KHUBEIRAH

AL HOSN

Sheikh Zayed the First St (7th St)

Khalidiyah
Garden

13th St

AL BATEEN

13th St

21st St

19th St

6th St

32nd St

AL KHALIDIYAH

Khalidiyah
Centre

AL MANHAL

Barunah St (34th St)

26th St

Al Khaleej Al Arabi Rd

Al Falah St

King Khalid Bin Abdel Aziz Saeed St

(9th St)

**AL
ZAAB**

9th St

Al Bateen
Mall

7th St

12th St

Al Karamah St (24th St)

Cemetery

(30th St)

Al Bateen St

(11th St)

2nd St

Khalifa Bin Shakhbout St

24th St
(26th St)

**AL
ROWDAH**

Khor Al Bateen

Delma St W (13th St)

10th St

AL BATEEN

32nd St

AL MUSALLA

Children's
Garden

1 Emirates Palace

2 UAE Heritage Village

3 Corniche

4 Qasr Al Hosn

5 Etihad Square

6 World Trade Center

7 Tarbouche

8 Al Maryah Island

9 Capital Gate

10 Sheikh Zayed Mosque

11 Between the Bridges

12 Aldar HQ

13 Yas Island

Al Saaha St (19th St)

Al Karamah St (24th St)

Previous page: Sheikh Zayed Mosque.

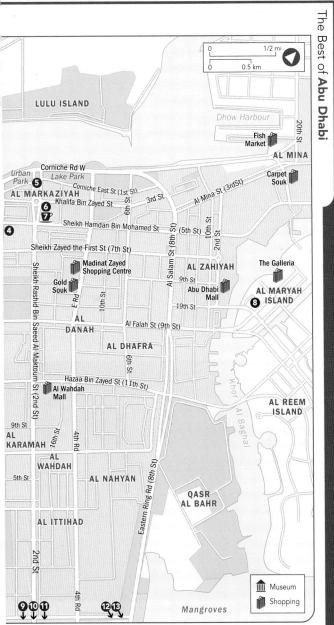

LULU ISLAND

Dhow Harbour

20th St

Fish Market

AL MINA

Carpet Souk

Urban Park

Corniche Rd W

Lake Park

Corniche East St (1st St)

AL MARKAZIYAH

Khalifa Bin Zayed St

3rd St

Al Mina St (3rd St)

6th St

5

6
7

4

Sheikh Hamdan Bin Mohamed St

10th St

2nd St

Sheikh Zayed the First St (7th St)

Al Salam St (8th St)

AL ZAHIYAH

The Galleria

Madinat Zayed Shopping Centre

9th St

AL MARYAH ISLAND

Gold Souk

E Rd

10th St

Abu Dhabi Mall

8

19th St

Sheikh Rashid Bin Saeed Al Maktoum St (2nd St)

AL DANAH

Al Falah St (9th St)

AL DHAFRA

6th St

Khor Al Baghal

AL REEM ISLAND

Hazaa Bin Zayed St (11th St)

Al Wahdah Mall

9th St

AL KARAMAH

16th St

4th Rd

AL WAHDAH

5th St

AL NAHYAN

2nd St

AL ITTIHAD

4th Rd

Eastern Ring Rd (8th St)

QASR AL BAHR

🏛 Museum

📦 Shopping

9 **10** **11**
↓ ↓ ↓

12 **13**
↓ ↓

Mangroves

0   1/2 mi
0   0.5 km

Few neighboring cities can be more different than Dubai and Abu Dhabi. Where Dubai is brash, glamorous, and cosmopolitan, Abu Dhabi is traditional and conservative. For some, Abu Dhabi's gentler pace of life and outlook have their own appeal, bolstered by such modern developments as the sumptuous Emirates Palace Hotel and the extraordinary Sheikh Zayed Mosque. START: Emirates Palace Hotel.

❶ ★★★ Emirates Palace. The most spectacular sight in central Abu Dhabi, the landmark Emirates Palace hotel lives up to every Western cliché about the petroleum-fueled opulence of life in the Gulf. Built at a cost of around $3 billion (possibly the most expensive hotel ever constructed), the entire place is a study in Arabian baroque and excess. The scale of the hotel is staggering: It's around a half mile long (guests are offered bicycles to circumnavigate the grounds) and equipped with more than 1,000 Swarovski crystal chandeliers, 150,000 cubic yards of imported marble, 114 domes, 102 elevators,

and more than 1,000 employees from around 50 countries. Fittings in the six Rulers' Suites (reserved for visiting heads of state) are made entirely of gold—including the sinks.

The hotel is open to the public, although nonguests are restricted to the main lobby area. Many people like to come for afternoon tea (see p 156), and there are plenty of top-notch restaurants if you really want to splurge. ⏱ *1 hr.* ☎ *02-690-9000. www.emiratespalace.com. For accommodations, see p 159.*

❷ ★ Heritage Village. Just down the road from the landmark Marina Mall (see p 153), the quaint

Emirates Palace and gardens in Abu Dhabi.

Abu Dhabi—Practical Matters

Abu Dhabi is more or less a 90-minute to 2-hour drive from Dubai along the super-fast Sheikh Zayed Road. There are regular buses from the Al Ghubaiba bus station in Bur Dubai and from the Ibn Battuta metro station, which arrive in Abu Dhabi at the main bus terminal in Al Wahdah, about 2km (1¼ miles) south of the city center.

Abu Dhabi's airport is on the mainland, roughly a 30- to 45-minute drive from the center (depending on traffic). A shuttle bus connects the airport and the city center. Alternatively, a taxi from the airport will cost around AED 70 to AED 80.

UAE Heritage Village occupies a pretty little complex of traditional coral-and-gypsum buildings and *barasti* (palm-thatch) huts. Local artisans can sometimes be seen at work here practicing traditional crafts, such as carpentry, pottery, and glassmaking. The slightly moth-eaten Al Asalah Restaurant offers superb views of the Corniche opposite. 🕐 *20 min. Breakwater, near the Marina Mall. Free admission. Sat–Thurs 9am–5pm; Fri 3:30–9pm.*

From Heritage Village, catch a taxi (around AED 12) to Al Markaziyah Gardens and walk northwest along the Corniche.

❸ ★★ **Corniche.** Running the length of Abu Dhabi's main waterfront, the city's breezy Corniche is a great place to stretch your legs and enjoy uninterrupted views of the city's modernist skyline. Parks and gardens line the waterfront, along with an attractive blue-flag beach stretching between the Hilton Hotel and Al Khaleej al Arabi Street. Looking over the water, you'll see the soaring Marina Tower (atop the Marina Mall) and an enormous flagpole just down the road—the second largest in the world. 🕐 *30 min.*

❹ ★ **Qasr Al Hosn.** More or less at the dead geographical center of the city lies the rambling

Corniche Road.

Soon to Come on Saadiyat

Long overshadowed by the spectacular success of neighboring Dubai, Abu Dhabi surprised the world back in 2006 by announcing the launch of the $27-billion Saadiyat Island development, centered on a series of spectacular museums, including an Abu Dhabi branch of the **Louvre,** a new Frank Gehry–designed **Guggenheim Museum,** and a spectacular **Sheikh Zayed National Museum,** in a building by Foster + Partners. Originally slated to be completed around 2012, the project has been far longer in the making than expected but looks finally to be bearing fruit with the opening in late 2016 of the new Louvre, in a spectacular new building by Jean Nouvel that resembles a kind of Islamic flying saucer. The event will doubtless give a massive boost to the city's cultural and touristic credentials. Construction work on the Louvre is already largely complete, although otherwise the island's attractions consist only of a couple of beachfront resorts and the fine **Saadiyat Public Beach** (AED 25). For an idea of what the whole island is eventually intended to look like, the **Manarat al Saadiyat** (daily 9am–8pm; free admission) exhibition has interesting models and pictures of future developments.

Qasr Al Hosn, the oldest building in Abu Dhabi. Built in 1793, the fort was extensively expanded in the 1930s and renovated in the late 1970s, acquiring a bright new covering of white-painted concrete— hence its popular name, the **White Fort.** The fort has been closed for renovations for several years, with plans to reopen the entire complex as a major new museum; right now, all you can see are enormous hoardings enclosing the building. ⏱ 10 min.

❺ ★★ Etihad Square. A few blocks north of Al Hosn Fort, workaday Etihad (or Al Itihad) Square is enlivened by a surreal series of five oversize sculptures that depict a small fort, a huge cannon, a pot cover, an incense burner, and what

World Trade Center Towers.

Al Maryah Island at dusk.

may well be the world's largest perfume bottle—an entertaining bit of sculptural whimsy amid the functional downtown architecture. ⓘ *15 min.*

⑥ ★★★ World Trade Center. A major new downtown landmark, the World Trade Center (designed by Foster + Partners) is visible from across the city, thanks to its two huge skyscrapers. The real interest, however, is at street level, where you'll find the gorgeous **World Trade Center Souk,** housed in an extraordinary wooden boxlike structure blending traditional Arabian motifs with stripped-back contemporary design—an architectural tour de force quite unlike anything else in the Gulf. The adjacent **World Trade Center Mall** over the road has a toned-down version of the same design but isn't nearly as memorable. ⓘ *30 min.*

⑦ Tarbouche. In the beautiful central courtyard of the World Trade Center Souk, this cheery Lebanese-style restaurant serves up a good selection of mezze to snack on, plus more substantial grills and kebabs. *$.*

Catch a taxi (around AED 15) to:

⑧ ★★★ Al Maryah Island. Nowhere encapsulates Abu Dhabi's new-found dynamism as dramatically as Al Maryah Island. A dusty, uninhabited island less than a decade ago, it's now being transformed into the city's new financial district. It's still very much a work in progress, but dozens of huge buildings have already risen from the sands. Its visually arresting centerpiece is the **Abu Dhabi Global Market Square** (or Sowwah Square,

Sheikh Zayed Mosque: Facts & Figures

The Sheikh Zayed Mosque may not be the largest in the world, but it does hold the world's largest carpet, made in Iran by around 1,200 weavers; the rug measures 5,627 square meters (60,500 sq. ft.), weighs 47 tons, and contains some 2,268,000 knots. Inside you'll also see the world's largest chandelier (from Germany), measuring 10m (33 ft.) in diameter and 15m (50 ft.) high and containing a million Swarovski crystals

as it was formerly known), a futuristic square overlooked by space-age skyscrapers, including the distinctive, anvil-shaped Abu Dhabi Global Market building and its swanky waterside Galleria mall (see p 153). ⏱ *30 min.*

Catch a taxi (around AED 30) to:

❾ ★★ Capital Gate. Popularly known as the Leaning Tower of Abu Dhabi, the Capital Gate skyscraper (home to the city's Hyatt Hotel) has been certified by Guinness World Records as the world's most tilted tower, with an 18° slant—more than four times that of its famous Pisan predecessor. ⏱ *15 min.*

Take a taxi (around AED 12) from Capital Gate to the:

❿ ★★★ Sheikh Zayed Mosque. The gargantuan Sheikh Zayed Mosque is a staggering vision of Islamic pride: a huge white edifice topped by 57 domes and flanked by four soaring minarets. Completed in 2007, the mosque took 12 years to build at a cost of around $500 million. It is named after Sheikh Zayed bin Sultan Al Nahyan, the first president of the UAE, who oversaw Abu Dhabi's transformation and is buried here.

Covering an area of 22,412 square meters (241,241 sq. ft.), the mosque is either the third or sixth largest in the world, depending on how you measure it (see the box above), with space for 40,000 worshippers. Inside, the mosque's extravagant design is a riot of gold leaf, marble, and elaborate stone work in an eye-boggling marriage of traditional and contemporary Islamic motifs.

The mosque is the only one in Abu Dhabi open to non-Muslims, although visitors must dress conservatively, and women should wear a headscarf. ⏱ *1 hr. Btw Al Maqtaa & Mussafah Bridges. Sat–Thurs 9am–10pm; Fri 4:30–10pm. Free guided tours lasting around 1 hr. Mon–Thurs at 10am, 11pm & 5pm; Sat–Fri at 5pm & 7pm.*

Take a taxi (around AED 10) from the mosque to:

⓫ ★ Between the Bridges. Just east of the Sheikh Zayed Mosque, no fewer than three bridges span the small sea inlet that separates Abu Dhabi from the mainland. The area between the southern (Mussafah) and middle (Al Maqtaa) bridges—Between the Bridges, as it's popularly known—has been recently developed into a

The Yas Marina Formula 1 Grand Prix Circuit.

dense cluster of restaurants and upscale hotels (including a Fairmont, Ritz-Carlton, and stunning Shangri-La; see p 160). For casual visitors, the highlight of the area is the attractive **Souk Qaryat al Beri,** attached to the Shangri-La, with a good selection of shops, restaurants, and a breezy waterfront promenade with sweeping views.

Nearby, the tiny Al Maqtaa Fort stands sentinel beside the northernmost of the three bridges (Sheikh Zayed)—a diminutive memento of the city's lawless past. ⏱ *30 min.*

Take a taxi (around AED 40) from Between the Bridges to Yas Island.

⓬ ★★ **Aldar HQ.** Driving along the Abu Dhabi–Dubai highway en route to Yas Island, you can't help but notice the extraordinary Aldar HQ building, the "world's first circular skyscraper" (as it's been described). It's one of the strangest and most striking buildings in the

UAE, looking like an enormous magnifying glass propped up by the side of the road. ⏱ *10 min.*

⓭ ★★ **Yas Island.** East of Abu Dhabi's city center, Yas Island's developments are populist rather than cultural. First there's the vast red **Ferrari World,** the world's largest indoor theme park, right next door to the dramatic **Yas Marina Circuit,** home to the annual Abu Dhabi Formula 1 Grand Prix (see p 101). Nearby you'll also find **Yas Waterworld,** with 45 slides and rides to rival anything in Dubai. The island's beautiful **marina** and idyllic public **beach** (AED 50) also pull in the crowds. *Ferrari World* ☎ *02-496-8000. www.ferrariworldabudhabi. com. AED 250, AED 205 children under 1.3m, free for kids 2 & under. Daily 11am–8pm (Thurs–Sat until 10pm). Yas Waterworld* ☎ *02-414-2000. www.yaswaterworld.com. AED 240, AED 195 children under 1.1m. Daily 10am–7pm.*

Abu Dhabi **Shopping**

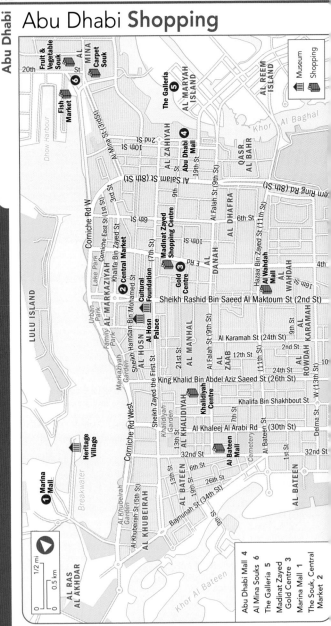

Legend:
- 🏛 Museum
- 🛍 Shopping

Map labels:

AL MINA, Fruit & Vegetable Souk, Carpet Souk, 20th St, AL, Fish Market, 6, Dhow Harbour

The Galleria, 5, AL MARYAH ISLAND, AL REEM ISLAND

Al Mina St (3rd St), AL ZAHIYAH, 10th St, 2nd St, Abu Dhabi Mall, 4, 19th St (9th St), Khor Al Baghal, QASR AL BAHR

Corniche Rd W, Corniche East St (1st St), 3rd St, Al Salam St (8th St), 9th, Al Falah St, 6th St, ...ern Ring Rd (8th St)

LULU ISLAND, Lake Park, Urban Park, AL MARKAZIYAH, Khalifa Bin Zayed St, Central Market, 2, Cultural Foundation (7th St), Madinat Zayed Shopping Centre, 3, Gold Centre, AL DHAFRA, AL DANAH, 10th St, Hazaa Bin Zayed St (11th St), Al Wahdah Mall, AL WAHDAH, 16th St, 4th

Family Park, Markaziyah Garden, Sheikh Hamdan Bin Mohamed St, AL HOSN, Al Hosn Palace, Sheikh Rashid Bin Saeed Al Maktoum St (2nd St)

Sheikh Zayed the First St, 21st St, AL MANHAL, Al Falah St (9th St), AL ZAAB, 12th St, Al Karamah St (24th St), 2nd St, 9th St, AL ROWDAH, KARAMAH, 10

Khalidiyah Garden, Khalidiyah Centre, AL KHALIDIYAH, 7th St, King Khalid Bin Abdel Aziz Saeed St (26th St), (11th St), 24th St, W (13th St), Delma St, Khalifa Bin Shakhbout St

Corniche Rd West, 13th St, Al Khaleej Al Arabi Rd (30th St), AL BATEEN, 32nd St, Al Bateen Mall, Cemetery, Al Bateen St, 1st St, 32nd St

Marina Mall, 1, Heritage Village, Breakwater, Al Khubeirah Garden, Al Khubeirah St (5th St), AL KHUBEIRAH, 13th St, 6th St, 26th St, 19th St (34th St), Baynunah St, 9th St

AL RAS AL AKHDAR, 1/2 mi, 0.5 km, Khor Al Bateen

Abu Dhabi Shopping A to Z

★★ Abu Dhabi Mall AL ZAHIYAH   Abu Dhabi's biggest and smartest mall has pretty much every store you'll need, ranging from posh designer outlets—Swarovski, Tiffany, and the like—to more workaday shops, plus a Virgin Megastore for Arabian music. There's a good food court on the top floor. *10th St. www.abudhabi-mall.com. Sat–Wed 10am–10pm; Thurs–Fri 10am–11pm. Map p 152.*

★ Al Mina Souks AL MINA   A lot of Abu Dhabi's old-style trading and wholesaling go on in the low-key souks dotted around Al Mina district. The **Carpet Souk** has a fair array of rugs—mainly factory-made rubbish, although you might find a few more interesting pieces. The main draw at the nearby **Fruit and Vegetable Souk** is the impressive line of date sellers, while the **Fish Market** buzzes in the morning with crowds of shoppers haggling over heaps of freshly landed catch. *Al Mina. Daily 10am–10pm; some shops closed 1–4pm & on Fri until around 2pm. Map p 152.*

Dates at the Food Souk in Al Mina.

★★ The Galleria AL MARYAH ISLAND   This super-swanky new mall is full of designer outlets and upscale restaurants. The airy architecture and water views make it well worth a visit. *Abu Dhabi Global Market Sq. www.thegalleria.ae. Sat–Wed 10am–10pm; Thurs 10am–midnight; Fri noon–midnight. Map p 152.*

★ Madinat Zayed Gold Centre AL DANAH   If not as pretty as Dubai's Gold Souk, Abu Dhabi's main gold market still stocks an impressive quantity of precious metal, along with lots of diamonds and other gems. *Al Sharqi St. (4th St.).* ☎ *02-631-8555. www.madinat zayed-mall.com. Sat–Thurs 9am–10:30pm; Fri 4–11pm. Map p 152.*

★ Marina Mall BREAKWATER   The sprawling Marina Mall is slightly cheerier (and fractionally more downmarket) than the Abu Dhabi Mall, with a massive Carrefour supermarket and a reasonable spread of designer shops. *Break-water. www.marinamall.ae. Sat–Wed 10am–10pm; Thurs–Fri 10am–midnight. Map p 152.*

★★ The Souk, Central Market AL MARKAZIYAH   A lot of the souvenirs sold here are kitschy junk, but some of the shops stock interesting collectibles, including crafts, carpets, and original paintings, plus spices and frankincense; one little place sells nothing but Arabian honey. *World Trade Center. www. wtcad.ae. Sat–Wed 10am–10pm; Thurs–Fri 10am–11pm. Map p 152.*

Abu Dhabi **Dining & Nightlife**

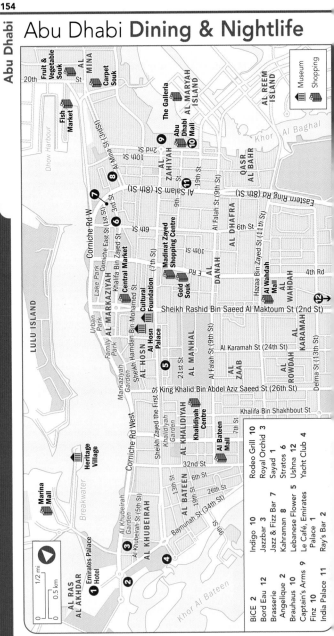

Fruit & Vegetable Souk

AL MINA

20th St

Carpet Souk

Dhow Harbour

Fish Market

The Galleria

AL MARYAH ISLAND

AL REEM ISLAND

Khor Al Baghal

QASR AL BAHR

Abu Dhabi Mall 10

AL ZAHIYAH

9

10th St

8th St (3rd St)

2nd St

8 Al Mina St (3rd St)

11 19th St

Al Falah St (9th St)

Eastern Ring Rd (8th St)

Corniche Rd W

Lake Park

Corniche East St (1st St)

7

3rd St (8th St)

6

Al Salam St (8th St)

9th

6th St

AL DHAFRA

6th St

Khalifa Bin Zayed St

5th St

Central Market

AL MARKAZIYAH

Urban Park

Madinat Zayed Shopping Centre

10th St

AL DANAH

Hazaa Bin Zayed St (11th St)

Family Park

ER Rd (7th St)

Gold Souk

Al Wahdah Mall

4th Rd

Cultural Foundation

9th

AL WAHDAH

Markaziyah Garden

Sheikh Hamdan Bin Mohamed St

Al Hosn Palace

AL HOSN

Sheikh Rashid Bin Saeed Al Maktoum St (2nd St)

LULU ISLAND

5

21st St

AL MANHAL

Al Falah St (9th St)

AL ZAAB

Al Karamah St (24th St)

AL ROWDAH

AL KARAMAH

Delma St (13th St)

12

King Khalid Bin Abdel Aziz Saeed St (26th St)

Khalifa Bin Shakhbout St

Sheikh Zayed the First St

Khalidiyah Garden

Khalidiyah Centre

AL KHALIDIYAH

7th St

Heritage Village

Corniche Rd West

Al Bateen Mall

32nd St

Breakwater

Marina Mall

Al Khubeirah Garden

13th St

6th St

AL BATEEN

Al Khubeirah St (5th St)

3

26th St

19th St

Baynunah St (34th St)

5th St

AL KHUBEIRAH

4

Khor Al Bateen

AL RAS AL AKHDAR

Emirates Palace Hotel

1

2

1/2 mi

0.5 km

0

| Museum |
| Shopping |

BiCE **2**
Bord Eau **12**
Brasserie Angelique **2**
Brauhaus **10**
Captain's Arms **9**
Finz **10**
India Palace **11**

Indigo **10**
Jazzbar **3**
Jazz & Fizz Bar **7**
Kahraman **8**
Lebanese Flower **5**
Le Café, Emirates Palace **1**
Ray's Bar **2**

Rodeo Grill **10**
Royal Orchid **3**
Sayad **1**
Stratos **6**
Ushna **12**
Yacht Club **4**

Abu Dhabi **Dining & Nightlife A to Z**

★★ **BiCE** CORNICHE *ITALIAN* The Abu Dhabi branch of the well-regarded Dubai restaurant (see p 90) serves fresh and inventive pastas and risottos, plus meat and seafood main courses, all reasonably priced. *Jumeirah at Etihad Towers.* ☎ *02-811-5666. http://bit.ly/ BiceEtihad. Entrees AED 75–AED 135. AE, DC, MC, V. Sat–Thurs noon–3pm & 7–11:30pm; Fri noon–11:30pm. Map p 154.*

★★★ **Bord Eau** AL MAQTAA *FRENCH* As good as it gets in Abu Dhabi, this sedate French-style fine-dining restaurant is full of old-school European style and charm. Delectable fish and meat classics—blue Brittany lobster, foie gras, rack of milk-fed lamb—satisfy even the most discerning gourmand. Sit

Bord Eau dining room.

inside or on the idyllic waterside terrace. *Shangri-La Qaryat al Beri, Between the Bridge.* ☎ *02-509-8511. www.shangri-la.com. Entrees AED 210–AED 370. AE, DC, MC, V. Daily 6:30–11:30pm. Map p 154.*

★★ **Brasserie Angelique** AL KHUBEIRAH *FRENCH* Once inside this ornate Paris-themed bistro, you may forget you're in the middle of the Gulf. The menu features elegant French classics ranging from veal cutlets to Toulouse-style cassoulet. *Jumeirah at Emirates Towers, Corniche Rd. W.* ☎ *02-811-5666. www.jumeirah.com. Entrees AED 75–AED 225. AE, DC, MC, V. Daily noon–3:30pm & 7–11:30pm. Map p 154.*

★★ **Finz** AL ZAHIYAH *CONTEMPORARY SEAFOOD* This chic seafood restaurant serves choice ocean catch flown in from across the world—think Dover sole, Alaskan king crab, and Maine lobster. Sit inside the stylish A-frame restaurant itself or out on the pleasant waterside patio, with its stunning views of Al Maryah Island. *Beach Rotana Hotel.* ☎ *02-697-9350. http://bit.ly/BRADRestos. Entrees AED 140–AED 220. AE, DC, MC, V. Daily 12:30–3pm & 7–11:30pm. Map p 154.*

★★ **India Palace** AL ZAHIYAH *NORTH INDIAN* A long-running Abu Dhabi stalwart, now with branches countrywide, the attractively decorated India Palace has plenty of subcontinental style. The menu features a well-prepared range of north Indian meat and veg curries and tandooris. *Al Salam St.*

Le Café, Emirates Palace.

☎ 02-644-8777. www.indiapalace.ae. Entrees AED 25–AED 60. AE, DC, MC, V. Daily noon–11:30pm. Map p 154.

★★ Indigo AL ZAHIYAH *NORTH INDIAN* One of the best-looking restaurants in the city, Indigo serves a well-prepared range of North Indian classics—tandooris, biryanis—plus some seafood options and a basic range of vegetarian dishes. Try the signature Sikandari raan (slow-roasted lamb). *Beach Rotana Hotel.* ☎ 02-697-9334. http://bit.ly/BRADRestos. *Entrees AED 80–AED 185. AE, DC, MC, V. Daily 12:30–3:30pm & 6:30–11:30pm. Map p 154.*

★★★ Le Café, Emirates Palace RAS AL AKHDAR *CAFE* The sumptuous lounge cafe in the Emirates Palace is deservedly popular for its beautiful high teas (AED 260), served either in traditional English or Arabian styles. *Emirates Palace.* ☎ 02-690-9000. http://bit.ly/LeCafeEP. *AE, DC, MC, V. Afternoon tea daily 2–6pm. Map p 154.*

★★ Kahraman AL MINA *ARABIAN* This unexpectedly upscale restaurant boasts chic decor and excellent contemporary Arabian-style meat and seafood dishes, along with (rather incongruously) a decent selection of sushi and maki (AED 38–AED 50). *Southern Sun Hotel, Al Mina St.* ☎ 02-818-4888. www.tsogosunhotels.com/hotels/abu-dhabi. *Entrees AED 95–AED 150. AE, DC, MC, V. Daily 7pm–midnight. Map p 154.*

★★ Lebanese Flower AL KHALIDIYA *ARABIAN* Popular and always packed, this no-frills Lebanese restaurant does a great line in grilled meat and fish dishes, accompanied by fresh salads and huge mounds of bread, plus lighter snacks, such as crispy falafel and creamy hummus. Unlicensed. *Off 26th St.* ☎ 02-665-8700. *Sandwiches & mezze AED 8–AED 25; entrees AED 45–AED 60. MC, V. Daily 8am–3am. Map p 154.*

★★ Rodeo Grill AL ZAHIYAH *STEAKHOUSE* This is the top steakhouse in town, dishing up such carnivorous classics as Josper-grilled Wagyu and Angus beef as well as some seafood. *Beach Rotana Hotel.* ☎ 02-697-9011. http://bit.ly/BRADRestos. *Entrees AED 150–AED 340. AE, DC, MC, V. Daily 12:30–3:30pm & 7–11:30pm. Map p 154.*

★★ Royal Orchid CORNICHE *THAI/CHINESE* One of the longest-running Asian restaurants in the UAE and still deservedly popular, this cozy and prettily decorated venue serves a wide range of tasty and very reasonably priced Thai and Chinese food. *Hilton.* ☎ 02-681-1900. http://bit.ly/HADRestos. *Entrees AED 52–AED 75. AE, MC, V. Daily 12:30–3:30pm & 7–11:30pm. Map p 154.*

★★ Sayad RAS AL AKHDAR *SEAFOOD* The flagship restaurant of the Emirates Palace, Sayad is the place to head for a big night out. The menu focuses on international seafood done with a flourish, from the superb fish creations to the caviar menu and fine French oysters. Sit either outside or in the restaurant itself, decorated in calming shades of underwater blue. *Emirates Palace.* ☎ *02-690-7999. http://bit.ly/EPRestos. Entrees AED 120– AED 295. AE, DC, MC, V. Daily 6:30– 11:30pm. Map p 154.*

★★ **Stratos** AL MARKAZIYAH *MODERN EUROPEAN* This revolving lounge bar and grill, perched on the summit of Le Royal Méridien, offers peerless views of the city below. The upmarket food consists of mainly seafood starters and Josper-cooked meat grills—or just come up for a drink or a sumptuous afternoon tea (3–6pm; from around AED 230). *Le Royal Méridien.* ☎ *800-101-101. www.stratos abudhabi.com. Entrees AED 190– AED 400. AE, DC, MC, V. Mon–Sat 3pm until late. Map p 154.*

★★ **Ushna** AL MAQTAA *INDIAN* Arguably the best of many restaurants in the pleasant Souk Qaryat al Beri, this smooth modern restaurant serves a well-prepared and sensibly priced range of meat, fish, and veg Indian standards in an attractive dining room. Take a seat on the beautiful waterfront terrace for added romance. *Souk Qaryat al Beri.* ☎ *02-558-1769. www.facebook. com/UshnaFineDining. Entrees AED 52–AED 115. AE, MC, V. Daily 12:30– 11:00pm. Map p 154.*

Pubs & Bars

★★ **Brauhaus** AL ZAHIYAH A refreshingly authentic German-style pub-cum-restaurant, Brauhaus has specialty Teutonic beers on tap or by the bottle, plus a food selection that includes Bavarian sausages

and suckling pig. *Beach Rotana Hotel.* ☎ *02-697-9011. Sun–Wed 4pm–1am; Thurs–Sat noon–1am. Map p 154.*

★ **Captain's Arms** AL MARKAZIYAH This cheery British-style pub offers cheap beer and nice outdoor seating overlooking the hotel gardens. *Le Méridien.* ☎ *02-697-4482. Daily noon–1am. Map p 154.*

★★ **Jazzbar** CORNICHE This long-running nightspot is particularly popular among a slightly older crowd, who come for the good live jazz (nightly) and Thursday comedy nights. Can get lively later on. *Hilton.* ☎ *02-692-4562. Sat–Wed 7:30pm–12:30am; Thurs–Fri 7:30pm– 1:30am. Map p 154.*

★★ **Jazz & Fizz Bar** AL ZAHIYAH At this sedate and svelte piano bar, cocktails and cigars are the order of the day (or, rather, evening). A live jazz band provides a pitch-perfect soundtrack most nights. *Sofitel Hotel, Corniche Rd. E.* ☎ *02-813-7848. www.facebook.com/JazznFizz. AE, DC, MC, V. Daily 6pm–2am. Map p 154.*

★★ **Ray's Bar** AL KHUBEIRAH On the 62nd floor of the Jumeirah at Etihad Towers Hotel, you'll find head-spinning views, cool decor, Asian tapas, and bespoke cocktails by the resident mixologists. Regular DJs add to the very chilled-out vibe. *Jumeirah at Etihad Towers, Corniche Rd. W.* ☎ *02-811-5666. Daily 5pm–3am. Map p 154.*

★ **Yacht Club** AL BATEEN A glam crowd of pretty young things gravitates to the Yacht Club, drawn by sleek modern decor, a gorgeous patio overlooking the marina, fancy cocktails, crisp Asian tapas, and regular DJs. *InterContinental.* ☎ *02-666-6888. Sun–Thurs 5pm–1am or later; Fri 7pm–2:30am. Map p 154.*

Abu Dhabi **Lodging**

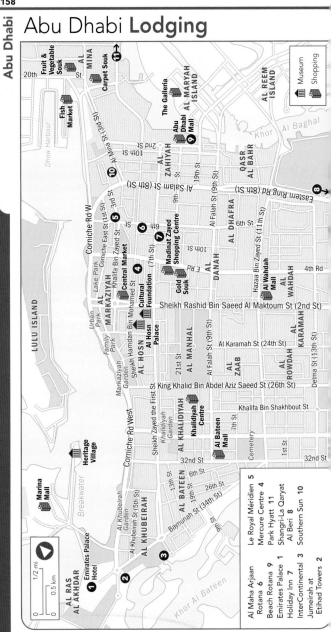

Al Maha Arjaan
Rotana **6**
Beach Rotana **9**
Emirates Palace **1**
Holiday Inn **7**
InterContinental **3**
Jumeirah at
Etihad Towers **2**

Le Royal Méridien **5**
Mercure Centre **4**
Park Hyatt **11**
Shangri-La Qaryat
Al Beri **8**
Southern Sun **10**

Abu Dhabi **Lodging A to Z**

★ **Al Maha Arjaan by Rotana** AL MARKAZIYAH This smart, modern, comfortably equipped apartment-hotel boasts spacious rooms and suites in a very central location and at competitive prices. Modest facilities include a rooftop pool and gym plus in-house cafe. *Hamdan St.* ☎ *02-610-6666. www.rotana.com. 288 units. Doubles from around AED 500–AED 700. AE, DC, MC, V. Map p 158.*

★★ **kids Beach Rotana** AL ZAHI-YAH This is one of Abu Dhabi's biggest and best-equipped hotels, with stylish rooms, a vast pool, a spa, and an excellent spread of restaurants. It's brilliantly located right in the heart of downtown but feels more like a resort thanks to its attractive waterside location with rambling gardens, a small beach area, and superb views of Al Maryah Island. *10th St.* ☎ *02-697-9000. www.rotana. com. 565 units. Doubles from around AED 750. AE, DC, MC, V. Map p 158.*

★★★ **Emirates Palace** RAS AL AKHDAR This "seven-star" über-hotel (see p 146, ❶) is one of the grandest and most luxurious places to stay in the entire Middle East, offering every facility you could possibly need in its vast, Arabian-style edifice. The only problem is finding the willpower to leave. *Corniche Rd. W.* ☎ *02-690-9000. www.emirates palace.com. 394 units. Doubles from* around AED 1,500–AED 2,500. AE, DC, MC, V. Map p 158.

★ **Holiday Inn Abu Dhabi Downtown** AL DANAH Dated but comfortable, this stalwart option has spacious, nicely furnished rooms and super-helpful staff. Facilities include a couple of bars and restaurants, plus a gym and tiny rooftop pool, and rates are usually decent value. *Zayed 1st St. (Electra Rd.).* ☎ *02-615-6666. www.holiday inn.com/abudhabidwtn. 257 units. Doubles from around AED 450–AED 500. AE, DC, MC, V. Map p 158.*

★★ **InterContinental** AL BATEEN One of Abu Dhabi's older five-star hotels, the InterContinental is still a good choice thanks to its location on the peaceful western side of town in a lovely waterfront setting, with fine views of the nearby Etihad Towers and Emirates Palace. The suave rooms come with sea or city views, while facilities include a huge pool, a big gym, a top-notch selection of restaurants and bars, and a fine swath of beautiful white sand. *Al Bateen St.* ☎ *02-666-6888. www. intercontinental.com. 390 units. Doubles from around AED 700–AED 850. AE, DC, MC, V. Map p 158.*

★★ **Jumeirah at Etihad Towers** AL KHUBEIRAH One of Abu Dhabi's top addresses, from the people who brought you Dubai's

The Beach Rotana Hotel.

Dinner on the beach at Shangri-La Qaryat al Beri.

Burj al Arab, this luxurious Jumeirah outpost in the futuristic Etihad Towers complex boasts all the amenities and contemporary style you'd expect at this price as well as marvelous views. Three pools and a private beach compete for your attention, along with a brilliant collection of restaurants and bars. *Corniche Rd. W.* ☎ *02-811-5555, www.jumeirah.com. 382 units. Doubles from around AED 1,100. AE, DC, V, MC. Map p 158.*

★★ **Le Royal Méridien** AL MARKAZIYAH The suave Royal Méridien strikes a good balance between slick downtown business hotel and relaxed resort, with spacious rooms plus a couple of pools and an attractive enclosed garden. Given the quality, rates are often a steal. *Khalifa St.* ☎ *02-674-2020. www. lemeridien.com/royalabudhabi. 276 units. Doubles from around AED 450– AED 500. AE, DC, MC, V. Map p 158.*

★ **Mercure Centre** AL MARKA-ZIYAH This decent, if uninspired, city-center business hotel ticks all the right boxes, and usually at ultra-competitive rates. Rooms are boxy but perfectly comfy, and amenities include a pool, three restaurants, two bars, and a nightclub. *Hamdan St.* ☎ *02-633-3555. www.mercure. com. 215 units. Doubles from around AED 300–AED 400. AE, DC, MC, V. Map p 158.*

★★★ **Park Hyatt** SADAIYAAT ISLAND An idyllic five-star beach retreat with sumptuous rooms, the ocher-colored Park Hyatt feels like a real hideaway even though it's only a short drive from downtown. The gorgeous pool with canopied loungers and wide unspoiled beach is Abu Dhabi at its most blissed-out. *Sadiyaat Island.* ☎ *02-407-1234. www. abudhabi.park.hyatt.com. 306 units. Doubles from around AED 1,300–AED 1,500. AE, DC, MC, V. Map p 158.*

★★ **Shangri-La Qaryat Al Beri** AL MAQTAA At the far eastern end of town, this luxurious Arabian-themed hotel enjoys a beautiful waterfront setting, with its own private beach and views of the Sheikh Zayed Mosque. Facilities include an excellent spread of restaurants, a gorgeous spa, and four pools dotted around the spacious grounds. Summer rates can be a real bargain. *Al Maqtaa, Between the Bridges.* ☎ *02-509-8888. www.shangri-la. com. 214 units. Doubles from around AED 950. AE, DC, MC, V. Map p 158.*

★★ **Southern Sun** AL MINA This smartly styled modern hotel offers close to five-star comforts at less than four-star prices. Excellent amenities include top-quality Arabian and steakhouse restaurants, plus a rooftop pool and gym, all backed up with superhelpful service. *Al Mina St.* ☎ *02-818-4888. www.tsogosun hotels.com/hotels/abu-dhabi. 353 units. Doubles around AED 450–AED 500. AE, DC, MC, V. Map p 158.* ●

The **Savvy Traveler**

Before You Go

Government Tourist Offices

USA: DTCM (Dubai Tourism and Commerce Marketing), 10th floor, 215 Park Ave. S., New York, NY 10003; ☎ 212-575-2262; www.visitdubai.com.

UK: DTCM, Ste. 201–206, 4th floor, Nuffield House, 41–46 Piccadilly, London W1J 0DS; ☎ 020-7321-6110; www.visitdubai.com.

The Best Time to Go

The best time to visit the Gulf is from November to March. Temperatures during these months are pretty perfect: a pleasant Mediterranean heat, never too oppressive (and sometimes surprisingly chilly after dark). Don't be surprised if there's the occasional rain shower, with heavier downpours and even the occasional thunderstorm not uncommon. By contrast, the months from mid-April to September/October are almost completely dry but scorchingly hot. These months are okay for lying under a parasol sipping fruit juice or going shopping in air-conditioned malls, but it's difficult to do anything more strenuous. Daytime temperatures often exceed 40°C (104°F) and remain high even after dark.

Festivals & Special Events

FALL–WINTER: All eyes turn to Abu Dhabi for the **Abu Dhabi F1 Grand Prix** in late November or early December, while back in Dubai there's rugger and parties aplenty at the **Dubai Rugby Sevens** (p 103) in early December. Also in December, the **Dubai International Film Festival** (p 101), Dubai's premier cultural event, attracts local and international cineastes.

The new year starts with sales and discounts galore in the city's malls with the **Dubai Shopping Festival** (p 101) from the beginning of January to early February. The sporting season begins in February with the international **Dubai Desert Classic** golf tournament, held at the Emirates Golf Club (p 79), followed by the **Dubai Tennis Open** (p 103) in late February in Garhoud.

SPRING: In March, the world's single richest horse race, the **Dubai World Cup** (p 103), is held at the Nad Al Sheba racecourse.

RAMADAN: The Muslim holy month is scrupulously observed across the UAE (p 102). Dates change every year.

SUMMER: The heat of summer sees things move indoors into the air-conditioned city malls, with the summer sales and child-friendly events of **Dubai Summer Surprises** (p 101) running from July to September.

Useful Websites

- **www.visitdubai.come:** The Dubai Tourism and Commerce Marketing website

- **http://tcaabudhabi.ae:** Official website of the Abu Dhabi Tourism & Culture Authority

- **www.timeoutdubai.com:** Comprehensive Dubai reviews and listings

- **www.timeoutabudhabi.com:** Abu Dhabi listings and reviews

- **www.thenational.ae:** Online version of the UAE's best English-language newspaper, the National, based in Abu Dhabi, with all the latest news from around the Gulf

- **www.gulfnews.com:** Another good source of news from the region

- **www.dubaiconfidential.ae:** Long-running expat Dubai blog, with reviews, listings, and news

DUBAI'S AVERAGE TEMPERATURES & RAINFALL						
	JAN	FEB	MAR	APR	MAY	JUNE
°C	19	19	22	26	30	32
°F	66	67	72	79	86	90
Rainfall in inches	0.5	1.5	0.9	0.3	0	0
	JULY	AUG	SEPT	OCT	NOV	DEC
°C	34	34	32	29	24	21
°F	94	94	90	84	76	69
Rainfall in inches	0	0	0	0	0.1	0.6

Cell (Mobile) Phones

Check with your home-based provider to see what it will cost you to use your phone while in the UAE. GSM phones will work in Dubai, but make sure any international call bar is switched off. CDMA phones will not work, so you'll have to either bring a non-CDMA phone from home or buy a phone locally—you should be able to pick up a cheap handset for under $25.

If you're going to be making a lot of calls, you might find it cheaper to buy a local SIM card from one of Dubai's two telecom companies, Etisalat (www.etisalat. ae) or Du (www.du.ae). Cards can be had for as little as AED 10 and rising to around AED 100, depending on the package—the Du Visitor Mobile Line (valid 1 month, with sim cards from AED 30) is a good deal. Sims are available from many phone and electronics shops around the city, and from the Etisalat and Du shops on arrival at the airport. You'll need to show your passport.

Car Rental

There are car-rental outlets all over Dubai (including plenty of places at the airport). All the big chains are represented (Avis, Budget, Europcar, Hertz, Thrifty), along with many smaller (and generally slightly cheaper) local companies. Rates start at around AED 100 per day. The better companies should offer free delivery and pick-up from your hotel or the airport.

Getting **There**

By Plane

There are numerous flights between the UK and Dubai; flying time is around 7 hours, and fares start at around £330. There are currently nonstop flights from Heathrow with Emirates, British Airways, Virgin Atlantic, and Royal Brunei Airways as well as indirect services with many other carriers. There are also direct services with Emirates from London Gatwick, Birmingham, Manchester, Newcastle, and Glasgow.

From North America, there are numerous nonstop services (all with Emirates, some of them code-sharing with JetBlue) from New York, Houston, Los Angeles, San Francisco, and Toronto, and, of course, there are many other one- and two-stop options. From New York and Toronto, flying time is roughly 13 hours, with fares starting at around $800; from the West Coast, count on 16 hours of flying time, with fares from $1,200.

By Land

The only relevant land border open to Western tourists is between the

UAE and Oman; there are numerous border crossing points between the two. It's about a 5-hour drive from Dubai to Oman's capital, Muscat.

Getting **Around**

By Metro

Far and away the easiest and cheapest way to get around Dubai is aboard the city's state-of-the-art new metro network. The backbone of the network is the 50km (30-mile) **Red Line,** running from Al Rashidiya (near the airport) through the city center and then down the length of Sheikh Zayed Road and on to Jebel Ali. The much shorter 20km (12-mile) **Green Line** loops around the city center between Festival City and Al Qusais (just east of the airport). Most of the network runs above ground, although sections in the city center go through tunnels (with nine underground stations).

Operating hours are Saturday through Wednesday 5:30am to midnight, Thursday 5:30am to 1am, and Friday 10am to 1am. There are departures roughly every 5 to 10 minutes. There are two classes on all trains, Regular Class and Gold Class. **Gold Class** tickets cost double the price of Regular Class and the carriages aren't much different, although they have the great benefit of generally being much emptier, meaning you can almost always get a seat—something of a rarity in the Regular Class carriages. All trains have one Gold Class carriage, always at the back or the front of the train. The carriages next to Gold Class are always reserved for **women and children** only and are often a lot less crowded than regular carriages. Note that the system is **driverless,** meaning that you can stand at either end of the train (one of which will always be Gold Class) for superb views. **Tickets** are covered by the **Nol** scheme—see below. Children **under 5** (or shorter than 90cm) travel free.

NOL CARDS & TICKETS Most transportation in Dubai, including the metro, tram, and bus networks (but not the Dubai Ferry or *abras*), is covered by the **Nol** system (www.nol.ae). You'll need to have a valid Nol card or ticket before getting on board any metro, tram, or bus—no tickets are issued on board.

There are three types of Nol cards (Blue, Silver, and Gold) and one type of Nol ticket (Red). **Nol Cards** are basically rechargeable plastic cards, valid for 5 years, which you can top up at any metro station (and many other places). You swipe the card as you enter and as you leave the metro/tram station or bus; when you exit, the correct fare is automatically deducted from the credit on your card. The **Blue Card** is available only to Emiratis and Dubai residents. If you intend to travel in Gold Class, you'll need to use a **Gold Card.** The **Silver Card** is valid only in Regular Class. The Silver Card and Gold Card both initially cost AED 25 (including AED 19 credit), although fares are double the price for Gold Class rides.

There's also the **Red Nol Ticket** (AED 2, no credit), intended for short-stay visitors. These are valid for 90 days and can be recharged for up to 10 journeys. You can't store a credit balance on a red ticket but have to recharge it with the exact amount needed prior to every journey—a bit of a pain, although having a red ticket does allow you to purchase the useful 1-day pass (see below).

Fares on all Nol transportation (metro, trams, buses) follow exactly the same pricing structure, based on a zonal system. Fares start from AED 3 (AED 6 in metro/tram Gold Class) for the shortest journey, rising to AED 7.5 (or AED 15 in Gold Class) for the longest journeys—a superb value. Fares are a fraction more expensive if you're using a **red Nol ticket,** running from AED 4 to AED 8.5 (or AED 10–AED 19 in Gold Class). Using a red Nol ticket lets you buy Regular and Gold Class **1-day passes** (AED 20/AED 40) valid for unlimited travel across the network (these and other passes are also available on Blue Cards, but not on Gold or Silver Cards).

By Tram & Monorail

In the south of the city, the metro system's Red Line connects seamlessly with the new **Dubai Tram** (with interconnecting stations at Jumeirah Lakes Towers and DAMAC Properties), making it a convenient way to travel around the Marina (although considerably slower than the metro).

Operating hours are Saturday through Thursday 6:30am to 1am, and Friday 9am to 1am, with **departures** every 8 minutes. **Fares** are covered by the Nol system (see above). As on the metro, trams also have **Gold Class** and **women-and-children-only** carriages.

The tram connects with the **Palm Monorail** (see p 18), which runs the length of the Palm Jumeirah island, from the mainland to the Atlantis resort.

By Car

Driving yourself around Dubai is eminently feasible. Traffic is often heavy and can be slightly chaotic during the rush hours, but it doesn't present too much of a challenge, assuming you're a reasonably confident driver. The main difficulty may be finding your route. Huge patches of citywide construction work mean that road layouts are constantly changing, and signage is often minimal. (Even the city's taxi drivers regularly get lost.) In addition, the city's convoluted one-way street systems present a challenge for the uninitiated.

By Taxi

Taxis are cheap, modern, and reasonably plentiful. All drivers (most of whom are Indian or Pakistani) are trained and licensed, although driving standards, fluency in English, and navigational skills do vary. There's currently a basic flag-fare of AED 5 (or AED 8/AED 12 if the taxi is booked by phone during regular/peak hours) plus AED 1.7 per kilometer and a waiting charge of AED 0.5 per minute after 10 minutes (all rates rise slightly from 10pm–6am). Note that there's a minimum charge of AED 12 and a surcharge of AED 20 if you catch a taxi at the airport (or AED 25 for family-size van taxis) or go out to Sharjah. Taxis are run by a number of firms, including Cars Taxi, Dubai Taxi, and National Taxis. Cars from all companies can be booked on ☎ 04-208-0808.

Taxis are usually fairly easy to find, at least in the newer parts of the city. The best places are at shopping malls or at large hotels. Taxi drivers prefer to avoid the congested city center, however, and finding a cab can be a pain in Bur Dubai and Deira, and a nightmare during the morning and evening rush hours. If you're traveling at those times, it's best to book on ☎ 04-208-0808.

By Bus

Dubai has an extensive and cheap bus network, but it's set up mainly for the needs of low-income expat workers living in the suburbs and isn't much use to tourists. The two main terminals are Deira's Gold Souk Station and Bur Dubai's Al Ghubaiba Terminal. In addition, regular intercity buses leave Al Ghubaiba for Al Ain (roughly every hour) and Abu Dhabi and Sharjah (roughly every 20 min.).

By Boat

The principal way of getting across the Creek in old Dubai is by **abra** (see p 8). There are two main routes: from **Deira Old Souk** station (by the Spice Souk) to **Bur Dubai** station (at the western end of the Textile Souk), and from Deira's **Al Sabkha** station (at the eastern end of the Dhow Wharfage) to **Bur Dubai Old Souk** station (at the eastern end of the Textile Souk). There's also a third (but much less popular) route from **Baniyas** station (between the Radisson Blu and Sheraton hotels) to **Al Seef** station opposite.

Boats leave as soon as they're full—usually every few minutes. It's well worth trying both routes at least once, if you've got time, and again by night, when the sight of the city lights seen from the water is especially memorable. The trip takes about 5 minutes and costs a bargain AED 1 (payable on board). Abras run on all routes from 6am to midnight and 24 hours on the route between Al Sabkha and Bur Dubai Old Souk.

Another great way of taking to the water is to catch the sleek new

Dubai Ferry. This runs three times daily between Bur Dubai and Dubai Marina (75 min.), and there are also once-daily journeys from the Marina out around the Palm Jumeirah toward the Burj al Arab and from Bur Dubai up the Creek. Fares are AED 50.

The city also boasts an extensive network of **water taxis,** with 32 stations around the city. You'll have to specifically charter a water taxi by calling ☎ 800-90-90—there are no regular timetabled services. Services run 10am to 10pm daily, and fares start at AED 60 per boat.

On Foot

Dubai is one of the world's less pedestrian-friendly cities. Distances are long, temperatures high, and sidewalks often nonexistent. Just crossing the city's many enormously wide and traffic-clogged highways can often be a challenge. Nice (mainly pedestrianized) places for wandering on foot include the Bur Dubai Creekside, around Burj Khalifa Lake in Downtown Dubai, around Madinat Jumeirah, along Marina Walk in the Dubai Marina Walk, or along the seafront-facing The Walk at the nearby Jumeirah Beach Residences.

Fast **Facts**

ARRIVAL The international airport is centrally located in Dubai, about 3km (2 miles) west of Deira and the old city center. There are several ways of getting to your hotel from here. The easiest is to pick up a taxi from the rank directly outside the arrivals terminal—if you don't mind the AED 20 surcharge (see above) levied by taxis picking up from here. It should cost around AED 40–AED 50 to reach the city center or Sheikh Zayed Road, AED 70–AED 80 to reach the area around the

Burj Al Arab, and AED 80–AED 90 to reach Dubai Marina. The Metro offers a considerably cheaper (and often faster in periods of heavy traffic) way of reaching your destination; it is directly connected to the airport, with dedicated stations for terminals 1 and 3. There are also frequent airport buses into the city center, although it's really much easier to take the metro.

ATMS There are innumerable banks across all parts of the city with 24-hour ATMs accepting Visa and

MasterCard (although Amex and Diners' Club are less widely recognized). There are also ATMs in all shopping malls, and in—or close to—all major hotels. Before traveling, check with your card issuer to make sure that your card will be accepted overseas.

BUSINESS HOURS Working hours in Dubai are a strange hybrid of Western and Arabian traditions. The standard working week in Dubai runs from Sunday to Thursday. Government offices are usually open Sunday through Thursday 7:30am to 2:30pm, while banks are generally open Sunday through Thursday 8am to 1pm. (Some are also open on Sat mornings.) Most malls are open daily 10am to 10pm (and most stay open until 11pm or midnight Thurs–Sat). Most independent businesses are open roughly Sunday through Thursday 9am to 5 or 6pm. Shops in souks generally open at the whims of their owners, usually from around 10am to 10pm, although many places close from 1pm to 4 or 5pm, and on Friday (and during Ramadan) some places (including some mall shops) stay shut until around 2pm or a bit later.

CONSULATES & EMBASSY Australia Level 25, BurJuman Business Tower, Khalifa Bin Zayed Road, Bur Dubai. ☎ 04-508-7100. www.uae.embassy.gov.au.

Canada Consulate, 19th floor, Jumeirah Emirates Towers (Business Tower), Sheikh Zayed Road. ☎ 04-404-8444. www.canadainternational.gc.ca.

UK Embassy, Al Seef Road, Bur Dubai. ☎ 04-309-4444. www.gov.uk/government/world/united-arab-emirates.

USA Consulate General, Al Seef Road, Bur Dubai. ☎ 04-309-4000. http://dubai.usconsulate.gov/.

CURRENCY EXCHANGE All banks will change major currencies and some still change travelers' checks (in the unlikely event that you're still carrying them). Many larger hotels also change foreign currency, although often at very poor exchange rates. There are numerous official bureaux de change across the city (including in all large shopping malls), many of them run by the leading UAE-wide Al Ansari chain.

DRUGS (see also **PRESCRIPTION DRUGS**). Travelers flying into Dubai (or even just transiting through the airport) should be aware of the Emirate's draconian customs regulations. Dubai operates a zero-tolerance policy on drugs. Anyone found entering with even a microscopic quantity of an illegal substance faces a mandatory 4-year prison term. This includes not only drugs carried on one's person but also drugs found in one's bloodstream or urine. Do not attempt to enter the country while under the influence, and ensure that your clothes and possessions are clean and drug-free if you have come into any contact with banned substances. In the eyes of the Dubai authorities, even a speck of contaminated dust or pocket fluff is enough to convict you—as several foreign nationals have found out, to their regret.

ELECTRICITY 220–240 volts AC, usually with UK-style three-square-pin sockets. Most U.S. appliances will require a transformer.

EMERGENCIES
Police/ambulance ☎ 999
Fire ☎ 997

GAY & LESBIAN TRAVELERS For all its cosmopolitan veneer, Dubai isn't a great place for same-sex couples on vacation. Homosexuality is illegal in the UAE, and although there is a scene, it's very well hidden, and gays and lesbians should exercise caution. Note, too, that gay- and lesbian-oriented websites will most likely be blocked in the UAE, so don't expect to pick up information online while you're in the city.

HOLIDAYS There are just three public holidays in Dubai with fixed dates:

January 1 (New Year's Day), Martyrs' Day (Nov 30), and December 2 (National Day). There are also six Islamic holidays with moveable dates:

Leilat al Meiraj (Ascent of the Prophet; May 5 in 2016)

Eid al Fitr (the end of Ramadan; see p 102; July 7–8 in 2016)

Arafat (Haj) Day (Sept 10 in 2016)

Eid al Adha (Feast of the Sacrifice; Sept 11–13 in 2016)

Islamic New Year (Oct 2 in 2016)

The Prophet's Birthday (Mouloud; Dec 12 in 2016)

All these dates fall about 11 days earlier in the calendar every successive year.

HOSPITALS Rashid Hospital Umm Hurair Street, Oud Metha. ☎ 04-219-2000. www.dohms.gov.ae/Hospitals-Clinics/MainHospitals/RashidHospital. **American Hospital** Oud Metha Road. ☎ 04-337-5500. www.ahdubai.com.

INTERNET Dubai is a very wired city, although it can be surprisingly tricky to get online if you don't have your own Wi-Fi device. Even the very cheapest hotels now have Wi-Fi (usually in-room)—usually free, although it's always worth checking before you reserve (hotels that do charge for Wi-Fi often charge extortionate rates). Elsewhere, just about all coffee shops offer free Wi-Fi when you buy a drink, as do many city malls and some other shops. Paid Wi-Fi can be found on the metro and in many places around the city using the various Eitisalat and Du "Hotspots" (usually around AED 10/hr.).

There are very few Internet cafes around nowadays. They can mainly be found in Bur Dubai—try **Aimei** (branches on the small road behind the Time Palace Hotel, and on Al Mussalla Rd. halfway between Bastakiya and Al Fahidi metro station), or visit the well-set-up **Mi Café** in the Al Ain Centre or **Futurespeed,** next to Dôme café in Burjuman. There are also a couple of places along Al Rigga Road in Deira—try **Frina,** near Al Rigga metro station.

Note that the Internet is heavily censored. This includes anything of an even slightly pornographic or politically sensitive nature—even mainstream sites, such as YouTube, Facebook, and Flickr have been partially or totally blocked in the past. Oddly enough, Dubai's two ISPs, Du and Etisalat, don't always block the same sites, so what's blocked on one machine or Wi-Fi connection may be viewable on another.

MAIL The most conveniently located post office for tourists is the Al Mussalla Post Office, directly opposite the entrance to Bastakiya. Mail takes about 7 to 10 days to get to Europe and the U.S. A postcard to either costs AED 3.5.

MONEY The UAE currency is the dirham, usually abbreviated as "AED" or "dh." Each dirham is divided into 50 fils, although these are seldom used nowadays. Coins come in AED 1, 50 fils, and 25 fils sizes. Notes come in denominations of AED 5, 10, 20, 50, 100, 200, 500, and 1,000. The dirham is pegged to the dollar at a rate of \$1 = AED 3.6725. At the time of writing, other exchange rates were roughly £1 = 5.5 AED, 1€ = 3.9 AED, C\$1 = 2.8 AED, and A\$ = 2.6 AED.

NEWSPAPERS & MAGAZINES Newspapers in the UAE are obliged to perform heavy self-censorship: No criticism of the government is permitted, and many editors feel obliged to print large photographs of various high-ranking sheikhs accompanied by flattering news bulletins on a daily basis. This makes for a very dull press. Easily the best UAE newspaper is the *National,* published in Abu Dhabi, while Dubai's leading newspaper, *Gulf News,* is also worth a look, as is the more tabloid-style *7 Days*. There's a far better range of local and international magazines on offer (although censors go through imported mags, laboriously crossing out any risqué shots with thick marker pens). For local listings and events, pick up the weekly *Time Out Dubai*.

PASSPORTS & VISAS Citizens of many Western countries, including citizens of the U.S., Canada, UK, Ireland, Australia, and New Zealand (for the full list, visit www.uae-embassy.org), are issued a free 1-month visa on arrival. Citizens of other countries should contact their nearest UAE embassy or consulate. You should have 6 months' validity left on your passport.

PHARMACIES There are pharmacies all over the place, including in every mall of any size.

PRESCRIPTION DRUGS Users of medically prescribed drugs should be very careful when taking medicines with them into the UAE—foreigners have been detained for carrying apparently innocuous medicines, including those freely available over the counter at home. If entering Dubai with any prescribed drugs, travelers are advised to carry a doctor's letter explaining the nature of the prescription and to keep the medication in its original packaging. A list of "controlled medicines" can be found at www.uaeinteract.com/travel/drug.asp.

SAFETY Dubai is an extremely safe city—the only significant risk is from road traffic accidents as a result of the sometimes-wayward standards of local driving. The possibility is often raised of terrorist attacks against the city, due to its extremely sensitive geopolitical location and (in the eyes of Islamic hardliners) supposedly freewheeling Western mores, but so far such a threat has failed to materialize.

SMOKING Smoking has been banned in all public transport, offices, shopping malls, and indoor restaurants. You can still smoke freely in almost all bars and pubs. Most hotels also now offer nonsmoking rooms or floors, and a few have banned smoking completely. If in doubt, don't light up—fines are draconian.

TAXES Most upmarket hotels in Dubai add a 10% service charge and a 10% municipality tax to the bill—a nasty surprise if you're unprepared. Always find out in advance what is and isn't included. On the other hand, most, but not all, restaurants and bars include these taxes in the prices quoted on their menus, although again check the small print or you'll be hit by the same 20% price hike come bill time.

TIME Dubai is 4 hours ahead of GMT. There is no daylight savings time.

TIPPING A 10% service charge is usually added to (or included in) most restaurant, bar, and hotel bills. It's up to you whether you want to tip more than this. Taxi drivers often attempt to round the fare up to the nearest AED 5 or AED 10—again, it's your choice whether to insist on getting your change back. Other than this, taxi drivers don't usually expect tips and will be pleasantly surprised if you give them one.

TOILETS Restrooms are available in all shopping malls, or you can just dive into the nearest plausible-looking hotel or restaurant.

TOURS & TOUR OPERATORS There are dozens of tour operators in Dubai, all running pretty much the same range of desert safaris, city tours, and Creek cruises. (There are also a couple of more unusual outfits in Bastakiya; see the box on p 26.) The following are some of the more reliable operators:

Arabian Adventures: ☎ 04-303-4888. www.arabian-adventures.com.

Dubai Private Tour: ☎ 04-396-1444. www.dubaiprivatetour.com.

Funtours: ☎ 04-283-0889. www.funtoursdubai.com.

Knight Tours: ☎ 04-343-7725. www.knighttours.co.ae.

Oceanair Travels: ☎ 04-358-2500. www.oceanairtravels.com/emirates.

Orient Tours: ☎ 04-282-8238. www.orienttours.ae.

Platinum Heritage Luxury Tours: ☎ 04-388-4044. www.platinum-heritage.com.

TOURS—BOAT CRUISES There are various ways of going for a boat tour of the Creek (also see the Wonder Bus, below). The most basic option is simply to hire an *abra* for your private use from any of the various *abra* stations. The official price is AED 120 per hour, although boatmen might attempt to get you to pay more.

Going for a **dinner cruise** aboard a traditional wooden dhow is another popular option. These tours can be arranged through all the tour agents listed above. One particularly classy boat is the **Al Mansour Dhow** (☎ 04-222-7171), run by—and departing from next to—the Radisson Blu in Deira. Another option is the **Bateaux Dubai,** a sleek, modern, glass-roofed vessel that also plies the Creek nightly (☎ 04-814-5553; www.jaresorts hotels.com; bookable through most travel agents). There are also dhow dinner cruises at Dubai Marina, although they are not as memorable as a trip down the Creek.

You can also go for short upscale *abra* trips around the waterways of **Madinat Jumeirah** (20 min.; AED 75, AED 40 children; Wed–Sun 11am–11pm, Mon–Tues noon–9pm), and around **Burj Khalifa Lake** (25 min.; AED 65; daily 5–11pm).

TOURS—CITY BUS TOURS
Big Bus Tours A good (if rather pricey) way to get a quick overview of Dubai, the Big Bus Company's open-top, double-decker buses run on three routes and 74 stops around the city and cover all the main areas.

You ride the bus as long and as many times as you like while your tickets lasts (24 or 48 hr.). ☎ 800-244-287. www.bigbustours.com. 24-hr. tickets AED 240, AED 100 children ages 5–15, AED 580 family of 4.

Dubai Trolley Free evening and after-dark trips around Downtown Dubai take place on an eco-friendly hydrogen-powered double-decker open-top trolley. The hop-on hop-off service follows a circular route, with stops at Dubai Mall, Burj Khalifa, Souk al Bahar and The Address, Vida Downtown, and Manzil Downtown hotels, with further stops to be added as the route expands. Daily 5pm–1am (although trolleys may stop running in summer).

Wonder Bus A bus tour with a difference, the Wonder Bus departs from BurJuman Centre, drives down to Garhoud Bridge, and promptly turns into a boat. You then sail down the Creek to Shindagha, return to dry land, and drive back to BurJuman. Fun for kids, although in truth it's really just an expensive Creek cruise-cum-bus tour. Ground Floor, BurJuman Centre. ☎ 04-359-5656. www.wonderbusdubai.net. AED 160, AED 115 children ages 3–12 (or AED 135/AED 115 for trip earlier in the morning).

TRAVELERS WITH DISABILITIES Many of the major hotels have facilities of varying standards for travelers with disabilities, including some specially equipped rooms, and most of the city's modern attractions are fully accessible—although, not surprisingly, most of the city's heritage properties are more difficult to access. Getting around the city is relatively straightforward: The metro is well set up for travelers with special needs, and Dubai Taxi has a number of accessible taxis (allow a few hours' notice when booking). Pavements are less easy to negotiate. Those in the old town are often narrow, congested, and frequently partly or wholly obstructed; in the newer parts of the city, sidewalks are frequently dug up for

construction projects. Drop-down curbs are not always to be expected, either.

A Brief **History**

C. A.D. 500 Extensive settlement of Jumeirah area is followed by trading links throughout the Gulf region.

C. 630 Islam gains a foothold in the area. The Ummayad Caliphate, based in Damascus, becomes the major political power in the region.

1095 First recorded reference to Dubai appears, in the Spanish-Arab geographer Abu Abdullah al Bakri's *Book of Geography*.

1587 First European reference to Dubai appears, as pearl merchant Gaspero Balbi mentions the presence of Venetian pearl divers working in the area.

C. 1800 Al Fahidi Fort is built, today the oldest surviving building in Dubai.

1820 The strategic significance of the Gulf on the sea routes to India attracts the attention of the British, who offer military protection to the sheikh of Dubai, Mohammad bin Hazza. Increasing numbers of Indians begin to settle in the town, while the Indian rupee is widely used as local currency.

1833 The Al Bu Falasah branch of the Bani Yas tribe leaves its former home in Abu Dhabi and takes control of Dubai, led by the Maktoum bin Butti, the ancestor of today's ruling Maktoum family.

1835 Dubai, along with other emirates in the region, signs a peace treaty with Britain.

1841 Settlement of Deira side of Creek begins. By around 1850, there are 350 shops in Deira, and the town has a mixed population of Arabs, Iranians, and Indians. The main economic activities are trade and pearl fishing.

1892 The Trucial States (or Trucial Oman), the forerunner of the modern UAE, is created.

1894 New tax incentives are introduced, diverting trade from Sharjah and Iran into Dubai, which becomes an increasingly important regional trading center.

1930S The development of artificial pearl culturing in Japan leads to the gradual collapse of Dubai's pearl industry. Trade, import-export, and smuggling become the town's economic mainstays.

1939 Sheikh Rashid, the father of modern Dubai, assumes power from his sick father (although he isn't made the official ruler until 1958). He implements the first of Dubai's major development projects, dredging the Creek to encourage shipping and developing new port facilities.

1947 Border disputes between Dubai and Abu Dhabi lead to brief fighting.

1958 Vast oil reserves are found in Abu Dhabi.

1960 Dubai International Airport opens.

1966 Oil is discovered in Dubai (although in much smaller quantities than in Abu Dhabi). Many foreign workers arrive, and the town's population triples in size within the next decade.

1971 The British leave the Trucial States, which are reformed as the UAE, a loose federation of partially autonomous emirates.

1970S AND 1980S Oil revenues are invested in a series of major new infrastructure projects aimed at boosting Dubai's commercial power, including the new Jebel Ali Port (opened in 1983) and the city's first skyscraper, the 39-story World Trade Center (1979). By the end of the decade, the population of Dubai is 500,000, a fifty-fold increase within 40 years.

1990 Sheikh Rashid dies. Sheikh Maktoum becomes the new ruler of Dubai, although power largely rests with his younger brother, Sheikh Mohammed, who is credited with further accelerating the pace of change and development in the emirate, including overseeing new projects, such as the Burj Al Arab hotel (1998) and the Palm Islands (2006 onward).

1996 First Dubai Shopping Festival is held.

2006 Upon the death of Sheikh Maktoum, Sheikh Mohammed becomes the ruler of Dubai. Falling oil revenues now account for only around 6% of the emirate's revenues, with the rest derived from a highly diversified range of trading, shipping, business, construction, financial, and other interests.

2009 Dubai is brought to the brink of bankruptcy as a result of the global financial crisis, with many major projects canceled or postponed in the wake of the crisis. First phase of the Dubai Metro opens.

2010 The Burj Khalifa, the world's tallest building, opens, despite a still-stalled economy.

2014 The Dubai Tram opens.

2015 Ongoing signs point to economic revival, with soaring property prices and the inauguration of new mega-projects, such as the huge Dubai Water Canal development, currently under construction.

Useful Phrases & Menu Terms

ENGLISH	ARABIC
Yes	Ay-wa/Na'am
No	La'
Thank you	Shu-kran
No thanks	La shu-kran
Please	Min fadlak/mini fadliki (to a m/f)
Let's go	Ya-allah
God willing	Insh-allah
Sorry/excuse me	Af-wan / muta'assif
Hello (informal)	Ya hala
Hello/welcome	Marhaba / Ahlan wa sahlan
Hello (formal)	Salam alaykoom
Hello (response)	Wa alaykoom salam
Good morning	Sabah el kheer
Good morning (response)	Sabah in nuwr
Good evening	Massa el kheer

Good evening (response)	Massa in nuwr
How are you?	Kay fahlak/fahlik? (to a m/f)
Fine, thanks	Zayn, shu-kran/Zayna, shu-kran (spoken by m/f)
What's your name?	Shuw ismak/ismik? (to a m/f)
My name is . . .	Is-mee . . .
No problem	Mish-mishkella
Where are you from?	Inta min-ayn?/Inti min-ayn? (to a m/f)
I'm from . . .	Anna min . . .
America	Ame-ri-ki
Britain	Brai-ta-ni
Europe	O-ro-pi
India	Al Hind
It's a pleasure to have met you	Forsa sai-eeda
I'm honored (response)	Anna as-ad
Goodbye	Ma-salama

Numbers

ENGLISH	ARABIC
0	sifr
1	wahed
2	itnain
3	talaata
4	arba'a
5	khamsa
6	sitta
7	saba'a
8	tamanya
9	tissa
10	ashra
20	ashreen
30	tala-teen
40	arba-een
50	khamseen
100	mia
200	mee-tain
1000	alf

Food & Drink

ARABIC	ENGLISH
Baba ghanouj	dip made from grilled eggplant (aubergine) blended with tomato, lemon juice, garlic, and onion
Bulghur	cracked wheat
Fatayer	small triangular pastries stuffed with spinach or cheese
Fatteh	tiny pieces of fried or toasted bread
Fattoush	tomato salad with fatteh
Foul madamas	dip made from beans (fava) mixed with lemon juice, oil, and chili
Jebne	white cheese
Hammour	common Gulf fish, with delicate white flesh

The Savvy Traveler

ARABIC	ENGLISH
Kibbeh	small ovals of lamb, mixed with spices and cracked wheat and then deep-fried
Labneh	creamy Arabian yogurt, usually flavored with mint or garlic
Moutabal	like baba ghanouj, but thickened with yogurt or tahini
Saj	Lebanese-style thin, round flatbread
Saj manakish	saj sprinkled with oil and herbs
Sambousek	small fried pastry filled with minced beef or cheese
Shawarma	chicken or lamb kabob sandwich, roasted on a vertical spit, sliced thinly, then wrapped in flatbread with ingredients that could include hummus, chips, salads, sauces, and chili
Shisha	waterpipe (or hubbly-bubbly), usually available in as many as 20 different flavored varieties
Shish taouk	chicken kabob, marinated in a mix of lemon juice, garlic, and other spices and grilled on a skewer
Sumac	spice made from the dried and ground berries of the sumac bush, with a distinctively tangy and intense flavor
Tabbouleh	finely chopped mixture of tomato, mint, and cracked wheat
Tahini	sesame seed and olive oil paste
Waraq aynab	vine leaves stuffed with rice and/or meat
Zaatar	popular fragrant Lebanese seasoning made from dried thyme, marjoram, oregano, and sesame seeds
Zatoon	olives

Airline & Car-Rental Websites

Airlines

AIR FRANCE
www.airfrance.com

AUSTRIAN AIRLINES
www.austrian.com

BRITISH AIRWAYS
www.britishairways.com

DELTA AIR LINES
www.delta.com

EMIRATES
www.emirates.com

ETIHAD AIRWAYS
www.etihad.com

GULF AIR
www.gulfair.com

KLM
www.klm.com

LUFTHANSA
www.lufthansa.com

MALAYSIA AIRLINES
www.maylasiaairlines.com

QATAR AIRWAYS
www.qatarairways.com

ROYAL BRUNEI
www.flyroyalbrunei.com

SINGAPORE AIRLINES
www.singaporeair.com

UNITED AIRLINES
www.united.com

VIRGIN ATLANTIC
www.virgin-atlantic.com

Car-Rental Agencies

ALAMO
www.alamo.com

BUDGET
www.budget.com

DOLLAR
www.dollar.com

EUROPCAR
www.europcar.com

HERTZ
www.hertz.com

NATIONAL
www.nationalcar.com

PAYLESS
www.paylesscar.com

SIXT
www.sixt.com

THRIFTY
www.thrifty.com

Index

See also Accommodations and Restaurant indexes, below.

Photo **Credits**

p i, left: © Nikita Starichenko; p i, middle: © Banana Republic images; p i, right: © ventdusud; p vii: © Ashraf Jandali; p 3, bottom: © Alexandr Vlassyuk / Shutterstock.com; p 4, top: © Rus S / Shutterstock.com; p 5: © Luciano Mortula; p 8, top: © outcast85; p 8, bottom: © Iryna Rasko / Shutterstock.com; p 9, top: Courtesy of Dubai Tourism; p 9, bottom: © TasfotoNL / Shutterstock.com; p 10, top: © bikeriderlondon; p 10, bottom: © Luciano Mortula; p 11, top: © David Steele; p 12, top: © Laborant / Shutterstock.com; p 13, bottom: © Guilhem Vellut; p 15, bottom: © Philip Lange; p 16, bottom: © Rus S / Shutterstock.com; p 17, top: Courtesy of Dubai Tourism; p 19, top: © Zhukov Oleg / Shutterstock.com; p 19, bottom: © Photobac / Shutterstock.com; p 20, top: © islavicek / Shutterstock.com; p 21: © Philip Lange; p 23, bottom: Courtesy of Dubai Culture Arts Authority; p 24, bottom: © Chris Howey; p 25, top: Courtesy of Dubai Culture Arts Authority; p 26, bottom: © Laborant / Shutterstock.com; p 29, top: © Sergemi / Shutterstock.com; p 29, bottom: Courtesy of Dubai Culture Arts Authority; p 30, top: Courtesy of Dubai Culture Arts Authority; p 34, top: © Patryk Kosmider / Shutterstock.com; p 35, top: © zeljkodan; p 35, bottom: © Elroy Serrao; p 36, top: © Darko Vrcan / Shutterstock.com; p 37, bottom: © TasfotoNL / Shutterstock.com; p 38, top: © Sirah Quyyom; p 39, bottom: © Denise Chan; p 41, bottom: © Francesco Dazzi; p 42, top: © Paul J Martin / Shutterstock.com; p 42, bottom: © dinosmichail / Shutterstock.com; p 46, bottom: © S-F / Shutterstock.com; p 47, top: © S-F / Shutterstock.com; p 48, bottom: © SHAHID SIDDIQI; p 49, top: © Tim Adams; p 51, bottom: © Goran Bogicevic / Shutterstock.com; p 52, bottom: Courtesy of Dubai Creek Golf Club; p 53, bottom: Courtesy of Dubai Tourism; p 54, bottom: Courtesy of Dubai Tourism; p 55, bottom: © SurangaSL / Shutterstock.com; p 56, bottom: © ISchmidt / Shutterstock.com; p 58, top: © S-F / Shutterstock.com; p 59: © Laborant / Shutterstock.com; p 60, bottom: © Kiev.Victor / Shutterstock.com; p 63, top: © Sirah Quyyom; p 63, bottom: © Tatyana Vyc / Shutterstock.com; p 64, bottom: © Xenon Flash; p 65, top: © Krista; p 66, bottom: © Fedor Selivanov; p 67, top: © Ritu Manoj Jethani / Shutterstock.com; p 68, bottom: © Ritu Manoj Jethani / Shutterstock.com; p 69, top: © Ritu Manoj Jethani / Shutterstock.com; p 69, bottom: © Sanchai Kumar / Shutterstock.com; p 70, top: © Ritu Manoj Jethani / Shutterstock.com; p 71: Courtesy of Madinat Jumeirah Hotel; p 73, bottom: Courtesy of Le Royal Meridien; p 75, top: Courtesy of One & Only Resorts; p 77, bottom: © Sakena Ali; p 79, bottom: Courtesy of Dubai Creek Golf & Yacht Club; p 80, top: © S-F / Shutterstock. com; p 81, bottom: Courtesy of Jumeirah Beach Hotel; p 83: Courtesy of One & Only Resorts; p 88, top: Courtesy of Four Points Bur Dubai; p 89, bottom: Courtesy of Asha's; p 90, bottom: Courtesy of Hilton; p 91, top: Courtesy of Grosvenor House/ NICOLAS DUMONT; p 92, bottom: Courtesy of One&Only Royal Mirage; p 93, top: Courtesy of Jumeirah Emirates Towers; p 93, bottom: Courtesy of Jumeirah; p 94, bottom: Courtesy of The Palace Hotel; p 95, top: Courtesy of Shakespear & Co; p 96, top: Courtesy of Dubai Creek Yacht Club; p 97: Courtesy of Jumeirah; p 101, top: © Nick Webb; p 102, bottom: © ZouZou; p 103, top: Courtesy of Dubai Tourism; p 104, top: © Panoramas; p 104, bottom: Courtesy of Jumeirah; p 106, bottom: Courtesy of One& Only; p 107, top: Courtesy of Jumeirah; p 108, top: Courtesy of One&Only; p 109, top: Courtesy of 360 Degrees; p 110, bottom: Courtesy of The Grosvenor House Hotel; p 112, bottom: Courtesy of Jumeriah Emirates Towers; p 113: Courtesy of Park Hyatt Dubai; p 117, bottom: Courtesy of Al lin Rotana; p 118, top: Courtesy of Arabian Courtyard Hotel & Spa; p 120, bottom: Courtesy of Dusit Thani Dubai; p 121, top: Courtesy of Hilton; p 122, top: Courtesy of Jumeirah; p 122, bottom: Courtesy of Jumeirah/ Victor Romero; p 123, top: Courtesy of One&Only Royal Mirage/ Douglas A. Salin; p 124, top: © Guilhem Vellut; p 126, top: Courtesy of Ritz Carlton Dubai; p 127: © Fedor Selivanov; p 129, bottom: © Philip Lange; p 130, bottom: © Philip Lange; p 133, top: © Susanne Nilsson; p 134, top: © Laborant / Shutterstock.com; p 134, bottom: © Susanne Nilsson; p 135, top: © Tatsiana Selivanava; p 137, top: © Philip Lange; p 138, top: Courtesy of Visit Abu Dhabi; p 139, bottom: © Philip Lange / Shutterstock.com; p 140, top: Courtesy of Visit Abu Dhabi; p 141, bottom: © Peter Fuchs / Shutterstock.com; p 142, top: Courtesy of Visit Abu Dhabi; p 143: Courtesy of Visit Abu Dhabi; p 146, bottom: © Kosmider / Shutterstock.com; p 147, bottom: © Sophie James / Shutterstock.com; p 148, bottom: © JoemanjiArts / Shutterstock.com; p 149, top: © Philip Lange; p 151, top: © muznabutt / Shutterstock.com; p 153, bottom: Courtesy of Visit Abu Dhabi; p 155, bottom: Courtesy of Shangri La Qaryat al Beri; p 156, top: Courtesy of Emirates Palace Hotel; p 159, bottom: Courtesy of Beach Rotana; p 160, top: Courtesy of Shangri La Qaryat al Beri; p 161: © RiumaLab / Shutterstock.com

Notes